Witchfinder
GENERAL

Witchfinder

GENERAL

The Biography of
MATTHEW HOPKINS

CRAIG CABELL

SUTTON PUBLISHING

First published in the United Kingdom in 2006 by
Sutton Publishing Limited · Phoenix Mill
Thrupp · Stroud · Gloucestershire · GL5 2BU

British Library Cataloguing in Publication Data
A catalogue record for this book is available from the British
Library.

ISBN 0-7509-4269-X

*For Jim Herbert,
a great friend who shares an interest
in the dark side of life.*

Typeset in 11/14.5pt Sabon.
Typesetting and origination by
Sutton Publishing Limited.
Printed and bound in England by
J.H. Haynes & Co. Ltd, Sparkford.

Contents

List of Illustrations   vii

Preface   ix

Acknowledgements   xiii

A Note on the Text   xv

Dramatis Personae   xvii

An Impression   xix

Prologue: The Plight of John Lowes   xxi

PART ONE: THE LIFE OF A WITCHFINDER

One   Birth and Death   3

Two   The American Connection   11

Three   European Influence   14

Four   Official Endorsement   18

Five   Witches in the Neighbourhood   24

Six   The Witchfinder and his Accomplices   35

Seven   Matthew Hopkins – Witchfinder General   39

Eight   The Witchcraft Trials   43

Nine   Wandering with the Witchfinder   49

Ten   Cromwell's Blind Eye   52

Eleven   The Burning of Mary Lakeland   56

Twelve   The Tide Turns Against Hopkins   59

Thirteen   Matthew Hopkins Retires   66

Fourteen   Death of a Witch-hunter   71

Fifteen   The Stigma of Matthew Hopkins   80

Sixteen   The Legacy of Matthew Hopkins   83

Seventeen   Paranoia and the Witch-Hunt   85

Eighteen   Afterword   88

Contents

PART TWO: THE CHARACTER OF A WITCHFINDER

Nineteen   *The Discovery of Witches* by Matthew Hopkins:
                The Text   93

Twenty   *The Discovery of Witches* by Matthew Hopkins:
                An Analysis   106

Twenty-one   *A Confirmation and Discovery of Witchcraft*
                by John Stearne: The Text   126

Twenty-two   *A Confirmation and Discovery of Witchcraft*
                by John Stearne: An Essay   193

Appendix One   *A True Relation of the Arraignment of
                Eighteen Witches*   199

Appendix Two   *A True Relation of the Arraignment of
                Thirty Witches*   207

Appendix Three List of the Condemned   213

                Notes   221
                Sources and Further Reading   231
                Index   234

List of Illustrations

The will of James Hopkins. (*Norfolk Record Office*)

Cover and illustration from Matthew Hopkins's pamphlet *The Discovery of Witches*. (*The Revd Montague Summers/Cayme Press, 1928*)

Woodcut showing the earliest known likeness of Matthew Hopkins as the Witchfinder.

Matthew Hopkins's signature from a conveyance document of 1641. (*Suffolk Record Office*)

Stearne's judgment about the marks found on Thomas Pye's body. (*EDR E12 Assizes, f.21*)

Portrait of William Lilly, astrologer.

Cartoon image of Matthew Hopkins.

Thorn Inn, 2006

The bank beside the Hopping Bridge, 2006.

Hopping Bridge at Mistley pond, 2006.

White Hart, Manningtree, 2006.

Peter Cushing in the film *Twins of Evil*. (*Hammer Film Productions Ltd*)

Vincent Price as Matthew Hopkins in the film *Witchfinder General*. (*Tigon British Film Productions Ltd*)

All images from the author's collection unless otherwise stated.

. . . the Witch-finder (as they call him) is coming . . .
Matthew Hopkins,
The Discovery of Witches

Preface

The work of Matthew Hopkins, self-styled Witchfinder General of the English Civil War, has entered folklore and legend. Little has been written about him in the past because little source material has been forthcoming. Only a handful of books exist and one of those is a work of fiction. What has been lacking is a direct biography of Hopkins, something that doesn't concern itself with lengthy asides concerning European Witch crazes and other irrelevant comparisons. This is a tall order because what is known of Hopkins's life is crammed into approximately three years (1645–7), his brief career as a Witchfinder. During that time Hopkins sent over 200 people,[1] mainly women, to their death for the crime of Witchcraft. Nowadays, such accusations would be laughed out of court, but in those paranoid, confused and God-fearing days, the charge of being a Witch and ruining people's lives was a very serious one and if brought before a Magistrate, could result in execution.

But what of Hopkins's life outside those three years? Was he a lawyer as some historians suspect, or was he a humble shipping clerk who dreamed of a higher station in life? We shall see. However, Hopkins capitalised upon the paranoia of his times, travelling across the east of England sourcing Witches (for a fee) and wallowing in his own self-glorification. There were other Witchfinders during the sixteenth and seventeenth centuries, but it was Matthew Hopkins who was the most sadistic and prolific.

It was only after Hopkins's death that people slowly began to see the error in their ways. Hopkins was a sadist who made money out of other people's misery. The 'War Guilt' (if you will permit the analogy) of the people pushed the character of Matthew Hopkins into a legendary rather than historic mindset. Parents would threaten children, 'If you don't go to bed, Matthew Hopkins will get you'.[2] And, indeed, children's fairy tales would take on characters with tall buckled hats, knee-length boots and long knotted staffs; adopting the style of Hopkins and the prevailing evil dictated by his image.

A classic example of this folklore image was even interpreted in Hollywood during the 1930s with the Laurel and Hardy movie *Babes in Toyland* (with its creeping man in black, complete with cloak and tall hat), and one could even suggest that the Child Catcher in *Chitty Chitty Bang Bang* had something of the Hopkins folklore image about him. Oddly in both movies, it is the children who are in danger from the Hopkins image not the adults; proof of the shift from true historical figure to folklore/children's fairy-tale creation. And, as importantly, doesn't today's image of the Witch fall in line with Hopkins's influence: the buckled hat, cloak and boots (maybe even the Wicked Witch of the West in *The Wizard of Oz*)?

Hopkins must have been a heady influence in the growing awareness of the British nation to achieve the cult status he enjoys today. He has been interpreted more directly in the cinema by two of the horror genre's most respected actors. First, in tenuous form, by Peter Cushing in Hammer Horror's *Twins of Evil*; but more classically by Vincent Price in *Matthew Hopkins – Witchfinder General*, dubbed one of the greatest horror movies ever made. Although the latter's storyline romanticises the true events surrounding Hopkins, it is extremely accurate in its interpretation of the accusation, torture and forced confession of Hopkins's victims. It also used some of the original locations for its more important scenes. For that reason alone, it is one of the few movies in the horror genre that could be called 'important'. With its 'Greensleeves'-like music throughout, it is a deeply macabre and unsettling film. However, there is a contradiction: I personally believe Peter Cushing's interpretation of the Hopkins *character*, with his posse of Puritan henchmen, is closer to the real-life person.[3] However, one thing both movies get very wrong is the fact that Matthew Hopkins was certainly in his mid-twenties when he started his Witch-hunt, and no more than 28 when he died; Cushing and

Price were much older men when they took on the character and for some bizarre reason both were finally thwarted by an axe!

The reason why I have chosen to write about Matthew Hopkins is because I wanted to read a full and serious biography of the man myself. I couldn't find one that addressed the issues that concerned me most about him, so I spent five years carrying out my own research and eventually found that I disagreed with much of what had previously been written about him (and his accomplices). Too many articles, reviews, biographical notes and websites rewrite hearsay and largely inaccurate material; while many historians' essays, lectures and books spread their nets too wide, taking in social history and examining Witchcraft throughout history. What of Matthew Hopkins himself? Surely more can be said about his character, his build, his dress sense, his moral standing, and his behaviour to both peasants and peers? This then became my motive: to write the first true biography of Matthew Hopkins, one that concentrated solely on the man himself – his character, his motives and what it was that made him do the things he did. This is most important because I truly believe that analysing social behaviour and Witchcraft in relation to Matthew Hopkins brings us no closer to the man himself. He was a loner, an isolationist, a man as far detached from the mindset of his society as Jack the Ripper was from his, but who so brilliantly exploited that society. The Jack the Ripper analogy is not an overblown one. Many wicked people have behaved according to their own moral codes. If one is to attempt to trace the real Matthew Hopkins, one must be bold, but in order to be bold in historical non-fiction one must provide a deep analysis of source documents and become immersed in the mindset that created them.

This source material is the watchword of this book. This has provided a solid base for my analysis of Matthew Hopkins's words and actions. Also, by offering transcripts (and supporting analysis) of some of the most important documents relating to Hopkins's work, the reader has more opportunity to form a truer and more personal picture of Hopkins for themself.

So here is the most comprehensive analysis of source material concerning Matthew Hopkins – Witchfinder General.

Acknowledgements

So many people assist in writing a work of non-fiction, from kind receptionists who try their hardest to be helpful when everybody else is at lunch, through to professional librarians and historians. Everybody has a significant role to play in the game of synchronicity that has fused this book together. I am most grateful for all the assistance, including the small players whose names I didn't pick up on but who referred my enquiry from one department to another on a hunch that it might somehow be helpful – it always was.

Of those people and establishments I did pin down, I would like to thank the following for their assistance, patience and professionalism: the British Museum, the British Library (London and online services), The National Archives (Kew), Cambridge County Records Library, Framlingham Parish Records (Suffolk), Framlingham Castle, Manningtree Tourist Point, Manningtree Library, Manningtree Local History Centre, Manningtree Wine Shop and Delicatessen, Essex Record Office (Colchester and Chelmsford), Colchester Castle, County Council Record Office (Ipswich), Suffolk Record Office (Bury St Edmunds), Bury St Edmunds Tourist Office, Moyse Hall Museum, Peter Backaraeh, David Bush.

I would also like to extend my thanks to the following whose help in many ways has been invaluable: my father Colin for the early proofread, Alan Hunter, Mark Ottowell, Andrew Chrysostomou. Also eternal thanks go to: Anita, Samantha, Nathan, Fern, Berny and Dave, all of whom have heard many rhetorical conversations about a certain Witchfinder – thank you for putting up with me; this was the one I *really* wanted to write. Also my posthumous heartfelt thanks go to Dennis Wheatley, for his well-researched non-fiction

Acknowledgements

The Devil and All His Works, which acted as an additional spur when I contemplated writing this book half a decade ago.

Also thanks are due to Christopher Feeney at Sutton Publishing for his undying enthusiasm for this project, Jane Hutchings for her ideas and persistence, and my good friends, James, Dave, Graham, Richard, Steve, Rick, John, Alan, Eamon, Jim and Tony, who also had to put up with my many Witchcraft revelations.

I would like to make a special thank you to the following people who have all helped in ways beyond their own comprehension: Terry Ward, Moira Sterry, Keith Arthurs, Vincent O'Mara, and also Mrs Jenkinson and Mrs Hood, people I could never forget and remain fiercely loyal to, despite the passing years.

Sincerely, many thanks to all.

Craig Cabell,
London, July 2006

A Note on the Text

To make this book accessible to a contemporary audience it has been the aim of the author to use as much contemporary spelling and punctuation as possible without disrupting the flow of the original narrative.

Translations of source documents were undertaken by the author from copies of the original text. Where a key word has no contemporary usage, it is explained by endnote; for less important areas of transcript, an edited version is supplied, '. . .' denotes a cut in the text. Original documentation is sourced at the end of the book for academic reference.

The use of capital letters for words such as Witches, Witchfinder Witch-hunt and Witchcraft, also God and the Devil, is deliberate, enhancing the reality of such manifestations within the criteria of the times in which the book is set. Conversely, the use of capital letters for titles such as Matron or Midwife are used to denote a 'commissioned' job instigated by the Witchfinder, rather than simply using the words as offhand job titles, which they were not.

COPYRIGHT NOTES

John Stearne's pamphlet transcribed from an original copy in the British Library; transcript used by permission of the British Library.

Matthew Hopkins's pamphlet and two Assizes pamphlets transcribed from copies of the original text in C. Cabell's private collection.

Dramatis Personae

(An alphabetical list of the influential players in the life and career of Matthew Hopkins)

Nathaniel Bacon	Counsellor/Recorder of Ipswich and friend of James Hopkins
Pricilla Brigs (Briggs[1])	One of Hopkins's first Matrons
Edmund Calamy	Puritan priest and part of a special commission of Oyer and Terminer
Oliver Cromwell	Lord Protector of England
William Dowsing	Biblical fundamentalist appointed Parliamentary Inspector of Church Artefacts
Samuel Fairclough	Puritan priest and part of a special commission of Oyer and Terminer
John Gaule	Reverend of Great Staughton and enemy of Matthew Hopkins
John Godbolt	Judge/Sergeant-at-Law; head of a special commission of Oyer and Terminer, formed by Parliament to monitor the Suffolk Witch-hunt
John Gurden	Friend of James Hopkins
James Hopkins	Vicar of Great Wenham and father of Matthew Hopkins
James Hopkins (younger)	Elder brother of Matthew Hopkins
John Hopkins	Elder brother of Matthew Hopkins
Marie[2] Hopkins	Mother of Matthew Hopkins
Matthew Hopkins	Son of James Hopkins: shipping clerk and Witchfinder

Dramatis Personae

Thomas Hopkins	Elder brother of Matthew Hopkins who supposedly left Britain for New England, USA
William Lilly	Noted astrologer and possible adviser to Matthew Hopkins
John Lowes	Vicar of Brandeston, executed by Matthew Hopkins for Witchcraft
Frances Milles	One of Hopkins's first Matrons
Mary Phillips	Female accomplice to Matthew Hopkins
Edward Purley	Predecessor to John Stearne – accomplice to Matthew Hopkins
John Stearne	Chief accomplice to Matthew Hopkins
John Thurlowe	Cromwell's Chief of Secret Service

An Impression

The landscape is flat and rural. A hazy autumn sun peers through the spidery silhouettes of tall trees gilding leaf-tips in liquid gold. A cold thick mist billows from the warming earth, not unlike a recently extinguished bonfire discharging its diminishing heat; but that phantom bonfire is everywhere, blinding white cataracts against inky-black trees. Excitable cloud-like plumes twist eagerly into the chilly morning sky, not unlike an extrovert Latin dancer spinning into an icy all-embracing mist – the real clouds themselves. And from these dizzy heights, remnants of early morning dew wink cheekily like tiny diamonds that know their worth.

Only the bland would suggest that there was something sinister about this scene, because peaceful, unspoilt landscapes hold as many suggestions of past, forgotten secrets, as a young girl's suitor suggests mystery and romance. But those spectral plumes and fairy-tale dewdrops dissipate and a chill breeze briefly whips in from the bleak River Stour; a river that watches with misty eyes – almost wistfully – creating a deeply Gothic feeling of melancholy. Yes, an ancient spell lost in a Blackwood fable; but that spell is soon broken, weak though it now is.

A deep rumble approaches as of horse's hooves falling heavily on the tranquil scene, but that tranquillity is finally shattered by the sound of the 0930hr from Liverpool Street as it pulls into Manningtree station. After a short stop, a whistle blows and the train moves on towards Ipswich.

Sunlight winks through a crack in the trees and the moment is lost . . .

This is Essex in the twenty-first century; still a beautiful, green and pleasant land. A perfect – healthy – atmospheric location to research one of the most feared and, until now, relatively unknown characters in English history: Matthew Hopkins – Witchfinder General.

It was always my intention to bring Hopkins back to life through the pages of this book. To visit the quiet, humble villages of Essex and East Anglia, the gently flowing rivers, bridges and whispering meadows, which languish beside quiet country lanes – all the locations where Hopkins worked his trade. Yes, the countryside is still quite unspoilt and there is still much to see of Hopkins's world, from All Saints Church, Brandeston, to Colchester Castle and beyond. And when one visits these places today, it is something more than imagination that leaves an unsettling feeling that infiltrates the mind and chills the blood.

So it is not just important to analyse the source material available – scarce as it is – it is also important to visit the places where Hopkins worked his trade to take that tiny wink of history that still prevails and form a deeper perception of the man and his times.

Just to take the train from Manningtree to Colchester, Ipswich, Bury St Edmunds, Great Yarmouth, brings home a geographical perspective between each major town in this story, which is impossible to get by simply analysing a map. The passion with which Hopkins executed his quest against Witches – maybe only for personal gain – was a deliberate one; one that brought him ill-health but also brought many people to the gallows.

No stone was left unturned in my search for Matthew Hopkins.

PROLOGUE

The Plight of John Lowes

Why, this is Hell; nor am I out of it.

Christopher Marlowe, *Dr Faustus*

Before we follow the traditional path of biography, it is right that
we take one isolated incident in the career of the Witchfinder
General in order to create the right setting.

It is appropriate to present, from the outset, an example of
Matthew Hopkins's cruelty, which will instantly give the reader a
perception of his methods and show why it is important to
document as much about this cruel man as possible. There is no
better example of Hopkins's work than the plight of John Lowes,
Vicar of Brandeston, Suffolk, who suffered so dramatically.
Although we will look at Lowes more closely in his correct place in
the Hopkins story, it is important to provide the reader with a spur
that can only come through early opinion.

All Saints, Brandeston, is a typical English church. Set in peaceful
grounds, flanked by whispering trees, one cannot imagine anything
but goodness and prosperity emanating from its white stone walls
and red-tiled roof. Sadly, like many such places of worship, All
Saints holds a dark secret.

Long before the quaint nineteenth-century roof was laid, Vicar
John Lowes received a visitor at his door. It was Matthew Hopkins.

Hopkins accused Lowes of Witchcraft. Lowes vehemently denied
the claim. He had been vicar of All Saints for more than forty years
and was himself approximately 80 years old; but Hopkins would
not be stopped from doing the 'Lord's' work. He told Lowes that he
had conspired with two Imps[1] to sink ships at sea.

Again Lowes denied the claim, but Hopkins had heard enough. He arrested the vicar in order to obtain a confession. Despite his age, Lowes was made of strong stuff. His inner courage, his faith in God, was unfaltering, but after four days and nights of beatings and sleep deprivation,[2] he was finally bullied into signing a confession to a crime he didn't commit.

Lowes was then taken to nearby Framlingham, where he was bound hand to foot and 'swam'.[3] He survived this treatment (thus proving his guilt) and was shortly taken to nearby Bury St Edmunds where he joined forty other innocents, all of whom would be hanged for their alleged crimes of Witchcraft.

In the summer of 1645, sentence was ruthlessly carried out. Grown men screamed like tortured children as their wives, mothers and even daughters were hanged. The townspeople looked on as the carnage took place in front of their eyes. Some took their execution peacefully; others screamed, struggled and spat their way to the grave. The Civil War had brought turmoil, paranoia and the decay of justice, and it was men like Matthew Hopkins who exploited the situation.

As a portly bag of cash was placed into Hopkins's hands that black summer's day in Bury St Edmunds,[4] locals watched John Lowes, loyal vicar of All Saints Church, Brandeston, read out his own Anglican burial service and quietly accept his death. He was allowed to read his own sermon so he could insist upon a Christian burial, which he duly received.

With his work in Bury St Edmunds complete, Matthew Hopkins moved on to the next town, to find more Witches and grow increasingly richer for the privilege.

Where did Matthew Hopkins come from? How did he get away with his crimes? And what were his motives? These are the three most important questions in the story of the Witchfinder General and, in order to try and answer them properly, we must build our arguments from the source material that provides us with the earliest known facts concerning him.

PART ONE

The Life of a Witchfinder

ONE

Birth and Death

So dear I loved the man that I must weep.
I took him for the plainest harmless man
That breathed upon this earth a Christian.
    William Shakespeare, *The Tragedy of King Richard the Third*

Unfortunately there are no surviving records of Matthew Hopkins's birth or baptism, so in order to find out where he came from one must work backwards from his death.

It is recorded in the Mistley Heath parish register that on 12 August 1647, Matthew Hopkins, son of James Hopkins,[1] Minister of Wenham was buried at Mistley. The register reads: '1647 Aug 12 Matthew s M: James HOPKINGS, Minister of Wenham, buried at Mistley.' The 's' here represents the word 'son' and 'M' represents 'Mr'. Not too much concern is expressed over the spelling Hopkings with a 'g'. There were many spellings of Matthew's surname, and indeed, he even signed his Christian name with one 't',[2] so we are happy that the Matthew Hopkins mentioned is the infamous Witchfinder General.

By studying the parish register we discover two major points: one, that Hopkins was the son of a vicar, and two, the location of his burial site. Taking the second point first, it isn't *that* exciting to discover where Hopkins was buried. The medieval church at Mistley was built around 1170 but was derelict by the onset of the eighteenth century; therefore the graveyard at Mistley Heath is now no more than a field for grazing sheep, with only a fragment of a wall surviving from the church and no clue as to where Hopkins is buried. Returning to the first point, James Hopkins, Matthew's father: if one consults *The Alumni Cantabrigienses*, it is clear that James Hopkins was a clergyman of the Church of England and vicar of Great Wenham. He died in 1634.[3] Indeed, his will still survives (unlike that of his son Matthew) and it makes a very interesting read:[4]

In the name of God Amen, I, James Hopkins, of Wenham Magna in the County of Suffolk, cleric, being weak in body but of perfect and good disposing mind and memory, I thank God, do make my last will and testament in the following manner. I first of all do freely surrender my soul into the hands of Almighty God, trusting that I shall be received to mercy only through the righteousness and merits of the Lord Jesus Christ my saviour and yield my body to the Earth to be buried according and where my executor shall think most [fit]; and whereas I am [expected] to [leave to] my heirs . . . certain lands and tenements in Framlingham at the Castle in the county aforesaid I give and bequeath all my said lands and tenements, unto Marie[5] my wellbeloved wife and her heirs paying and discharging the portion ensuing bequeathed to my children; that is to say paying unto each of my six children severally when and so soon as they or either of them shall accomplish the age of two and twenty years the sum of one hundred marks of current money of England. Nevertheless as touching my son Thomas my mind and will is that my executor shall as soon as she can find opportunity send him over the seas to such our friends in New England as she shall think fit and that he shall there abide until he shall accomplish the said age of two and twenty years and so soon as he shall have accomplished the said age, then I will that my executor shall pay him the said sum of one hundred marks, deducting there-from the charge which she shall disperse in sending him over the seas, by the direction of my said wife; and shall not also stay there until he shall accomplish the age aforesaid, then I will that he shall not have any benefit of this my said will nor of the said one hundred marks formally bequeathed to him and furthermore if any of my said children shall depart their present life before they severally shall accomplish their ages of two and twenty years as aforesaid then the portion of such child or children so dying shall be equally divided between the survivors of them at there several ages aforesaid . . . I will that my executor shall pay unto my sister Lane at Ely forty shillings yearly during her life and into Anne Lane my servant twenty nobles . . . I give to my eldest James all my books, and all the rest of my goods and chattels I give them to Marie my loving wife who I do make my sole executor for my last will requiring her to take advice of my true worthy friends Mr John Gurden of Wenham aforesaid, and Mr Nathaniel Bacon [aka Nathaniel Bacon] and praying them to give their best furtherance and advice unto her in all difficult matters, that do or may concern the executing thereof. Lastly I leave my children to the direction and government of my wife requiring them to yield unto her all dutiful respect as they shall answer yet to God and also requiring her to look to their education according to her best skill that they may be brought up in the fear of God and in such honest calling as shall best suit with their dispositions and estates; and I do declare this to be my last will and testament; hereby revoking and annulling all former wills or writings in the nature of wills, or writings tending thereunto and in witness hereof I do here adjoin my hand and seal this twenty fifth day of December in the year of our Lord one thousand six hundred and thirty four in the presence of John Gurdon Roger, London.

Before analysing this will – the fullest document to shed light on the youth of Matthew Hopkins – we must first admit that his name doesn't appear in it. This suggests that Matthew was one of the six children and not either of the two eldest boys, James or Thomas, who were not even 22 themselves in 1634.

So was Matthew Hopkins still attending school in 1634? It seems so and, when we use that hypothesis in line with another document, it appears highly probable. Although the parish records have not survived from Great Wenham (from James Hopkins's time), the will of Daniel Wyles (dated 1619) does. In this document Wyles states: 'James Hopkins, preacher of the word of God at Great Wenham, and to his wife . . . 6s 8d each to their children James, Thomas and John when able to read a chapter of the New Testament, to buy a bible.'[6]

This document at least reveals categorically that Matthew Hopkins was not born before 1619 and so, if he is one of the six children[7] (which seems highly likely when viewing the entry of his death, i.e. who his father was), then he couldn't have been more than 28 when he died. If he came into his money at 22 and immediately started to plan his trade as a Witchfinder (say at the earliest date of 1644), then he would only have been barely 25 when he died (born 1622). It is therefore reasonable to assume that Matthew Hopkins died in his mid- to late twenties, so overall we are looking at a short but 'colourful' life.

So now we have the parameters of Matthew Hopkins's life, let us look more closely at his father's last will and testament and see what we can piece together with regard to the Hopkins household and the children's upbringing and opportunities in life. This is crucial if we are to understand what made this son of a vicar one of the most notorious of men during the English Civil War.

It is apparent that the family are financially comfortable and the 'certain lands and tenements' at Framlingham Castle are of particular note (especially when viewed in context of the fate of John Lowes).[8] However, much has been made of the 'New England' context in the past,[9] where it has been hypothesised that Hopkins 'faked' his own death by some means, or maybe his mother somehow made an entry in the parish register announcing his death, and then he fled the country to New England with the help of some friends in the shipping world. To me this is sheer nonsense, especially when it is suggested that he could have had something to do with the Salem Witch Trials (if still alive he would have been in his seventies by then). Marie Hopkins is noted in James's will as his 'wellbeloved wife' and 'my loving wife', in whom he put his complete trust concerning the future of his children and his estate.

To suggest that she could 'doctor' the parish register is doing her a great injustice. She was the wife of a faithful vicar who – according to the will of Daniel Wyles – was 'a preacher of the word of God', an endearing and respectable title for somebody to use. In the same will, mention is made of Hopkins's wife and children and the gift of a Bible for each: surely the Hopkins family was a respectable household. So what happened to Matthew?

We can surmise from the source documentation – short though it is – that James's eldest two boys had a decent education. The words, style and perception of Matthew's pamphlet *The Discovery of Witches*,[10] suggest that he was astute and educated too, so what happened to him? Was he simply a bad egg? Did he have a political motive? All that is for discussion later, but his youth appeared to be comfortable although, for the teenage years at least, fatherless.

An important question here is: if Matthew died young – mid- to late twenties as previously suggested – did his father also die young (i.e. was there a hereditary illness that prompted early death)? If the eldest sons were not 22 in 1634 when the will was written, it could suggest that the father was quite young when he died. It is also apparent from the will of Daniel Wyles (1619) that the two eldest boys were but mere babies at the time (not being able to read).

So did James Hopkins die young? It would certainly provide more evidence against the New England life of Matthew Hopkins. But then again, people didn't live so long at that time, or read at a very early age, so we have a strong contradiction. Or do we?

James Hopkins was a vicar, so it can be surmised that his life was documented before he died. Indeed, a 'James Hopkins' was awarded a Perne scholarship at Peterhouse in 1597, as mentioned in *A Biographical Register of Peterhouse Men* by Thomas Alfred Walker. However, Walker stated that James Hopkins was a royal Chaplain and the author of *A Sermon on Ezna* (1604), which seems unlikely; however the dates of his time spent at Cambridge University's oldest college do seem plausible. So, if we take the earlier statement to be correct and judge that the Cambridge James Hopkins was 20 years old in 1597, then if he is indeed the same James Hopkins, he would have been in his late fifties when he died in 1634.

A study of *The Alumni Cantabrigienses* shows quite categorically that James Hopkins was Vicar of Great Wenham from 1612 to 1613, and if that was his first parish and he was just married, then his children were born after several years of marriage. Suddenly we have a picture of the Witchfinder's father: a man educated at Cambridge and who came into his church and married at approximately the same time (1612) and had up to six children before dying in his late fifties. We also know this man to be well liked/respected in his community, and who wanted the best for his wife and children.[11]

So with this new information, what then went wrong? If the boys were fatherless when young, how did they all fare with no father figure around them, only a mother? Did the boys run amok? There is no evidence to suggest so, but if Matthew's career as a Witchfinder is anything to go on, they all certainly developed their own individuality and self-justifying moral code. It is easy to form a credible hypothesis of the Hopkins family both before and after the death of the father, but how much of that rationale is true?

A document sourced by Richard Deacon for his short 1976 study of the Witchfinder General sheds more light on the early life of Hopkins. Deacon writes, 'In September 1645, one John Hopkins (almost certainly James' son) of Wenham is described in parish records as being . . . appointed "Minister of South Fambridge" in Essex. There is an additional note of a year later – June, 1646 – stating that there had been complaints that John Hopkins had neglected his work and he had been replaced.'[12]

This evidence supports my hypothesis because if one brother is both dangerous and cunning (Matthew) and one 'neglected his work' despite 'complaints', it does imply misdirection after what seemed a very promising start. So with no father figure, and despite the mother's best endeavours, the boys became lazy – and in the case of Matthew, destructive and manipulative.

I don't consider this to be a stab in the dark. If one looks at the behaviour of certain privileged children in today's society, once the balanced family unit is broken, especially within a large family (and without adult support from other branches of the family[13]), cracks will show.

James does make reference to his 'worthy friends' of Wenham in 'different matters'; but in the context of carrying out the wishes of the will this cannot be interpreted as a pledge of being second father to six children. These 'worthy friends' surely had their own lives to lead. Indeed, Nathaniel Bacon was a very influential man in his day and we will discuss him later.

It can be surmised by the work John Hopkins was entrusted with (for a year at least) and the position Matthew acquired before becoming a Witchfinder (he worked as a shipping clerk), that the children observed their education in accordance with their father's wishes and obviously continued to know their Bible (as Matthew would later expertly twist to his advantage). An important point to make is that in the seventeenth century some children underwent private tuition instead of attending a formal school and, quite possibly, that is how Matthew and his siblings were taught.

An important question is raised at this juncture: when looking laterally at the Hopkins children in relation to their adult lives, it is only Matthew and John we find evidence of. Did the others die? There are no surviving records stating so, and no surviving documents concerning their burials or wills.[14] We can accept the fact that Thomas went to New England and probably didn't come back. It is also not difficult to believe that one or two of the younger children followed him there when they were old enough, especially if he was doing well. But I don't accept that Matthew went to America. He had his own agenda and, as we will see, came unstuck. What about his brother John?

When researching this chapter I found that a John Hopkins emigrated to Hartford, CT, USA in 1636 with his wife Jane (formerly Jane Strong), whom he married after inheriting 4 acres of land in Cambridge on 4 August 1634. He was born in either 1614 or 1615 and died at a young age (approximately 40), leaving his two children money and land, which they would inherit at the ages of 18 (girl) and 22 (boy). Could this be the elder brother of Matthew who maybe followed his elder brother Thomas to the promised land? The approximate date of birth seems a little early to me, especially if he was the third brother, but it would explain what happened to John

Hopkins of South Frambridge after being discredited at almost exactly the same time.

The evidence is very tenuous but is tantalisingly close to what we know/assume of John Hopkins. To be more comfortable we would probably like to see his date of birth being 1617 or 1618 and coming into an inheritance of land in 1635 rather than the precise 4 August 1634 (James Hopkins made his last will on 25 December 1634, hence the date of August is a little early).[15] It might be argued that the dates could still be correct, but not without supporting documentation.

We will analyse the USA connection of the Hopkins family a little more closely in the next chapter, but there is a final interesting aside: a John Hopkins website (from the USA) that specialises in tuberculosis. It is said by some sources that Matthew Hopkins died of such a disease in his late twenties. If the British Hopkins family died young, could it have been through such a disease: chest infections/breathing problems, especially in those cold bygone days with no central heating? Could that complaint still be endemic to the family today? And could John Hopkins be the link with that American legacy? Possibly not; but perhaps more credibly than brother Matthew having anything to do with Witchery in Salem.

If we have forgotten the name of our God, or stretched out our hands to a strange God; Shall not God search this out? For he knoweth the secrets of the heart.

Psalm 45, King James Bible

TWO

The American Connection

> Here is all the invisible world, caught, defined, and calculated. In
> these books the Devil stands stripped of all his brute disguises.
> Here are all your Familiar spirits – your incubi and succubi; your
> Witches that go by land, by air, and by sea . . . Have no fear now
> – we shall find him out.
>
> Arthur Miller, The Crucible

In the previous chapter I mentioned a John Hopkins who
emigrated to America in the 1630s (a namesake of one of
Matthew's brothers). We cannot rule out that the 'American' John
Hopkins is not the brother of Matthew Hopkins, because an
American connection has been authenticated through James
Hopkins's will. The lack of documentation of the marriages and
deaths of the Hopkins family also suggests that some of the children
went to America, but the existence of an entry of death for Matthew
Hopkins is testament that he didn't follow family members there.

Also, and quite importantly, we find that the 'American' John
Hopkins came from Coventry, nowhere near Matthew Hopkins's
East Anglia. This is rather disappointing news, because all we are
left with is a namesake and Hopkins is not the most obscure of
names – then or now. It is easy to be taken in by supposition.

There was a Stephen Hopkins who sailed on the *Mayflower* with
his wife Elizabeth Fisher and four children (one born en route), but

again, further study shows that Stephen did not come from East Anglia and his will holds no secrets as to an English legacy or indeed living family there.

I am loath to say that 'no evidence has so far come to light', because I simply believe that none exists today. So many romantic writers are eager for a connection between Matthew Hopkins and the Salem Witchcraft Trials, that they will hold court with any flimsy evidence.

One of the few things I do find interesting is the coincidence of American Witchcraft at the same time as Matthew Hopkins's tyranny. Between 1645 and 1662 over 100 Native Americans and 58 European immigrants in New England colonies were accused of Witchcraft. More intriguing, in 1647 Alse Young became the first person hanged in New England for being a Witch (the same year as Matthew Hopkins's death). However, we then find that Dutch colonists in New York accuse George Wood and Ralph Hall of Witchcraft. Now some may argue that Hopkins had a connection with European Witchcraft, i.e. he learned his trade there, so could he have joined his Dutch colleagues for such wild antics in America? No, of course not. For him to flee England and take up the same trade so quickly afterwards in America, and most probably under an assumed name, is a monstrous suggestion and one that only serves to fuel the ambiguity and mystery over the basic facts. One can live with the fact that Hopkins may have studied shipping or some other trade in Europe – possibly Holland – in his teens (see Chapter Three), one can possibly accept that there may be a European family connection and that he stayed with relations on the Continent and picked up his knowledge of European Witchcraft before working the trade, but all these hypotheses are conjecture, nothing more.

To learn more about the Hopkins family in America, one must go backwards in time not forwards, and that is where any real new evidence could be gleaned; especially as to the social position of the family and its structure/relationships with other families up to the time of Matthew's birth. However, if that evidence exists it can never be proved, because the source material that opens the door to America in James Hopkins's will states that 'friends' not 'relations' lived in America and the eldest son had been chosen to go there to make his fortune, not the whole family. It is implied that a hard life awaited Thomas Hopkins in America but James was adamant that his son should go there until he was at least 22 years of age. So if we are *not* looking for the name Hopkins in American records, what should we look for? We can only really look for names that appear in the will and compare them to the well-documented shipping list for the *Mayflower*, but the only name that crops up there is Hopkins! And there is no logical connection between that Hopkins and James/Matthew Hopkins, no clues, no leads. But does it matter to this biography? I believe not, because any American connection has little to do with Matthew Hopkins. It seems that the American connection didn't influence his life in any solid way, so let us move on.

From here on, I shall abandon the American connection of Matthew Hopkins because I truly believe that there was no opportunity for Matthew *himself* to go there. I do not believe that the note of his burial was faked. I believe that he died in England in his mid- to late 20s.

But evil belongs to the individual and, as any one marching soldier can upset a platoon's rhythm, so individual evil can disrupt the purpose of the whole.

James Herbert, *Shrine*

THREE

European Influence

And he said, that which cometh out of the man, that defileth the man.

Mark 7: 20 (King James Bible)

The most elusive part of Matthew Hopkins's story is his teenage years, from schooling to apprenticeship. There are no documents that explain what he was doing during his formative years and, because of that, many people have constructed their own theories built around the odd quote from Hopkins himself, or made an educated guess based upon the fashions of the time. In fact, I will go further and state that too much subjectivity has been brought to this part of Hopkins's story.

As this book adheres to source documentation, the applicable quotes from Hopkins must be given fair trial but only with a warning caveat: many people believe that the reason why there is no trace of the 'teenage' Hopkins is because he wasn't in the country. It is thought that rather than making a trip to America he instead ventured to Holland where he learned about the shipping trade and ostensibly (but inadvertently) the European Witchcraft craze. It is this later idea that many people place an emphasis on; however, it must be accepted that there is no evidence to suggest that he ever left England. I believe that Hopkins's Continental Witchcraft influence came from the writing of King James. It is known that Hopkins was familiar with the popular text of King James and it lended some kind of authority to his future work as a Witchfinder. King James was greatly influenced by Continental ideas appertaining to Witchcraft and, indeed, embraced the European notion that torture should be employed as an aid to achieving confessions from supposed Witches (also the Swimming test). This fact should not be understated, since works such as *Daemonologie* and the King James Bible were considered important texts because they had been written by the monarch and, ostensibly, that made them learned and lawful.

Acknowledging this and understanding a little more about the personality of Hopkins through his writing provides a safe base to suggest that Hopkins probably never went to Holland to study Witchfinding methods first hand. In *The Discovery of Witches* he stated quite early on in the text that he 'never travelled far' to gain his experience. He then gives a story concerning a local coven of Witches close to where he lived; there is no hint of a European influence.

So can we now dismiss a European visit (and consequent European influence of Witchfinding methods) by Hopkins? Not entirely. Hopkins told Lady Jane Whorwood: '[I] studied maritime law in Amsterdam and learned there much about the problems of ensuring ships.'[1] This quote – if believed – does make sense. It is known that Hopkins spent some time as a shipping clerk in Mistley. Also, if friends/family had travelled to America it can be suggested that the family had a strong sea connection so, in short, he had every advantage to travel abroad. Also, Hopkins's words to Lady Jane are not used in a flattering or justifying way, which lends them more providence (what would he hope to gain by lying?).

There was a strong dose of synchronicity coming into Hopkins's life during his teenage years. Having possibly studied shipping in Amsterdam and consequently learned something of a seaman's superstitions (mermaids, sea-monsters, bad omens), he may have picked up little nuggets of information that would serve him well in his future trade as Witchfinder. In juxtaposition to all this are the King James Bible and *Daemonologie*, and the familiarity of Holland and its customs.

The Dutch influence on Hopkins should not be overplayed. Understanding that he was a shipping clerk in Mistley (and not a lawyer in Ipswich as sometimes thought) brings more perspective to the claims of a Dutch education: he learned a basic trade in Amsterdam and came home to be a shipping clerk in Mistley. That is all. If he saw anything of Dutch Witchcraft trials we shall never know, but I suspect little or none at all. What is important to note are the facts concerning Hopkins's teenage years: the writings of King James I, and the basic shipping skills learned during a stay in Amsterdam. This is all we can rely upon and, frankly, it is enough. The evidence is scant, but the facts are there. So much has been incorrectly assumed in the past, that one must go back to the basic facts and make a logical deduction. Hopkins had a methodical and unglamorous education. His schooling must have been good. His father had provided for him (through his will) and at the onset of his twenties he would receive his inheritance. There is no evidence of him being anything grander than a shipping clerk in Mistley, but he must have pined for other things.

Looking at his life and writings during his work as Witchfinder General, we clearly see a scheming, cold-hearted Puritan. Hopkins was overtly perceptive and therefore never lost an opportunity to better himself, with the King James Bible in his back pocket and the Dutch climate in his soul.

It is interesting to note that Hopkins accused people of sinking ships at sea and a sea-connection does follow through some of his most famous Witchfinder cases (such as John Lowes and Mary Lakeland); he stuck with what he knew.

In his book *Matthew Hopkins – Witch Finder General*, Richard Deacon suggested that Hopkins could have had Huguenot blood (probably on his mother's side), which would add weight to the Dutch connection somewhat and the possibility of relations living in Holland but, again, this cannot be proved.

What made Hopkins stand out from other Witchfinders? His extreme measures? No, not really, but rather his prolific crusade and his ability to work in many contemporary European styles of

Witchfinding. He was truly a law unto himself. His methods made him stand out from the crowd and his influences must have come from somewhere: the shipping apprenticeship and learned reading (noting also that the King James texts were subject to influences from Scottish Witchcraft, the King being Scottish, as well as European). Also, as we will discover, the work of William Dowsing was almost instrumental in providing Hopkins with his final spur. With this last aspect assimilated Hopkins would start to plan his career as Witchfinder.

While analysing the early stages of Matthew Hopkins's life, it is not good to assume too much. So far we have discovered that Hopkins was the son of a vicar, probably the middle to youngest of the family. He was well provided for after his father died. He was brought up well, his family life was comfortable, he wanted for little, and his life was the Bible and good schooling until he could take an apprenticeship in Holland, coming back to work in Mistley as a shipping clerk (probably after receiving his part of the inheritance).

But why was the job of shipping clerk not good enough for him, and where did it all start to go terribly wrong?

You must cast the scholar off.

Christopher Marlowe, *Edward II*

FOUR

Official Endorsement

> Once upon a time the devil stayed at an inn, where no one knew
> him, for they were people whose education had been neglected.
>
> Robert Louis Stevenson, *The Devil and the Innkeeper*

American anthropologist Leslie A. White once said: 'Only where
one knows so little can one write so much . . . the absence of
facts gives the imagination free reign.' White wasn't writing about
Matthew Hopkins but the Amarna historiography (Egyptology). But
the comparison is the same. It doesn't matter how many years have
passed; if the documentation is not there for analysis then
supposition is bound to creep in.

The origins of British Witchcraft are filled with much
supposition, no area more tangled with good ideas or keen
perception than the years surrounding Matthew Hopkins and the
English Civil War. In 1966, Ronald Bassett wrote a fictional history
of Matthew Hopkins, which quickly became the acclaimed Vincent
Price movie. In Bassett's book, Hopkins started off as a soldier and
then things got more ludicrous from there on. The book was
followed in 1976 by Richard Deacon's slim volume, *Matthew
Hopkins – Witch Finder General*, documenting Hopkins against the
backdrop of British/European Witch trials. This is no heavy
criticism of Deacon's book as it has become the benchmark for
Hopkins researchers ever since, although some of his research is

deemed unreliable by certain scholars. Conversely, Malcolm Gaskill's work, *Witchfinders*, concentrated on both Hopkins and Stearne, adopting a storytelling prose and perception from the writer's knowledge of Witchcraft and the English Civil War years. As examples of in-depth analysis, these are the works that stand out. We could add the Reverend Montague Summers's analysis of Hopkins's pamphlet, but its tone and perception are a little out of date and it offers no new insights into Matthew Hopkins; it also takes on wider issues.

So let us not stray from the path here. How did Hopkins get away with murdering 'Witches' for so long? This is a very important area to explore as analytically as possible, because every killer needs a motive, including the Witchfinder General.

In the 1640s the belief in Witchcraft was endemic in British society; people believed in God and feared the Devil. What Hopkins and his accomplices did was police the towns and villages they visited and were paid (by the local Magistrate) for quelling the fears of an increase in local Witchcraft. This may seem a fantastical notion today, but 400 years ago, especially during the English Civil War, fear and paranoia were rife, local Magistrates (or Sticklers) were given 'martial law' and cold, calculating men such as Matthew Hopkins took advantage of the situation.

Obviously, there were Witches and Witch-hunters before the Civil War,[1] but this chapter concentrates on how Hopkins got away with *his* crimes. In order to understand this, one must accept that the conception of the extreme Witchfinder such as Hopkins was a natural progression from events of the time. I do believe that Matthew Hopkins was influenced by William Dowsing.

In 1643, Dowsing, a Puritan farmer, was appointed[2] to smash stained-glass windows and decorative images in the churches of Suffolk. This was the year before Hopkins began to work his trade,[3] finding a 'Witch living in the Town where he lived.'[4] It is coincidental that Dowsing was conducting his work in the east of England where Hopkins lived and that Dowsing was a farmer. Hopkins worked his trade among the local middle and lower classes, the farmers and peasants: those more paranoid about local Witches and gossip.

19

Furthermore, William Dowsing visited Hopkins's father's old church at Great Wenham in February 1644, one month before Hopkins claimed to have witnessed the first Witches in his town.[5]

It is perhaps not so surprising that the form of religious cleansing conducted by William Dowsing should mutate into Hopkins's work. Hopkins turned Witch-hunting into a work of art. He found more Witches in a shorter time than anybody else and consequently slaughtered more people. To begin with, people believed in his crusade, because it was an extension of Dowsing's work. Hopkins compounded lessons learned from Dowsing with his knowledge of the King James Bible and the excuses/loopholes in the law at that time.[6]

By reading *The Discovery of Witches* we may perceive that Hopkins had some knowledge of law – and a keen perception – but in order to dig deeper, we must explore the possible 'official' capacity of Hopkins's work. If we are using Dowsing as a role model for Hopkins then it would be prudent to understand how a farmer such as Dowsing was 'appointed' to his religious duties and, more importantly, consider whether Hopkins was appointed in a similar way. Was he indeed given the mantle of Witchfinder General rather than appointing himself to the role?

Let us look at Dowsing's appointment and follow Hopkins's providence from there. Briefly, the Parliamentary instruction of 1641, 'Resolution of Ecclesiastical Innovation', was followed in 1643 by another that essentially banished from churches any ornaments, pictures, decorations or inscriptions that were evocative of papal influences. The responsibility of carrying out this work was placed on many people, one of whom was William Dowsing, perhaps the most famous because he kept a diary of his activities.

Dowsing was appointed by Parliament; but what of Hopkins and his activities? In *The Discovery of Witches*, Hopkins mentioned King James's *Daemonologie*. This, coupled with the King James Bible, gave Hopkins a sound learned base for his antics. Hopkins quoted from *Daemonologie*, so we know the source he used as justification for his work; but was that work officially recognised? After a study of *Calendars of State Papers, Domestic 1625–1649*[7] it seems unlikely, but Hopkins didn't need a direct endorsement from the government.

There is an interesting theory connected to the justification of an official endorsement to the 'rank' of Witchfinder General.

In 1645 Parliament granted a special commission of the Oyer and Terminer[8] to monitor the Suffolk Witch-hunt (namely Hopkins's work). Judge John Godbolt (Sergeant-at-Law) presided over the court, which included several Justices of the Peace, along with two respected ministers from Suffolk, Edmund Calamy and Samuel Fairclough.[9]

John Godbolt was MP for Bury St Edmunds and it is possible that Hopkins presented himself to the Judge for official endorsement of his self-appointed title.[10] If the Judge failed to respond, Hopkins could claim that he 'presented the title to Judge Godbolt (the special commission) and met no resistance'. A lavish assumption? Not really, because Hopkins did publicise the title Witchfinder General and would not have left himself open to criticism by personally overblowing his status. There had to be some tenuous providence.

In *The Discovery of Witches*, Hopkins stated: 'The Witchfinder, as they call him . . .' As who call him? Peasants? Farmers? Judges? Maybe the special commission? If indeed Judge Godbolt didn't respond to Hopkins's request but Hopkins used the 'endorsement', then Godbolt was probably embarrassed that he didn't either endorse or refuse the title. Overblown analysis? No. There are certain inconsistencies in the way Hopkins worked in relation to what the commission endorsed, such as the 'swimming test'. This test was unlawful according to the commission, but strangely Hopkins continued to get away with it. Why? Hopkins started off as a celebrity doing good not bad; but surely his high profile wasn't strong enough for such a commission to turn a blind eye?

Admittedly there was something within the commission that Hopkins did abide by and that was 'voluntary confessions of Witchcraft with supporting evidence' and 'compact with the Devil, or upon evidence of the use of Imps'.[11] If one acknowledges that Hopkins obeyed this aspect of the commission's ruling, so for the most part satisfying the priests' criteria, then a decision appertaining to Hopkins's conduct would be escalated to the Judge. It is interesting to note that John Gaule would attack Hopkins through the Judges of the Assizes approximately one year later (1646); and let us not ignore another interesting point here. If Hopkins had been economical with the truth when promoting his 'status' as Witchfinder General, i.e. claiming an endorsement from Godbolt, then perhaps covertly he had lost favour with the Judge. Perhaps Godbolt felt used by Hopkins. Hopkins was certainly unscrupulous but did he dare attempt to manipulate or use people in such a way?

That remains to be seen, but what is known is that Judge Godbolt's commission was not very effective, even though Fairclough (for one) had a very good reputation. However, for them to ignore any bending (or total breaking) of the rules is still hard to believe. Why? Because it would leave such respected men open to criticism themselves. There had to be a reason for their negligence.

Furthermore, 'Sergeant Godcold [Godbolt], Old Calamy and Fairclough',[12] condemned John Lowes on Hopkins's evidence. Did they really want to be seen to be at odds with Hopkins's work after such a high-profile hanging? One would think not. However, Judge Godbolt did warn Hopkins and Stearne, in August 1645, against the practice of swimming without receiving the victim's permission first. Although no further noises were made concerning that, to be fair, they did abandon the test before the end of the year.

The commission did not seem very strict with Hopkins; but Judge Godbolt's sentencing of John Lowes and overall sympathy with the Witchfinder's methods cannot be denied.

What does all this mean? That Hopkins was dealt with delicately by his peers and was very much the right man at the right time to take advantage of the Witchcraft Act. There was also a phoney endorsement of his title of Witchfinder General, and although it ultimately suggested official backing, it was never endorsed by Judge Godbolt or anyone else. However, I'm sure Hopkins would gladly have argued the case if approached, with a horde of villagers (from places he had patronised) calling him such.

Between King James, William Dowsing, local support and tenuous endorsements, Hopkins continued to hunt Witches throughout 1645, 1646 and, for the most part, 1647, so there had to be some kind of authenticity to what he did.

I wish to emphasise the Dowsing connection, because it is no coincidence: Dowsing visited Wenham Magna (Great Wenham), James Hopkins's former parish, on 3 February 1644, a month before Hopkins saw his coven of Witches and was inspired to become a Witchfinder (see *The Discovery of Witches*). Dowsing noted in his diary that 'There was nothing to reform.'[13] However, at Wenham Parva (Little Wenham) later the same day, 'We broke down three superstitious pictures; and gave orders to take down 31, which the church warden promised to do; and to take down a stone cross . . .'

So what picture of Matthew Hopkins do we have thus far? I see an angry young man. An idealist. Cold-hearted and, quite possibly, introverted. Until he found his vocation in life, a vocation that would cost him his life. In his pamphlet *A Confirmation and Discovery of Witchcraft*, John Stearne stated that people who malign Hopkins and himself, do so because they don't know them and their motives. At the end of his pamphlet Stearne stated that he took no bribes during his Witchfinding career and only took what money was owed to him for his work, nothing more.

This raises an interesting point: was Hopkins's (and Stearne's) crusade against Witches truly evil? By today's standards it definitely was but back in the 1640s maybe not so. Hopkins was a Puritan but Stearne (as we can judge through reading his pamphlet in Part Two) was an extreme Puritan with a wife, child and house. I do feel that Stearne believed in what he was doing;[14] while Hopkins began his crusade for nothing short of personal profit.

So the spur for Hopkins to become a Witchfinder was a financial one. If that is true, how did Hopkins turn his money-making idea into reality? Before we explore Hopkins's broader work as a Witchfinder, it is important to analyse the conception of that work.

Let us now go back to Manningtree in the early 1640s and find out.

> In sixteen hundred and forty three,
> William Dowsing came to Badley.
> He did not like what he saw that day,
> So he went to work, then went away.
>
> Anon

FIVE

Witches in the Neighbourhood

But he interrupted me with a savage outburst. 'The People?' he cried. 'What people? There are neither men nor women in that house of Satan's! What? Have you lived here so long, and never heard?'

Robert Louis Stevenson, *Olalla*

So Hopkins found his inspiration for a career as Witchfinder through William Dowsing: to perform an extreme act of brutality with religion as his justification. And this would allow him to make lots of money; his incentive for being such a prolific Witch-hunter.

It is important to be furnished with that information before we analyse Hopkins's career as a Witchfinder from its conception because, most importantly, I believe that Hopkins's only motivation for Witchfinding was financial reward. However, money did not drive John Stearne, nor for that matter did sadism.[1] Stearne believed wholeheartedly in Witchfinding. Furthermore he was conned into joining Hopkins's company by Hopkins himself. Let us now go back and analyse Hopkins work from its beginning.

In his pamphlet *The Discovery of Witches*, Hopkins speaks of a 'horrible sect' of seven or eight Witches living in his home town of Manningtree, who together with other Witches met once every six weeks close to where he lived.

Even though *The Discovery of Witches* is a vital source text for any biographer of Matthew Hopkins, it is accepted that he twisted the story of his crusade to convince people that what he was doing was true and just. However, this text cannot be written off. Perhaps he did (as stated in *The Discovery of Witches*) overhear a woman mumbling something that could be construed as Witchery and with the sudden revelation of knowing what his vocation was going to be, followed the Witch until she met with another; then built his evidence from that meeting and denounced them to the local Magistrate.

This theory is more plausible than it might appear, because all Hopkins could be accused of is being a local citizen doing his duty to his community. When he found that the local Magistrate accepted it, he found more Witches. He then, perhaps, instructed his local friends and acquaintances to find more Witches, and that is when, according to Hopkins's pamphlet, twenty-nine people were condemned 'at once' and another four were brought 25 miles to be hanged at the first Assize. These latter four people are interesting because they had simply conspired against Hopkins's work and had to be quietened (they were possibly relations of a just person he had condemned for Witchcraft!).[2]

This is an important point, because in order to be able to conduct his work, Hopkins would have had some high-ranking support, for example a local Magistrate who thought he had performed a loyal service and perhaps recommended him to another town or village.

There must be a reason why Hopkins was so confident and managed to become so prolific so quickly. Perhaps he was cunning enough to have a Magistrate suggest that he take up Witch-hunting (because he had a natural aptitude for it). Could his mother have endorsed his quest; surely he was doing the Lord's work?

If we use the above as a working hypothesis, we can deduce some important answers concerning Hopkins's style:

1. He built his reputation unofficially in his local town.
2. He brought in accomplices that were like-minded.
3. He obtained an official endorsement for his work (from local

Magistrates) and was recommended to another town (and word of mouth became an important tool).

4. His mother may have praised him for doing the Lord's work.
5. He quickly adopted a mechanism for covering any unjust or unsavoury actions by using supernatural cover stories that condemned the 'guilty'.

This last statement is very important because if we look further into it we deduce that Hopkins was not a deeply religious man himself, otherwise how could he commit such sacrilege (he would have feared God too much if he had religious beliefs). Hopkins simply knew that what he was doing was wrong (there are too many supernatural cover stories in *The Discovery of Witches*, so he could not have believed in the justification of his extreme measures).

We now know how Hopkins became a Witchfinder and consequently how he became so respected so quickly. And if a Magistrate did endorse his work, then word would travel and so would Hopkins.

Although Hopkins conceived his form of Witch-hunting in 1644, it took him approximately a year to plot his work and build up the respect and reputation needed to implement it outside the comfortable parameters of Manningtree.

Now we understand the how and why of Hopkins's campaign against Witches, let us focus on his first victim and ascertain more.

It is Manningtree, 1645. The winter had been long and bleak, especially for the town's tailor John Rivet. His wife had been suffering terrible fits and after confiding in friends Rivet decided that the reason for his wife's ailments was Witchcraft.

The previous summer, Richard Edwards's son died after a series of fits. Edwards was a respected local man, a staunch Puritan and, when his tragic loss was analysed alongside the death of Henry Woolvett's young daughter, a pattern emerged.

Rivet could clearly see the same pattern and consulted a 'cunning' (wise) woman 8 miles away in Hadleigh, who informed him that two women conspired against his wife. She did not name the two women, but Rivet believed them to be Anne West and a toothless 80-year-old one-legged woman known locally as 'Mother [Elizabeth] Clarke'. Why did Rivet suspect Clarke? Simply because she had a reputation of being an evil woman whose mother had been executed for Witchcraft.

Rivet, wracked with concern for his wife, spread his rumours about the two women and, because her symptoms were similar to those of the poor children who had died the previous year, the word spread that Witchcraft was being practised.

Matthew Hopkins, a respected local figure, quickly cried 'Witch', and in March 1645 started to work his trade as Witchfinder.

It is interesting to note here that at the Lent Assizes at Chelmsford in 1641, Anne West 'the elder of Lawford' had been accused of using Witchcraft against a man's (Thomas Hart) sow. Due to lack of evidence she was eventually acquitted (see Jail Delivery Roll for 6 August 1641), but would she be so lucky the next time?

Hopkins was determined to convict both Clarke and West of Witchcraft, and found that since the acquittal a feud had broken out between the Hart family and Anne West, and Anne's daughter Rebecca. Hopkins tried to build up a case against Anne and Rebecca but the evidence was scant. But he secured a confession from Rebecca. This was done by compiling evidence from locals and twisting what the accused women said. John Edes (possibly one of Hopkins's associates) testified that: 'a few weeks since she [had] confessed familiarity with the Devil in the likeness of a young man, he promising [Rebecca] her revenge and all her desires if she would deny God and wholly trust in him. Having requested the Devil to revenge her on John Start [Hart], who lived in the same house, he sickened and died and she then thought that [the Devil] could do like God.'[3]

Hopkins wanted Rebecca to denounce her mother and he visited her on a number of occasions over March and April 1645 to achieve this. Was that the only reason for Hopkins's visit? Maybe not.

The beginning of Hopkins's work as Witchfinder is quite well documented and, on the face of it, largely taken for granted. What I find most extraordinary about the story, especially in the early stages, is Rebecca West's role. I use the word 'role' quite deliberately, because if it wasn't for her denouncing her own mother as one of five Witches (with Elizabeth Clarke as the ringleader), Hopkins job would have been much more difficult. He needed a little bit of luck in order to get his Witch-hunting antics up and running, and what more could he want than a girl confirming his 'fears', confessing to Witchcraft and castigating her mother and another already suspected of the crime. This was an incredible turn of events for its day. But what's more, when the women were brought to trial, Rebecca West was acquitted.

And there lies the rub. Why? Hopkins would have been exclusively involved in that acquittal. As a staunch, respected member of the Manningtree community, his voice counted. So why did Hopkins spare Rebecca West? Looking at his career as Witchfinder as a whole, there are far too few acquittals, most of which are not necessarily linked with Hopkins himself. I believe the young Matthew Hopkins found the 15-year-old Rebecca West open to seduction, and so he was instrumental in saving her life if she did his bidding.

If we look closely at her confession, there are many clues as to the circumstances of what happened. A Gentleman is mentioned in West's confession; could this be Matthew Hopkins? If Hopkins confronted Rebecca West several times while she resided in Colchester Castle, then it strongly suggests that for the return of certain favours, Hopkins would spare her. The applicable segment of the confession follows:

> And being asked by the Judge whether she ever had carnal copulation with the Devil, she confessed that she had. And being asked diverse questions by a Gentleman that did speak several times with her before and afterward (giving her godly and comfortable instructions) she affirmed that so soon as one of the said Witches was in prison, she was very desirous to confess all she knew, which accordingly she did, whereupon the rest were apprehended and sent unto the Jail. She further affirmed, that when she was going to the Grand Inquest with one mother Miller (indicted for a Witch) she told mother Miller that she would

confess nothing, if they pulled her to pieces with pincers: and being asked the reason by the Gentleman, she said she found herself in such extremity of torture and amazement, that she would not endure it again for the world: and when she looked upon the ground she saw herself encompassed in flames of fire: and presently the Grand Inquest called for her, where they admit but one at a time, and so soon as she was thus separated from this mother Miller, the tortures and the flames began to cease: whereupon she then confessed all she ever knew, and said that so soon as her confession was fully ended, she found her conscience so satisfied and disburdened of all her tortures, that she thought herself the happiest creature in the world: withal affirming that the Devil can take any shape, and speak plain English.[4]

When one reads the whole of Rebecca West's confession it is fantastic to believe that she escaped the noose. But she did, as John Stearne complained: 'I saw . . . one of the greatest agents in Colchester business . . . labour and endeavour all he could to keep this woman whom he so much held withal from her legal trial, and likewise heard him threaten both me and all that had been given against her, or informed what manner of woman she had been in her life and conversation, to their knowledge, or as they had heard: yes, as I since have heard she was condemned at that Assize and by his procurement reprieved. Since which time, on her behalf, this has been done.'

To me 'one of the greatest *agents in Colchester* [my italics]' was Matthew Hopkins (although through *his* agent as I shall explain presently). So there he was, battling to save Rebecca West's life, while condemning her mother and her acquaintances. It doesn't matter whether his intentions were noble or not, Hopkins's credibility would have been enhanced by showing compassion to this young girl, because he brought her to justice in the first place and extracted the confessions from her. He was unquestionably a most noble gentleman for doing such a thing.[5] And note Stearne's words too: 'threaten both me and all that had been given against her . . .' Where is Hopkins mentioned? He isn't, but then again Stearne's pamphlet has little pockets of self-glorification.

Another interesting point is raised in John Stearne's pamphlet. When he describes Rebecca's Imps entering the room (while he and other witnesses watched and extracted her confession to Witchcraft), he mentions one that looked like a greyhound.[6] There is evidence to suggest that in 1645 Hopkins kept a greyhound.[7] I always found Hopkins's 'pet' a little odd as it left him open to the possibility of having Imps himself. But only one document seems to relate to Hopkins's greyhound. Could this be because he didn't have it for long and that it was probably acquired for the purpose of becoming Rebecca West's Imp in a theatrical show of 'Witchcraft', which, when one reads John Stearne's description of West's Imps presenting themselves, was laid on to convince Stearne (an extreme Puritan) that the Devil's work was occurring in the real world? This is feasible, because Hopkins had a motive: he wanted his new acquaintance John Stearne to accompany him in pursuit of Witches, to lend more authenticity to his work. But why? Because Hopkins had been working for a year on launching his crusade, and was possibly failing miserably. Hence the theatrical show.

Stearne did not know Hopkins that well at the time; he called him one of the 'greatest agents of Colchester' because that was where Hopkins was when called upon:[8] visiting Rebecca West in Colchester Castle. He would have mentioned this in his diary (which we will discuss later) and that is how he would present it in his pamphlet in 1648.

So Stearne was duped by Hopkins and Rebecca West. And the success of this hoax started England's greatest Witch-hunt, because after the initial prosecution of the five Witches the floodgates opened and Hopkins began his crusade against Witches across the eastern counties.

Further evidence can be obtained by reading and understanding the undertone of both Hopkins's and Stearne's pamphlets. Hopkins is clearly being manipulative and economical with the truth in his pamphlet (see Part Two for a further analysis), while Stearne (see Part Two for transcript and analysis) leans heavily on scripture and justifies his actions through the words of God. Where is God in Hopkins's work?

Stearne also documented the people he had met and accused of Witchcraft. His condemnation of 'the reader' who passes judgement on both himself and Hopkins is done overtly with nothing to hide. After reading Stearne's pamphlet one must conclude that he was either an extreme Puritan who believed in what he was doing, or he was a highly dangerous criminal. After reading everything connected with John Stearne and his part in the Witch-hunts I opt for the former rather than latter conclusion. He was a family man with a home he never strayed too far from while working; conversely, Hopkins would travel further away from his home, in both the dark biting winter of 1644–5 and the snow of 1645–6.

But going back to the key figure of Rebecca West: why was she never tortured? Why she was never 'swum'? Why did Hopkins visit her in prison so often? Was he taking food to her? Was he reassuring her? Did he make love to her? His treatment of Rebecca West is completely different to that of other so-called Witches; was it because she was terribly young? There are so many threads hanging from the Rebecca West story that when one begins to tie them up the only coherent conclusion that can be arrived at is that Hopkins was seducing her. And when her work was over, Hopkins discarded her.

Surely Rebecca was taking a huge risk? Maybe not. Hopkins had a rudimentary knowledge of the law. He knew that if Rebecca acted as an informer for the Crown – against the other accused – she would escape the noose. It must have sounded a simple plan to the young Rebecca, but her naivety vanished on her acquittal and she disappears off the map of history, never to return into Hopkins's life.

This, in itself, is interesting because it suggests that maybe Rebecca left Essex because of broken promises from Hopkins. Did Hopkins agree to save Rebecca's mother? We don't know, but her mother was executed in May 1645 for Witchcraft.

The truth may be more revealing than that. I believe that Rebecca was horrified at the living conditions in Colchester Castle, the urine, excreta, the beatings and torture, the vermin, death and disease. She may have threatened Hopkins that she would turn on him unless she was released immediately.

How long was Rebecca in prison? There is evidence to suggest that she was imprisoned in early March and then examined in Manningtree on 21 March 1645. Hopkins stated in his pamphlet that he interrogated Rebecca (and five others) in Colchester on 18 April. The Assizes were not until July, but she was acquitted, so she was imprisoned for at least two and a half months, a long time to suffer such conditions, especially for a girl of 15. Surely, it is something more than love that makes someone endure this. All this is however complete conjecture, but it does stand to highlight one of the most important parts of Hopkins's crusade: its conception through the confession of a woman who showed her Imps, admitted sleeping with the Devil, avoided torture and punishment, and then was acquitted and disappeared.

What we do know is that Matthew Hopkins was a shrewd man; he most definitely conned John Stearne into joining him (but the price was too high for Rebecca West). He was on his way. The quest he had planned for almost a year, culminating with the first Assizes, had given him the stamp of official recognition, something he could use as a badge of respect. The acquittal itself was an example of compassion or fair play to a young girl who was clearly corrupted by her mother into practising Witchcraft.

As I make some rather large assumptions in this chapter, which have a bearing on the rest of the book and therefore the path of Matthew Hopkins's life, it is important to look closely at the providence for my claim of a 'relationship' between Matthew Hopkins and Rebecca West.

Should one use the words of John Stearne as evidence? Why not? However, in his book *Witch Finder General*, Richard Deacon quoted from a supposed unpublished document entitled the *Tendring Witchcraft Revelations*. Unfortunately, the document has not come to light since Deacon's book and, indeed, Malcolm Gaskill accuses Deacon of an elaborate hoax concerning the document. However, one passage from Deacon's book purporting to be from the Tendring document falls in line too nicely with one of my theories. The quotation runs thus: 'Master Stearne had many words to say a little and in doing so misled his readers. The Colchester business he speaks of was moreover but an oblique manner of name [*sic*] a group of Royalists intent on protecting those of their agents persecuted or prosecuted by Hopkins and Stearne as Witches. Thurlowe once again had a lawyer's hand in all this as indeed did he with so many imbroglios of this time in Essex long before he was appointed Argus Number One.'

On the face of it this doesn't appear to help my argument, because it seems to discredit my main source documentation. In fact it does not. Hopkins needed official blessing to get Rebecca West acquitted. He never liked the blame to be apportioned to him (which is why there were always other witnesses to his work as Witchfinder). Thurlowe was an acquaintance of Hopkins from late 1644 to early 1645, while using the Thorn Inn in Mistley. The time was perfect for Hopkins, West and Thurlowe to stage a show of Witchcraft.

It is possible that Thurlowe knew Hopkins before 1644. There is no sure evidence but if Hopkins did study law in Britain as some have suggested, then they could have studied together. Also of interest, Thurlowe was Cromwell's head of the Secret Service; so there is suddenly a suggestion of covert schemes, especially with the mention of Royalists being condemned for Witchcraft.

Furthermore, in the same document it is noted that Hopkins had, 'an intimate knowledge of the Rosicrucian Cipher'. This cipher was used by parliamentary spies and Thurlowe would have been acquainted with it; but why would Hopkins, if he had no official backing?

The evidence of the Tendring document, if true, adds a layer of conspiracy that makes a lot of sense. The very idea of a liaison between Hopkins and Thurlowe conjures ideas of using Witchfinding as an excuse to cleanse Cromwell's England of Royalist agents.

So let us indulge that theory for a moment, look more deeply into the friendship of Hopkins and Thurlowe, also consider the use of the cipher. Hopkins and Thurlowe would plot their schemes during meetings at the Thorn Inn (see Chapter Seven). According to local legend, Hopkins had an office on the first floor. Could this have been his office as a shipping clerk? Unlikely, but the idea of a private place for Hopkins and his Company to talk in a local inn seems logical. And the cipher? While searching for Witches, Hopkins's Company would write the code on a building or tree in a village to leave vital intelligence for Hopkins and Stearne concerning local Witches.

All of this suggests a more covert operation which may have been in sympathy for Cromwell, as we shall explore in more depth later. Also, the code was unknown to Royalists, thus enhancing the possibility of an unofficial Parliamentary crusade and an unofficial endorsement of the supposed self-appointed Witchfinder General.

If we look at what people were saying at the time of Hopkins's first Assize, the above hypothesis is confirmed: 'Some of them [Witches] confessed they had been in the King's army . . . His Majesties army it seems beholding to the Devil; you may be sure it is just cause where the Devil takes part . . .'[9]

Does all this validate the Tendring document? Whether Deacon invented the document or not, it does prove one thing: his research and theories appertaining to Matthew Hopkins were taking him in the same general direction as mine have. Also, and most importantly, other source documentation, which I have incorporated above, suggests the same thing.

I wish to emphasise this point, because it is important to ask how Hopkins got away with hanging Witches while apparently breaking the law (by using illegal methods) for two and a half years. The answer is official backing, albeit covert.

So now we know whose side Hopkins was on and actively so. We also know what skulduggery he employed to coerce Stearne to join him and authenticate his Witchfinding tactics through eyewitnesses. Things were about to take off on a grand scale.

And he went out from thence, and came into his own country; and his disciples follow him.

Mark 6, King James Bible

SIX

The Witchfinder and his Accomplices

> A wonderful fact to reflect upon, that every human creature is
> constituted to be that profound secret and mystery to every other.
>
> Charles Dickens, *A Tale of Two Cities*

This chapter is probably the most pivotal in the book, because in
my opinion the source material appertaining to it has never
been studied correctly before. There are hidden secrets still to
discover about Hopkins's life story, if one cares to look deep enough
and if one is able to extract the relevant material.

While researching this book, I kept returning to the simple question:
why? Not just why did Hopkins get away with it? But why was he not
stopped? Why was he accepted wherever he went (until the Revd John
Gaule took the faith and rose up against him)? The answers are quite
simple if we accept that Hopkins had a powerful group of men
supporting him. Not just 'officials', but a hand-picked body of men
and women – a Company – who rode with him from place to place.

I suggested in the Introduction that the Peter Cushing movie
Twins of Evil was a close interpretation of the character of Matthew
Hopkins. Now it is important to qualify that bold statement. The
religious mania displayed by Cushing in the movie, and that of his
Company, provided the excuse for the atrocities perpetrated. And
that is exactly how Hopkins qualified his actions, through religious
beliefs. John Stearne's pamphlet (reproduced in Part Two) shows

clearly the boiling Puritan blood bursting from every page. Stearne was the adrenalin of Hopkins – but not the greed. This is important because a character by the name of Edward Purley is deemed to have been Hopkins's number-one accomplice before Stearne, and perhaps a lack of supporting passion from Purley was the reason why Hopkins's Witch-hunt did not start in 1644.

Let us look closely at the evidence concerning Hopkins 'Company', because this evidence has never been analysed before. Starting with Hopkins's own pamphlet, *The Discovery of Witches* shows the path of time and the consequences of Hopkins's fall from favour. Near the beginning of the document (query 4) Hopkins states that ten people were in the room while a confession was being sought from an assumed Witch. At the end of the document he states that his fees were simply to 'maintain his company with three horses'. Note his word 'company'. Taking this literally, Hopkins went from a large Company to just a trio over the course of his Witchfinding career.

Is this correct? Did Hopkins ride with ten accomplices to begin with? He certainly rode with three, and as his pamphlet stated in the answer to query 5: 'any man tried by search of his body, but commonly a dozen of the ablest men in the parish or else where, were present, and most commonly as many ancient skilful Matrons and Midwives present when the women are tried.' This statement makes things clearer, as Hopkins acknowledged that he called upon local people to assist him: people who spread gossip, who had an axe to grind with a certain 'Witch'. Obviously, Hopkins couldn't finance a large regular Company, so how does the Company theory work? Did three people call upon ten to a dozen others to assist with their work? In his pamphlet, Hopkins mentions specific jobs within his 'Company': Matrons/Midwives, Watchers, Walkers, Swimmers and, although he wouldn't admit it, Torturers. Hopkins must have had a loyal band of people he could call upon for this work, otherwise he wouldn't state: 'any man else may find them as well as he and his Company, if they had the same skill and experience'.[1]

Hopkins had to show he had the skills to carry out his work, so he had to have learned people to hand; or, as he calls them, his

'Company'. The obvious deputies in the Company were John Stearne and Mary Phillips but there were others: Edward Purley (still?), Pricilla Briggs and Frances Milles, Elizabeth Hunt; these we know of. These accomplices would lead 'Torture' and 'Matron' duties and silence any subordinates if anything untoward occurred (such as bribing confessions from the victims). Also, the leaders within the Company were needed in order to add professional authenticity to Hopkins's claims. Lesser accomplices would do the dirty work and be called upon like loyal soldiers. It is because of this code of seniority in the Company that other members were not named: they were simply workers. But what if those workers turned upon Matthew Hopkins? This will be addressed later.

Looking at the mechanics of Witchfinding, trusted accomplices *had* to oversee the confessions, because if the accused had to be kept from sleep for two or three days, shiftwork had to be applied and somebody with authority was needed to preside over the proceedings. It is difficult to believe that Hopkins and Stearne would do this themselves. In his pamphlet Stearne admits as much.

It should also be remembered that William Dowsing had people who rode with him; further proof that Hopkins did indeed copy Dowsing's style to begin with. He then sought official endorsement, like Dowsing. Although he was indeed recognised, he was never commissioned Witchfinder General.[2] Here, Hopkins got it the wrong way round. While Dowsing was appointed to his duties and then carried them out, Hopkins appointed himself, set to work and then sought endorsement. Unfortunately for Hopkins, this was part of his downfall.

When we read Stearne's pamphlet we find that he received the warrant to arrest Elizabeth Clarke for Witchcraft and Matthew Hopkins accompanied him. Knowing what we do of Hopkins and Stearne's position in the proceedings, I cannot accept that as truth. Obviously, Stearne could say what he wanted in his pamphlet as Hopkins was dead at the time of writing, and I do feel that he gave himself a grander – although moderately so – position in the proceedings. He does admit to not being present at the confession of Elizabeth Clarke (and the Watching). Edward Purley was Stearne's predecessor so was very much a part of the Elizabeth Clarke confession. Stearne quickly became involved and, strangely, Pricilla Briggs, who inspected Clarke, seems to have been pushed out at the same time and replaced by Mary Phillips.[3] Indeed, the three (Hopkins, Stearne and Phillips) would become known as 'the three unspotted Lambs of the Lord'. Stearne and Phillips are the two other 'horses' in his Company mentioned at the end of his pamphlet, but we know of three other named accomplices – Edward Purley, Frances Milles and Pricilla Briggs (see Dramatis Personae) – proof of others who could be called upon and who, quite possibly, might be angry at missing out on some of the bounty towards the end.

Stearne's writing should be treated with some caution. Many people believe his words but I don't accept everything he put down in his pamphlet. Hopkins was the schemer; if it wasn't for him, Stearne would not have become a Witchfinder. He clearly jumped on the bandwagon, albeit very early on, but he was a local man, a family man too, so his authority and strength of character became an asset to Hopkins. Why? Because although Hopkins was a schemer, he was of a weak disposition. He was slight of build and prone to chest infections. A basic analogy would be to say that Stearne was the muscle. When Hopkins's Witchfinding days were over and he and Stearne parted company, he was almost certainly lynched, and he was lynched because he didn't have Stearne to protect him – or his diminished Company.

There was reason and structure behind Hopkins's Company. He formed it and Stearne (and Phillips) came in and tweaked it. They were a brilliant double act. Matthew Hopkins was a cunning man. He plotted carefully, took advice from people like Thurlowe and then implemented his plans as systematically as a well-trained soldier. But the trouble with any large group of people who form a Company with one clear ideology is, they will also develop tensions, have issues among themselves or with their peers, and this would prove to be a chink in the armour of Matthew Hopkins.

The parties so judging can justify their skill to any, and show good reasons why such marks are not merely natural.

Matthew Hopkins, *The Discovery of Witches*

SEVEN

Matthew Hopkins – Witchfinder General

It appears that God hath appointed (for a supernatural sign of the monstrous impiety of the Witches) that the water shall refuse to receive them in her bosom, that [it] has shaken off them the sacred Water of Baptism, and wilful[ly] refused the benefit of [it].

King James I, *Daemonologie*

So there was structure and calculating menace to Matthew Hopkins's crusade. He needed a loyal team, people who could temper the Sticklers[1] and work the long shifts he wasn't prepared to do himself. But what was the significance of the Thorn Inn?

The Thorn Inn was yards from his alleged house at The Green, Mistley, and where he possibly had an office. Although the current building only dates back to the eighteenth century,[2] there has been a Thorn Inn on the site since the 1500s. It is a local landmark. Here Hopkins held court, took in the idle talk and formulated plans, and from this a loyal 'Company' was formed. Richard Deacon's *Tendring Witchcraft Revelations* states: '[at] the Thorn also there came such celebrated persons as the Number One Argus, John Thurlowe and William Lilly, the astrological prophet and almanacker.' Hopkins clearly had influential friends and, as we will see in relation to Oliver Cromwell, there are sound arguments to support this.

Let us then learn a little more about the two gentlemen mentioned in the Tendring document. John Thurlowe was the son of Thomas

Thurlowe, an Essex rector. He studied law at a young age and could quite feasibly have studied with Hopkins whereupon they forged a friendship. As Number One Argus, Thurlowe was also Cromwell's Chief of Secret Service. In 1645 he was approved as one of the secretaries to the commissions of Parliament at the Treaty of Uxbridge.

By 1645, William Lilly was one of the country's leading astrologers. He had well-placed friends within the aristocracy and was an incredibly influential man who nearly came unstuck when he predicted the Great Fire of London so accurately he was suspected of starting it. He was later acquitted of the charge. Interestingly, William Lilly published his first *Almanack* in 1644, which does suggest that Hopkins could have been introduced to Lilly's work by reading the bestselling publication. As the Civil War continued, Lilly was consulted by Parliamentary forces and used as an Intelligence Officer. However, some people believe that he was a double agent working for both Puritan and Loyalist. Indeed, this idea does hold some weight when we realise that his clients were the wealthy (and the aristocracy), a group of people with different beliefs. His astrology predictions were published in newspapers from the outset of the Civil War and in order to be accessible to both camps Lilly exercised a diplomacy akin to Hopkins in the way he spoke to anyone in authority: graciously.

What I find most relevant about Lilly from the point of view of a biographer of Hopkins is Lilly's secret association with Parliamentarians. This brings Lilly and Thurlowe together. But then there is the darker side of Lilly's association with Hopkins. Hopkins had to be more aware of the occult, and that could only come through Lilly. In his novel *Witchfinder General*, Ronald Bassett got the balance right when Hopkins speaks to a magistrate concerning his experience: 'You will understand sirs, that any practical inquiry into occult matters requires gravity and sincerity, probity and impartial spirit – these in addition to an intensive legal training.' Hopkins wanted to authenticate every aspect of his work as Witchfinder. In so doing, his critics could be answered. However, in practice, it didn't quite work out that way.

Looking broadly at the two respected gentlemen possibly advising Hopkins on political and astrological data, we begin to see from where Hopkins gathered his expert skills and, also, the authority behind them.

In his study of Matthew Hopkins (sub-headed *A Study of Master Matthew Hopkins commonly call'd Witchfinder General*), the Reverend Montague Summers stated that Hopkins was not acquainted with the scholarly works of the great demonologists, such as Bodin, Grilland, Godelman, Boguet, Remy, Guazzo 'and the rest'. Summers also stated that Hopkins was not familiar with the *Malleus Maleficarum* ('the supreme authority' of demonology).

Summers knew this because he had studied the historical works himself, but the subtle point he missed is that Hopkins relied upon Lilly to fill that gap in his knowledge. Lilly wasn't there simply to tell Hopkins the current political situation or future astrological reasoning, he was there as a scholar of some note who could advise Hopkins on the occult, in an official sense. Lilly was known as the Merlin of his day, and part of Hopkins's downfall was probably not listening to the minutiae of what Lilly said. Summers instantly identified Hopkins's lack of knowledge but failed to realise that he was relying upon somebody else to furnish that knowledge, but when he became too 'powerful' he ignored Lilly (who seems to disappear from Hopkins's life after a while). However, what Summers did get right, and which has seldom been said before, is that Hopkins was very familiar with Richard Bernard's *Guide to Grand Jurymen* (1627), having read it during his professional (legal?) training. One could argue that Hopkins was not 'legally' trained, but I strongly suggest that the writing is his pamphlet *The Discovery of Witches* reflects a legally trained mind and that he did undertake some study. In simple terms, Hopkins was an expert in the legal system with regard to Witches, and Lilly was an expert of the occult and astrology. This is further evidence of job distinction within Hopkins's Company or among those whose skills and services were called upon.[3]

Looking deeper into the Thorn Inn meetings, we can see that Hopkins was building a foundation of providence for his prolific Witch-hunt. With Hopkins's Company (and their associates) we have a group of experts who could be called upon for whatever occasion presented itself. The meetings at the Thorn Inn were the life's blood of Hopkins's plans. He would assemble all the people he needed, hear the rumours, requests, superstitions, and then lay down a course of action. The Inn was a think-tank for plans to be made. The fact that there seems to be no surviving documentation from the Thorn Inn meetings suggests that there was little structure to the proceedings. The Inn was where Hopkins held court and gathered the knowledge he needed to conduct his work, but nothing was written down that could be used as evidence against him at a later stage.[4]

So was this Hopkins's tried and tested way of conducting his trade? Not quite. According to local Manningtree gossip – up to today – Hopkins held his early meetings at The White Hart in Manningtree High Street and procured his confessions in the extensive cargo cellars that ran the length of Manningtree, which, interestingly, were originally for holding goods for shipping.

It could be suggested that Hopkins's more secretive meetings (with the gentry) were held in Mistley (at the Thorn Inn), with people like Thurlowe and Lilly (who wanted to keep the blood off their hands), while the more public meetings were held at The White Hart in Manningtree with his Company. It was Manningtree shipping cellars that provided him with a dungeon to carry out initial questioning of suspected Witches, and some Witches were hanged in Manningtree in August 1645 after the first Assize next to The White Hart, halfway up a hill, so again, there is evidence to bring the location into the story.

So we know how Hopkins developed the idea of Witchfinding (on his own grand scale), how he surrounded himself with a loyal and impressive Company, how he organised his plotting and built his increasing reputation as an authentic Witchfinder – the Witchfinder General. Once these things were firmly in place, it was time to search for Witches beyond Manningtree. There was much work to be done.

Hopkins was, so to speak, a mere quack; a mountebank. He had neither the training nor the knowledge to deal with the hideous anarchy of Witchcraft; his motive was vilest lust for gains, and this swept both innocent and guilty alike into his net.
The Revd Montague Summers, *The Discovery of Witches – A Study of Master Matthew Hopkins commonly call'd Witchfinder General*

EIGHT

The Witchcraft Trials

> Aldeburgh and Stowmarket were behind them. The first they had
> visited three times, in September, December, and finally in January
> of the new year, reappearing on each occasion without warning,
> questioning, prying, accusing, until the fishing-folk and weavers
> of the small town and its adjacent hamlets walked in terror.
>
> Ronald Bassett, *Witchfinder General*

Why write a biography of a man such as Matthew Hopkins?
What do we get from the analysis today? Taking the second
question first, we get a picture of a manipulative underachiever. A
man who almost single-handedly murdered more than 200 people
on a charge of Witchcraft, no longer accepted today as the reality it
was during the Civil War.

In answering the first question, Matthew Hopkins is the sore
thumb in the history of British Witchcraft. He employed different
tactics to his predecessors, he hanged more people in a shorter space
of time and his notoriety – but obscurity – has attracted many
people to his legend. So it is right that we examine this man and try
to separate the fact from the fiction.

In order to do this, we must now look more closely at the
Witchcraft trials perpetrated by Hopkins, in order to get a picture of
the effect and impact his trials had upon the British Witchcraft circuit.
For a detailed account of the personalities accused, how confessions

were obtained, the various acts of torture and an 'authentic' list of victims (those who died and those who were acquitted), I refer the reader to Part Two which contains the source documentation.

Matthew Hopkins, according to his own pamphlet, decided that he would become a Witchfinder in March 1644. The first victim was Elizabeth Clarke, an elderly one-legged widow, whom Hopkins reported to the authorities. The woman was 'apprehended and searched by women who had for many years known the Devil's marks, and found to have teats about her, which honest women have not'. These 'learned' women would become allies of Hopkins in his wide-reaching search for Witches. In March 1645, Clarke confessed to Witchcraft after being kept awake at night (a process called 'Watching'). After this confession, her so-called associates from her 'coven' were rounded up, underwent a similar process of Watching and, on confession, were thrown into gaol. In July and August 1645, the first group of Witches were tried at the Assizes. later in the year, Hopkins and his now credible Company had crossed into Suffolk where at least 117 Witches were examined or tried before the end of the year. That is a lot of work in a short space of time, bearing in mind that confessions had to be obtained, the Witches imprisoned and then brought to trial.

During 1646, Hopkins and Stearne gained a heady reputation, and the successful accusation and subsequent trial of Witches began to increase further. They travelled into Huntingdonshire, Cambridgeshire, Northamptonshire, Bedfordshire and Norfolk. In total, nearly 250 Witches were investigated in the east of England during Hopkins's two-and-a-half-year reign, and it is largely believed that at least 75 per cent of them were hanged for the crime. Although begun by Matthew Hopkins, John Stearne finished the campaign when Hopkins fell ill in mid-1647. This whole sad episode is known as the 'East Anglian Witchcraft Trials' and is widely accepted as the most serious outbreak of Witch-hunting in British history.

Religion is blamed for this outbreak, and Hopkins, a Puritan, as the mastermind. However, I prefer to look upon Matthew Hopkins as an atheist (see Part Two for further analysis) who allowed John

Stearne – an extreme Puritan – to justify the antics of the Company through *his* Puritan beliefs. Indeed, the Oyer and Terminer (Judge Godbolt along with Fairclough and Calumy) were Puritans and Hopkins would make Stearne play to that audience. However, it was the Protestant John Gaule who would preach against Hopkins (after the successful trial and execution of Vicar John Lowes) and hasten his downfall.

The 'disease' of Witchcraft was not endemic in Hopkins's day. During the Civil War, the east of England had by far the largest number of supposed Witches, not because more Witches lived there but because Matthew Hopkins with his individual and perverse imagination lived there. An analysis of Witchcraft in Britain during the sixteenth and seventeenth centuries reveals a distinct decline in Witch trials running up to the East Anglian Witchcraft Trials, so logically, Matthew Hopkins can be held completely responsible for them.

With this in mind, what route did Hopkins and his Company take to round up his Witches and how did he split the 'team'? The Witches captured by Hopkins's Company came from small villages such as Lawford, Chattisham and Brandeston, rather than towns such as Norwich or Ipswich. This may provide clues as to how Hopkins planned his route, especially to begin with. He had to build up his reputation by playing the small arenas first; he would then build up to larger theatres as time went on. Unfortunately for him, he eventually became too unwell (as a result of the harsh winters of 1645–6 and 1646–7) and met too much opposition to venture into towns.

By analysing the gaol Calendar and Delivery Roll (plus *A True and Exact Relation* and *A Confirmation and Discovery of Witchcraft*), a picture of the accused and their homesteads emerges. We can tell from the first Assizes on 29 July 1645 that Hopkins and his Company first travelled south into Essex, to Ramsey, Thorpe-le-Soken, Kirby-le-Soken, Walton-le-Soken, Great Holland, Great Clacton, St Osyth, Alresford, Wivenhoe, Langham and back to Mistley via Manningtree. This is a very telling tour. The places are in a horseshoe arc from Mistley to Langham, following the coast as far as Great Clacton and then rising up past Colchester via Langham to Manningtree and home. The route is too contrived not to have been planned, probably at the Thorn Inn. The victims would be held in their local town of Colchester while awaiting trial, and once that had been successfully completed (July and August 1645), Hopkins would move on to pastures new.

The Suffolk trials took a route that followed another, more circular, arc from across the Stour: Polstead, Sudbury, Lavenham, Hitcham, Rattlesden, Wetherden, Westhorpe, Bacton, Framlingham, Linstead, Halesworth, Glemham, Blaxhall, Wickham, Creeting, Stowmarket, Hintlesham, Chattisham, Copdock . . . (see Appendix Three for full listing). The one thing that becomes apparent from this list is that although an arc is followed again (leading across the Stour and west, then returning comfortably inland away from any land breaks), the route seems a little more haphazard. This is because Hopkins and Stearne split the county into two, Hopkins taking a western path, while Stearne took an eastern path (and remained in close proximity to his family at all times). This particular campaign probably started in July 1645, shortly after the Assizes, or maybe August. Again, this was probably planned at the Thorn Inn but endorsed by a higher authority, possibly through the Assizes. For Hopkins and Stearne not to be arrested as spies in the various locations they needed some kind of official endorsement. As their work seemed to pass without a hitch, one can conclude that the endorsement was impressive.

The work continued even further away from home in September to December 1645, taking in King's Lynn and Yarmouth for the Norfolk trials (bad weather hindered Hopkins's fragile frame). Huntingdonshire followed in April/May 1646. In 1647 the Fens were chartered but due to Hopkins's waning health Stearne took over the commission.

The Company covered much ground between mid-1645 and mid-1647. Two years of trekking and on average 100-plus people tried and executed each year. The Company travelled by horseback by invitation or via some other (higher?) commission. The self-belief of the Witchfinders appears staggering today, especially if Hopkins suffered from weak lungs. The bitter winters and generally damp conditions did not help his health but continue he did until at least the middle of 1647, the year his pamphlet was published (to answer his critics), and the year of his young death.

What do Hopkins's travels tell us?

1. He was single-minded.
2. He had great and powerful friends in order to influence so many local Magistrates and Sticklers and not be accused of spying.
3. He had – at least until the tide turned against him – a loyal Company to assist in the persecution of Witches.
4. His influencing skills and arguments held depth; he was very perceptive and convincing.
5. His 'official' endorsement was rated highly and he must have been recommended by one village to another on occasion.

We can get a more personal picture of Matthew Hopkins by observing his travels and how the various campaigns were split up and planned. To examine here the various accusations and Witches found would detract from the importance of Hopkins's travels. We must see the man who plotted this work in order to draw a larger picture of him.

The personality would be cool, perhaps even charming. Methodical and persuasive. He was from a good family, well educated and that brought a great deal of local respect. So he was self-assured. He was short to medium height, slight of frame, with possibly fair or blond wavy hair and a beard that circled his mouth and peaked at the chin but did not extend up the face to his hairline. He wore extravagant clothes. A seventeenth-century engraving shows him wearing a three-quarter-length cloak, shirt and high-buttoned waistcoat, with tall bucket boots and spurs. A wide-brimmed hat may have shaded his eyes. He also carried a tall staff. He was most definitely right-handed, although in two different illustrations his left hand is seen in a raised manner, which gives a sense of self-consciousness, possibly even conceit. He was concerned about his clothes not being soiled or out of place, thus exerting superiority over his lower-class quarry.

This is the best image we have of Matthew Hopkins against the backdrop of his crusade against Witches. And it is enough. The temerity of his trek, the organisation of his Company, the professionalism of the legal aspect to the work give us a very clear picture of this manipulative man and how he built such a weighty argument against Witches in the eyes of the law.

Beyond Holton St Mary, Hopkins shaded his eyes and started across the green countryside that fell away to the eastward, where he could just see the small clutter of rooftops he knew to be Wenham – his birthplace – but he neither paused nor made comment, and the small cavalcade passed on.

Ronald Bassett, *Witchfinder General*

NINE

Wandering with the Witchfinder

I intend to give your town a visit suddenly.

From a letter written by Matthew Hopkins

In order to provide an authentic account of Hopkins's work as a Witchfinder, one must examine the methods he used, and also the 'authentic' texts and how he interpreted them.

When Hopkins started his campaign in Essex and Suffolk, he did so in his local area, listening to local gossip and assisting (exploiting?) those who bore a grudge against their neighbours. His Company – and also Stearne and himself – would hear the local gossip and then set to work, approaching the 'Witches' and directly confronting them about their Covenant with the Devil. To begin with, the suspected Witches were examined by the Midwives and Matrons in the Company. If 'teats' were found for Familiars/Imps to suckle upon then the accused was certainly a Witch and would be Watched by Hopkins's people. More often than not, Imps would come into the room at some stage, probably an insect that crept under the door or a pet cat or dog, it didn't really matter what. With the aid of sleep deprivation (for up to three or four days) and Pricking by Torturers, the Witch would make a confession. Most of these confessions would be denied once in court (for example John Lowes), but by then their Imps had been seen by members of Hopkins's Company, who were also witnesses to the confession, and then there were the local villagers/townspeople who were 'witnesses' to the Witchcraft perpetrated by the accused. All this evidence was surely enough and gathered in a legally prescribed manner. The only thing frowned upon was the Swimming test, but Hopkins used this less as time went on, though simply because he was told not to.

It is safe to say that Hopkins accused many old people who couldn't endure much Searching, Watching, Torturing or even Swimming. Some people were mentally challenged (either through old age or mental defect) and would confess willingly. A case mentioned by the Witchfinders concerned 'Meggs the baker' who apparently travelled 12 miles in December 1645 willingly to be searched for Witches' marks. He was later charged and hanged. Surely Hopkins couldn't believe his luck on that occasion.

For every Witch found and charged, Hopkins took a set fee, and with it his reputation and list of powerful contacts grew. And judging by the tone of a letter he sent to an unknown official in 1646 (see Chapter Thirteen), he was swollen with confidence and his own self-importance.

So Hopkins had all the evidence required for trial. His Company, those he 'employed', and also locals from the villages and towns he visited, would testify for him in court, and it is suggested through certain documentation, that Stearne seemed to appear in court more than Hopkins (the latter being always keen to move on to the next town or village and take more money and hospitality from the locals).

But how did Hopkins morally and lawfully authenticate his crusade? The answer is through learned text. I have already mentioned the King James Bible and the King's own *Daemonologie*, but what else did Hopkins use for providence? Certainly books like Michael Dalton's *Countrey Justice* (1618), which stated: 'Devil's marks . . . being pricked, will not bleed, and be often in their secret parts and therefore require diligent and careful search.' So Hopkins took his Pricking from there, but what about Swimming?

One book that seems to echo Hopkins's techniques is William Perkins's work *Discourse* (edited by Thomas Pickering in 1602). However, interestingly, Perkins discredited Swimming by stating that water had no sacred qualities to warrant such trial. But it was re-accredited by King James in his *Daemonologie* – Hopkins simply took the ideas that suited him.

Hopkins, then, took the King's work as his essential guide, perhaps with certain European Witchcraft techniques thrown in. But what were the European techniques? Mainly these centred on accusations that the Devil had intercourse with women. This simple idea would enrage a Puritan (it certainly enraged John Stearne who used many examples in his pamphlet) and Hopkins knew that it would lend itself well to his exploitation of God-fearing magistrates and Sticklers.

However, one interesting document sourced by Richard Deacon in *Witch Finder General* (1976) is a news pamphlet (anon., dated 1647), which makes the following revelation: 'Witnesses have spoken concerning about the Devil who talks not in an unknown tongue, but in English, and in a low hoarse strange manner . . . the deaths of many entitled Witches have been wrongly caused by the malice and imposture of one Matthew Hopkins who has procured evil men to impersonate the Devil and to mimick his voice.' A weighty accusation indeed. Did Hopkins have a 'mimick' as part of his Company? It is difficult to say, but what is important to realise when reading the testimony of Watchers and even some witness reports is that people only see what they want to see. If a beetle enters a so-called Witch's cell then surely it is an Imp, if an old lady has teats under her arms for the sucking of Imps they are surely not spots, boils or the crustations of unkept old age. And if Hopkins did employ someone to seduce would-be Witches and then admit after laying with the woman that he was the Devil, then surely the Witchfinder's work was much simpler: the woman really did have something to hide.

The more we look into Hopkins's work the more devious he seems to become; but strangely, I don't see John Stearne as a smooth schemer like Hopkins. They were two very different people.

I was sick – sick unto death with that long agony; and when they at length unbound me, and I was permitted to sit, I felt that my senses were leaving me. The sentence – the dread sentence of death – was the last of distinct accentuation which reached my ears.

Edgar Allan Poe, *The Pit and the Pendulum*

TEN

Cromwell's Blind Eye

> The abhorrence in which I held the man, the dread I had of him,
> the repugnance with which I shrank from him, could not have
> been exceeded if he had been some terrible beast.
>
> Charles Dickens, *Great Expectations*

So what of the Lord Protector of England? Where does Oliver
Cromwell fit into the story of Matthew Hopkins? As the most
prominent figure in the English Civil War, and one of the most
respected and feared men of his day, surely he voiced his opinion on
the work of the Witchfinder General? He did not. But like many things
connected with Hopkins's story, silence speaks a thousand words.

It is my belief that Cromwell was scared of Hopkins. In 1644, as
Governor of Ely, Cromwell marched into the cathedral and
dismissed the congregation because of offensive choir members.
Cromwell's brutal disregard of anyone who stood in his way (when
he believed he was acting in everyone's interests) raised hatred
against him on all sides. Also, Ely had been seen as a Witch stronghold since the early 1630s (coincidentally the time Cromwell had
moved into the area). Cromwell knew that belief in Witchcraft and,
later, the work of the Witchfinder General, was very strong, so like a
good politician he did little to oppose it.

But there is a deeper tie between Cromwell and Witchcraft: a few
years before Cromwell was born there was a story of Witch-hunting

in his own family. In 1593, the wife of Sir Henry Cromwell, Oliver's grandfather, had died and, the doctors not feeling dogmatic enough to name a sufficient cause, some local people were accused of using Witchcraft to cause her death. John Samwell and his wife Alice, also Ann their daughter, were charged at the Huntingdon Assizes and, in the words of the Noble:

> they were, therefore, all three publicly murdered, suffering amidst the acclamation of a barbarous and rude populace . . . their goods were forfeited to Sir Henry as lord of the manor; but he unwilling to possess himself of the supposed felon's goods, gave them to the corporation conditionally, that they procured from Queen's College in Cambridge a doctor or bachelor of divinity to preach every day of the Annunciation of the Blessed Virgin, a sermon against the sin of Witchcraft in one of the churches of Huntingdon.

As G.R. Stirling Taylor wrote in his biography of Oliver Cromwell:

> such was the atmosphere of the Cromwell house; and the reader who has any respect for the scientific value of environment will agree that it cannot be left unrecorded in Oliver's biography . . . Cromwell had now been instructed, on the unimpeachable authority of the judge of the High Court of Justice, that it was a proved fact that evil men and women could, at the unlawful order of the Devil, bewitch their victims to death; and this alarming knowledge of the spiritual world must have singularly confirmed the young Oliver in his growing conviction that he, on his side, could be an agent of the lawful commands of the Almighty.

Stirling Taylor went on to state that, 'If one man could obey Satan, it was his [Cromwell's] part to counteract him in obeying the voice of God.'[1]

Cromwell had allegedly been accused of Witchcraft himself,[2] and because he was a highly superstitious man, he obviously ignored Hopkins. Also, if Cromwell was acting as a soldier at that time (1645/6) he would not wish to talk of Witchcraft.

There was also a more sinister reason for Cromwell's silence. If we turn to the case of John Lowes, we see a vicar with presumed Catholic leanings hung by evidence initially presented by his hostile parishioners and later, authenticated by his own torture-induced confessions. Now if Cromwell was opposed to the Church and monarchy, then he would probably take delight in the curbing of Catholicism through Witch-hunting. Also the special commission of the Oyer and Terminer headed by Judge Godbolt was set up by Parliament, so Cromwell had an excuse to ignore Hopkins (somebody was doing the work for him).

Cromwell had family ties with East Anglia; he must have heard of Matthew Hopkins and therefore would have developed an opinion of him, but whereas there is much documentation concerning Cromwell and his battle with the monarchy, we find nothing concerning him and Matthew Hopkins. Surely this is telling in itself and I for one take it as an endorsement of the theory that Cromwell was *worried* about Hopkins's work, if only for his own selfish reasons. He did not want to get involved because by doing so he would leave himself open to criticism and further accusations of Witchcraft (it was there in his past and Hopkins had a good knack of digging up the past). Cromwell wanted to win the people over – like a good politician – and if he opposed Hopkins, not only could he leave himself open to claims of Witchcraft, he could also lose the confidence of those who thought that Hopkins was doing a good job. Let us remember that to begin with Hopkins was known as a good and God-fearing man; it was only later that people wised up to his agenda. What has to be fully appreciated is that ordinary people believed in the Devil as a physical disturbance in their day-to-day lives; they also believed that certain people – mainly women – could be corrupted into doing his dirty work. Worst of all was that the accused 'Witch' had a terrible job attempting to prove her or his innocence once the accusation had been made, and this was what scared virtually everyone who came into contact with Matthew Hopkins and his Company.

Hopkins provided a moral dilemma for Cromwell and when such difficulties present themselves the best thing for any soldier or politician to do is to turn a blind eye, which is exactly what Oliver Cromwell, Lord Protector of England, did. But there is one more thing: John Thurlowe, Cromwell's head of the Secret Service. It is thought he was a confidant of Matthew Hopkins, so perhaps instead of turning a blind eye, Cromwell kept one good eye on Hopkins through Thurlowe.

So Thurlowe had a reason for being with Hopkins. Not just to curb Royalist spies but to protect Cromwell. Obviously, it could all be coincidence. Thurlowe was possibly in the right place at the right time when Hopkins started plotting his crusade; but that doesn't seem to hang together for me. It is more convenient to say that Hopkins and Thurlowe were acquainted with each other before 1644. The one thing that does seem plausible is that Thurlowe wanted to keep 'in' with Hopkins so that Royalist spies *were* caught by Hopkins and tried as Witches. There is evidence to support this. The Witch of Newbury (1643) was mentioned in the Tendring document which states, 'who espied upon the Parliament Forces with the intention of destroying their armoury'.[3] In short this woman was arrested while making her way across a river. She was condemned and executed as a Witch.

Further evidence of the 'Royalist-Witch' theory actually comes via William Lilly, who stated that 'much astrological intelligence contributed to the apprehension of Witches and it was not entirely by accident that most of these were outside the Parliamentary pale'. I find those words very interesting, because if both Lilly and Thurlowe patronised the Thorn Inn and had similar motives for 'advising' Hopkins, then they could have been there to steer Hopkins into capturing and executing Royalists. The successful hanging of such people would be good propaganda for the Parliamentarians.

There was good reason for Hopkins to be so active in Cromwell's East Anglia domain.

Things are not what they seem; nor are they otherwise.

St Padmasambhava (Tibet)

ELEVEN

The Burning of Mary Lakeland

Who weeps for these, weeps for corruption.

Arthur Miller, *The Crucible*

Before we look closely at the hanging of Vicar John Lowes and show how opinion turned against Hopkins, we need to look at another important incident.

A famous myth has grown up around Matthew Hopkins that he burned most of his victims. This is totally inaccurate. In fact, only one burning can be proved out of a total of 200-plus hangings. However, because of the severity of this form of execution, the horrific image gained a hold on the public conscious which has persisted over the centuries. Death by burning was a punishment reserved for women who killed their husband – or actively conspired to do so – and was called Minor Treason by the Court.

A pamphlet concerning the burning of (Mother) Mary Lakeland was released in late 1645 entitled *Confessions of Mother Lakeland of Ipswich, who was arraigned and condemned for a Witch at Ipswich in Suffolk*. This pamphlet described Lakeland as 'a professor of religion and an admitted Witch for nearly 20 years . . . [who bewitched her] husband . . . whereby he lay in great misery for a time and at last died.'

Richard Deacon compiled some evidence suggesting that Hopkins was sent to Ipswich deliberately to accuse Lakeland of Witchcraft

(Minor Treason) because she was a Royalist agent. This is possibly true. What is also interesting about the Lakeland burning is that four other people were accused of Witchcraft and murder at the same Assizes: James and Mary Emmerson, Rose Parker and Margery Sutton, all of whom were acquitted. So why was Lakeland burned?

Like most of the important incidents in Hopkins's campaign as Witchfinder, little evidence can be found. Perhaps though, the evidence as laid down in pamphlet form is the only kind we need on this occasion, because not only had Mother Lakeland killed her husband, she had apparently taken revenge on a man who had broken his courtship with her granddaughter: 'Because he would not have her, she sent and burnt a new ship that had never been to sea, that he was to go master of; and sent also to torment him and take away his life.' There is much to learn from this piece of text. Suddenly Lakeland has conspired to kill another man. But the interesting thing here is that he has ties with shipping, as did Hopkins. Did this man know Hopkins and ask him to dispose of an unwanting (or unwanted) future mother-in-law? We may never know, but it is interesting to speculate concerning this most famous burning.

The historical story is inevitably confused by a folk-tale conclusion typical of all Hopkins's trials:

One thing that is very remarkable, and to be taken notice of: that upon the very day that she was burned, a bunch of flesh, something after the form of a dog, that grew upon the thigh of . . . Mr Beale, ever since the time that she first sent her Imp to him being very hard but could never be made to break by all the means that could be used, break of itself without any means using. And another sore that at the same time she sent her Imp to him rose upon the side of his belly in the form of a fistula, which ran and could not be broken for all the means that could be used, presently also began to heal, and that there is great hope that he will suddenly recover again.[1]

Lakeland also sent her dogs out to kill a Mr Lawrence of Ipswich and also his child. This was apparently because Lawrence asked her for repayment of a debt of 12 shillings. Then there was Mrs Jennings (also of Ipswich) who had a mole sent to her by Lakeland to kill her for not lending her a needle. Do these stories expose a wicked women at the least?

Mary Lakeland, widow of Ipswich barber John Lakeland, was burned to death in September 1645. Before the execution, Mary did not appear to try and retract her confession (forced by Walking); she seemed to be 'very penitent for her former lewd and abominable endeavours, and acts, and desires to have petitions put up to diverse Godly Ministers that they would be pleased to pray in their several congregations that her said Imps may have no further power, to do any more such like hurt neither by sea nor land, as they have diverse times formerly done, to the destruction, loss, or utter undoing of many sundry good and honest people.'[2]

Does all this suggest that Lakeland was guilty of conspiring – or actually carrying out – murder? It cannot be ruled out. Was every one of Hopkins's victims totally innocent? I would argue that most were, but in the case of Mary Lakeland there seem to be so many local witnesses, and extreme crimes that did, on this occasion, actually result in death. What would a modern court of law make of Mary Lakeland? Don't forget that her husband had died a painful death and that she had at least threatened others with extreme measures. She did nothing to save herself from such a terrible end. Was there then something abominably just in Hopkins's methods?

Religious men say Devils are wiser than men but why then is it that Devils should choose to be conversant with silly women. If the Devil be so wise and wise to do evil why should he not choose to deal with wise men and great men. Yet as appears by the news we receive this day from Suffolk he meddles with none but poor old women. Life is precious and there is need of great inquisition before it is taken away.

The Moderate Intelligencer, London, 1645

TWELVE

The Tide Turns Against Hopkins

I have hated them that hold superstitious vanities: but I trust in the Lord.

Psalm 31

To whet the reader's appetite I briefly related the sad fate of John Lowes, Vicar of Brandeston, at the beginning of this book. Hopkins forced Lowes to confess to Witchcraft and then had him executed on 27 August 1645[1] (not 'the Autumn' of 1645 as is often incorrectly stated). It is now important to look very closely at the story of John Lowes and understand the intricate details, because it was Hopkins's success in executing Lowes that contributed to his own downfall.

Like most criminals, Hopkins finally overstretched himself. Thus far he had worked his trade among the lower-middle class and below (farmers and villagers), who were all too happy to complain about the Witchcraft perpetrated by their neighbours. However, when Hopkins rode into Brandeston and accused John Lowes of being a Wizard, he was suddenly upgrading his antics to involve the Church (and the perception of Lowes's friends, associates and contemporaries therein). With hindsight, this was a mistake. But Lowes was an easy target because of his personal history.

In his youth, Lowes appeared before the Bishop's court at Ipswich on a charge of refusing to conform to the rites and ritual of the

59

established Church; shortly afterwards he was convicted of 'Common Imbarritor' (one who maliciously incites litigation).[2] It was this very flaw in his personality that would later annoy his flock and lead to his downfall; however, according to the Reverend Montague Summers, Lowes had already been arraigned for Witchcraft. He was a prime target for Matthew Hopkins.

John Lowes had been the Vicar of All Saints Church, Brandeston, for more than half his life.[3] Now approximately 80 years of age, he was cantankerous and set in his ways. This is implied in the Brandeston parish register where an unknown chronicler wrote of him: 'a neighbour Justice of the Peace and a Doctor in Divinity, who both knew him [Lowes] very well, altogether acquit[ted] him of that crime [Witchcraft] as far as they could judge, and did verily believe the truth is, that he was a contentious man, and made his parishioners very uneasy, and they were glad to take the opportunity of those wicked times and get him hanged.'

Lowes' parishioners are viewed as a hostile bunch,[4] but there is perhaps reason for this. His sermons were slow and vindictive, therefore his parishioners probably saw him as a menace, which is why they were happy to support Hopkins's claim that Lowes practised Witchcraft and sank ships at sea. This charge and perception are substantiated by a study of *An Historical Essay Concerning Witchcraft* by Francis (Bishop) Hutchinson.[5] His narrative begins: 'It is said, that he [Lowes] was a painful preacher for many years . . . [but] it is a monstrous tale, without any tolerable proof to support it.' Hutchinson clearly supported Lowes, and related his 'crime' thus:

> there happened in sight [of] a man that had nothing else to do but observe this ship. He could have no particular malice, no temptation of gain; for he knew not whose ship [it] was, nor was likely to get anything by the loss of it; only an Imp that he had with him had a mind to destroy it, and without acknowledgement of God, asks leave of this man, as if ships sailed by his permission his Imp, he gives consent for the wreck, and the Imp sunk it before his face. Men believe wonderful things, they take care that

the proof be as extraordinary. But in this case, we have no corroborating circumstances of time, or place, or the ship, or any witness, in a case that requires vast numbers, that could depose (or could name a ship), or at least a ship particularly described, did sink when it had a calm sea and a fair wind, without either rock or tempest. Instead of probabilities, we have an intimation of another nature [that] some wandering scandalous people, that took up a trade to get their bread amongst the rabble, by finding out Witches, swore that under their trials, he confessed such a thing against himself.

A more detailed version of Lowes' confession is found in *A True Relation of the Arraignment of Eighteen Witches* released in 1645 (see Appendix One for an abridged transcript). However, what is quite interesting is Hutchinson's choice of words at the end of the above passage: 'some *wandering scandalous people*, [my italics] that took up a trade to get their bread amongst the rabble . . .' Although a contemporary source, this backs up the claim that Hopkins had a Company who rode into villages with him, men and women who perhaps were better educated and ostensibly richer than the people they terrorised.

But why did Lowes confess to such a crime? The answer can be found in Hutchinson's work. He transcribed a letter from 'Mr Rivett' who was 'a worthy gentleman, who lived lately in the same place [Brandeston], and whose father lived there before him', so here we have a first-hand account of the circumstances of Lowes' confession. The letter reads:

Sir, In answer to your request concerning Mr Lowes, my father was always of the opinion, that Mr Lowes suffered wrongfully, and hath often said, that he did believe he was no more a Wizard than he was. I have heard it from them that watched with him [local people and a Marshal from Hopkins's hand-picked Company] that they kept him awake several nights together, and run him backwards and forwards about the room until he was out of breath: then they rested him a little, and then ran him again:

and this they did for several days and nights together, till he was weary of his life, and was scarce sensible of what he said or did.

This was one of Hopkins's usual methods of prompting a confession. It is no wonder the old man confessed to Witchcraft. His fate was sealed, as Mr Rivett continues: 'They swam him at Framlingham, but that was no true rule to try him by; for they put in honest people at the same time, and they swam as well as he.'

Hopkins initially held a trial for Lowes in the ditch of the Old Castle at Framlingham. This may not seem to have much significance on the face of it, but when we observe that the castle was once a home to staunch Catholics and Lowes had Catholic sympathies, the exercise represents a Puritan victory. This surely was Hopkins's finest hour.

Lowes was hanged at Bury St Edmunds. Beforehand, he had recovered enough to 'stoutly' maintain his innocence. Hutchinson confirmed this in *An Historical Essay Concerning Witchcraft*: '[Lowes] challenged them to make proof of such things as they laid to his charge. I heard this from a person of credit [who heard his trial] . . . I have never heard anyone speak of him, but with great compassion . . . and their belief of his innocence. And when he came to his execution, because he would have [a] Christian burial, he read the office himself, and that way he committed his own body to the ground, in sure and certain hope of the resurrection to eternal life.'

It was Hopkins's style to get local support because it added weight to his wild claims of Witchcraft. It was all valid evidence in front of the local Magistrate (especially the Oyer and Terminer) and, indeed, the weight of many eyewitnesses is what convinced certain Magistrates of the guilt of the accused (Lowes in this case). But never before had Hopkins rallied around the local peasants to condemn a member of the Church. Instead of working his way up to such a figurehead of the community, Hopkins took a big step.

In order to make a watertight case against Lowes, Hopkins didn't need one confession but several, as the following bears out:[6]

after his swimming at Framlingham [Lowes] confessed . . . [and showed] his marks . . . [and] that the biggest of his Imps [for he had seven] did suck at his teat . . . being asked how long these Imps had sucked, [he] said five years and he said to Ton [Imp] who came first to him [and] asked if he should suck he said when goody . . . tester Daniel Rayner [said] that Lowes confessed he employed his yellow Imp to do all the hurt he could at sea between Yarmouth and Winterton and that he had been the death of many cattle and that these Imps did force him to employ them about some evil action. Nathaniel Man of Brandeston [said] that upon falling out with Mr Lowes and Mr Lowes threatening him he went for a warrant to bind him to the peace and that immediately after Mr Lowes came to this deponents[7] wife who having a child with her gave her 2s 6d to buy something and immediately after this money was received the child fell sick, languished and . . . died.

The above confessions and additional witnesses and evidence were enough to seal Lowes' fate.

Lowes was a big fish to catch but catch him Hopkins did, although at what cost? In order to understand how the tide turned against Matthew Hopkins, we must look at the people who supported Lowes,[8] their respected positions and influence: Bishop Hutchinson was amazed at how anyone could accept the evidence against Lowes. And it wasn't just Lowes; forty other innocent people were hanged at Bury St Edmunds in 1645–6 for Witchcraft[9] at the hands of the Witchfinder General. Instead of an ever-decreasing list of Witches, it appears that the list of the accused, and consequently condemned, was on the increase.

But what did Hutchinson make of this in his book? He was disgruntled but he did not try and clear Lowes' name. His book was published a lifetime later and was in answer to a book supporting Witchcraft, and it only mentioned Lowes in the context of many other victims. Bishop Hutchinson knew the weight of evidence against Lowes was considerable, because it was backed by many people – churchgoing individuals who knew the vicar well, thus tempering his argument. Hopkins was still a respected figure and the Church was in a delicate situation, as Roland Parker wrote: 'villages in the neighbourhood had little sympathy for the Crown, they had even less for the Church, and for this the attitude of the Church was partly to blame. Not the parson; he, poor chap, was doing his best to live in tune with his parish and make do on a stipend of less than £5 a year. But the Bishop and his Archdeacon waged a campaign of purification, which only resulted in antagonising their flock.'[10]

It must be remembered that the Church was in a very awkward position during the Civil War. It tasked itself to keep some semblance of order within its parishes, but that proved very difficult with bloodshed and uncertainty an everyday occurrence, especially for the lower classes. It is said of John Lowes[11] that he associated himself with the Laudian[12] party, which obviously didn't sit well with his parishioners. And the parishioners' hatred towards Lowes could have stemmed chiefly from his beliefs.[13]

Obviously, in the heart of Cromwell's England, Lowes was in a minority, and Hopkins could use this to his advantage, quickly whipping up support, not least of which from John Godbolt who probably would not want to be seen sympathising with a Laudian. It is my belief that this is the true reason why Lowes was found guilty despite his vehement claims of innocence at his trial.[14] John Lowes was murdered for his Catholic beliefs. Let us remind ourselves that William Dowsing, a staunch Puritan, attempted to banish all traces of Catholicism from Suffolk churches (he destroyed nearly 300 in a year) and had as a sympathiser Matthew Hopkins. This adds weight to the claims that Hopkins's activities were politically motivated in favour of Cromwell and not the Crown and ostensibly the Catholic Church.

However, the Church did speak out against Hopkins in the form of Reverend John Gaule of Great Staughton, who wrote a pamphlet in 1646 entitled *Select Cases of Conscience Touching Witches and Witchcrafts* in which he castigated Hopkins's methods. Indeed, he even preached that Hopkins was a Witch himself. As a powerful and influential speaker, people listened to Gaule's arguments and the tide truly started to turn against Hopkins, prompting him to write his own pamphlet, *The Discovery of Witches*, as a response. Then Parliament began to criticise Witchfinders, perhaps in response to Hopkins's pamphlet. So Hopkins, as the most feared of all Witchfinders, then became the example who had to be crushed. Matthew Hopkins would be dead within two years of John Lowes' execution.

The hanging of a great number of Witches in Suffolk and Essex, by the discovery of one Hopkins in 1645 and 1646, is famously known. Mr Calamy went along with the Judges in the circuit, to hear their confessions, and see that there were no fraud or wrong done them. I spoke with many understanding, pious and credible persons, that lived in the Countries,[15] and some that went to them to the prisons. Among the rest, an old Reading Parson named Lowis [Lowes], not far from Framlingham, was one that was hanged; who confessed that he had two Imps.

Richard Baxter, *The Certainty of the Worlds of Spirits*[16]

THIRTEEN

Matthew Hopkins Retires

When there are any mighty winds and thunders with terrible lightning, it is common opinion that the Devil is abroad.

The Revd George Gifford, *A Discourse of the Subtill Practises of Devilles by Witches & Sorcerers*

Let us now look more closely at the circumstances that forced Matthew Hopkins to retire, and begin with the Revd John Gaule, who was probably the most outspoken and forceful of Hopkins's enemies.

Parishioners in Great Staughton had, for some time, blamed Witches for their own sins. This infuriated John Gaule. He did not believe in the superstitions and accusations of his flock. He could detect jealousies and unneighbourly behaviour and knew that Witchfinders such as Matthew Hopkins and John Stearne only exaggerated the problem.

By May 1646, Gaule was preaching quite vehemently against Hopkins and his work. Hopkins heard of this and wrote to a man, known only by the initials M.N., to ask if he would be welcome at Great Staughton to conduct his work (did he hope to accuse Gaule of Witchcraft?).

M.N. was probably a local Magistrate and no record of a reply exists, though one may have been written. However, of interest is the fact that Gaule castigated Hopkins in his 200-page pamphlet

Select Cases of Conscience Touching Witches and Witchcrafts, and he did so most vehemently. What is also interesting is that Gaule printed the whole of Hopkins's letter after his preface. Was this to show Hopkins that M.N. was indeed on the side of the Church and would not stand for any Witchfinding in his town? It is an interesting idea and, as we are fairly sure that Hopkins never visited the town, a very telling one as well, because it is concrete proof that Magistrates and the Church were working together in small towns in order to throw out the Witchfinders; Hopkins letter ran thus:

My service to your Worship presented, I have this day received a letter, &c – to come to a town called Great Staughton to search for evil disposed persons called Witches (though I hear your minister is farre against us through ignorance). I intend to come (God willing) the sooner to hear his singular judgement in the behalf of such parties; I have known a minister in Suffolk preach as much against their discovery in a pulpit, and forced to recant it (by the Committee) in the same place. I much marvel such evil members should have any (much more any of the clergy who should daily preach terror to convince such offenders) stand up to take their parts against such as are complainants for the King, and Sufferers themselves with their families and estates. I intend to give your town a visit suddenly. I am come to Kimbolton this week and it shall be ten to one but I will come to your town first, but I would certainly know afore whether your town affords many Sticklers for such cattle, or willing to afford as good welcome and entertainment, as others, where I have been, else I shall wave your shire (not as yet beginning in any part of it myself) and betake to such places, where I do, and may persist without control, but with thanks and recompense, so I humbly take my leave and rest.
Your servant to be commanded,
Matthew Hopkins

The original letter does not exist (only one document baring Hopkins's signature is known to exist today). Suffice to say, Gaule was determined to discredit Hopkins, and the publication of his pamphlet on 30 June 1646 did much to achieve that.

But Gaule didn't stop there. He continued to preach against the Witchfinders and specifically against Matthew Hopkins. Hopkins had already retaliated before Gaule wrote his pamphlet, as Gaule wrote that he had received hostile remarks about his preaching 'from one I never saw before', obviously Hopkins.

So the slanging match was in full flow. Gaule preached, Hopkins spoke out by return, then Gaule wrote his pamphlet after being told that Hopkins wanted to Witch-hunt in Great Staughton. Gaule would probably have been worried about Hopkins's threat to come to Great Staughton but he must have had some strong support. He was indeed a worthy adversary of Hopkins.

Gaule did not just speak out against Hopkins, he also preached about the sins of parishioners who put their faith in Witchfinding rather than in God. In his pamphlet he writes: 'The country people talk already, and that more frequently, more affectedly, of the infallible and wonderful power of Witchfinders, [than] they do of God, or Christ, or the Gospel preached.'

Because Gaule did not graduate from either Oxford or Cambridge, biographies have not been too praiseworthy of him over the years. This is unfortunate because his contribution to the discrediting of Witchfinding and astrology (see his 1652 pamphlet *ThecMaq-Astro-mancer*, printed by Joshua Kirton) was contemporary, bold and furthermore correct. As he wrote perceptively in *Select Cases*: 'It is strange to tell what superstitious opinions, affections, relations, are generally risen amongst us since the Witchfinders came into the country.'

Although Hopkins continued his predatory Witch-hunt for approximately another year after the publication of Gaule's pamphlet, the art of Witchfinding became more difficult to pursue because of it. Hopkins (and Stearne) certainly made less money. Even splitting up and travelling across the Fens during a wet summer and into a bitter winter, the duo had a much more miserable time than they had the previous year.

When we analyse Hopkins's letter to the mysterious person at Great Staughton, we notice that he was concerned about local Sticklers. These people were increasingly worried about Witchfinding and as more was said against the infamous Matthew Hopkins, the Sticklers began to dig their heels in, more so after the publication of Hopkins's pamphlet and Parliament's new stance against Witchfinding.

Did it all become too difficult for Matthew Hopkins, leading him to retire? Not quite. There is more too it than that. We know for certain that Hopkins suffered from poor health. He was prone to chest infections and in 1647, suffered from the consumption that finally killed him in August of that year. This consumption was apparently 'a long sickness' according to John Stearne (see his pamphlet). It could have started during his long and fruitless treks through the snow of the previous winter, and was aggravated by his frustrating tour of 1647.

We will speak more of Hopkins's death in the next chapter. However, suffice to say that he was a sick man throughout 1647 but despite this he tried hard to find Witches, although their prosecution became increasingly difficult. However, I am convinced that there is more to Hopkins's retirement than that.

In Stearne's pamphlet he doesn't mention being with or visiting Hopkins during his 'long sickness'. His words are cold. There could be many reasons for this, such as not wanting to be associated as a 'friend' to the discredited Witchfinder, but I believe there is something more within these words and, as a consequence, they expose the reason why Stearne wrote his own pamphlet: he had worked Hopkins out himself. He knew that if Hopkins didn't have to be at an Assize then he wouldn't go. There was no profit in it for him. He wasn't that interested in seeing justice done, he wanted to move on to the next village or town and make more money by finding Witches, but the money began to dry up, Hopkins became more desperate and Stearne finally began to suspect that he had been duped. Did Hopkins and Stearne argue about the lack of funds in their Witchfinding pot? At the end of Hopkins's pamphlet *The Discovery of Witches* (written and published in 1647, shortly before his death), he makes a closing remark that provides us with much information: 'he demands but 20s a town, and doth sometimes ride 20 miles for that, and hath no more for all his charges thither and back again (and it may be stays a week there) and find there 3 or 4 Witches, or if it be but one, cheap enough, and this is the great sum he takes to maintain his Company with 3 horses.' How the mighty had fallen. Hopkins's words sound like a certain amount of sour grapes. His Company had diminished. There was but Stearne and Mary Phillips left, and the documentation seems to reveal that Phillips was riding more with Stearne.

In the above extract Hopkins confirms that the number of Witches he had found had indeed dwindled from thirty plus to as lowly a figure as one. And in the latter stages of his quest, money became an issue. This, together with his ill-health, led him to give up. Stearne and Phillips continued for a while until they too grew tired with the amount of work they had to put in for such little gain.

One last point though: did Hopkins and Stearne fall out over other matters? With all the criticism bandying around, did Stearne pick up on something and confront Hopkins about it? Was there an observation that left Stearne open to as much criticism as Hopkins? But Hopkins was Swum for his unethical methods was he not (see next chapter)? Stearne suddenly felt very exposed and tried to distance himself from Hopkins, thus isolating the accused ringleader. He does this openly in his pamphlet, indeed taking the credit for any official advice they had to gain from local magistrates (even though Stearne had not turned up in court once when he was meant to). Yes Stearne must certainly have felt quite exposed. He knew deep down that he had not always acted appropriately, so he went back to his wife, had another child and drifted into obscurity.

I am not ignorant how dangerous it is for me to put myself so far forth into the sea of common opinion.

John Stearne, *A Confirmation and Discovery of Witchcraft*

FOURTEEN

Death of a Witch-hunter

Shall the dust praise him? Shall the worms declare the truth? Go to him, take his shame away!

Arthur Miller, *The Crucible*

The death of Matthew Hopkins is something of conjecture and legend today. Unfortunately, the problem with a legend is that the story distorts through time. However, it can still hold elements of the truth.

In this chapter we shall analyse every source document that mentions Hopkins's death and evaluate their authority and providence. Unfortunately there is no other way to write about Matthew Hopkins's death. There is no officially recognised document appertaining to his demise (apart from the parish register), so it would be wrong to make a bold statement without first analysing the material available to us.

The Mistley Heath parish register notes that Matthew Hopkins was buried on 12 August 1647. Whether he died that very day is unclear but it is suspected that that was the case.

Legend has it that Matthew Hopkins was deemed too successful as a Witchfinder and therefore accused of Witchcraft himself.[1] After undergoing the Swimming test and floating – thus proving his guilt by his own favoured method – he was hanged. A fitting allegory to the story, and one favoured by Ronald Bassett in his work of fiction *Witchfinder General*, but is it the truth?

No, it is not. So let us now explore the historical documentation. Working backwards, let us first look at Bishop Hutchinson's version of Hopkins's death. *An Historical Essay Concerning Witchcraft* was first published in London in 1718, a lifetime after Hopkins died. However, Hutchinson did conduct extensive research and, despite some small errors, managed to transcribe some first-hand accounts concerning the characters of Matthew Hopkins and John Lowes. So Hutchinson's account holds some weight. Hutchinson wrote: 'I have often heard; that Hopkins went on searching and swimming the poor creatures till some gentlemen, out of indignation at the barbarity, took him and tied his thumbs and toes, as he used to tie others, and when he was put into the water, he himself swam as they did. That clear'd the country of him; and it was a great pity that they did not think of the experiment sooner.'[2] Hutchinson also wrote a few pages further on: 'I have heard that it was time for Hopkins to leave the country when he did, for the people grew very angry at his discoveries.'

There is much to glean from the above, but it must be remembered that the legend of Matthew Hopkins was established by the time Hutchinson wrote his book, as seen in his words: 'I have often heard . . .' What is interesting is that there is no mention of Hopkins being hanged as a Witch. If Hutchinson had 'often heard' about hanging, then he would have mentioned it. He either didn't hear of it or he didn't take the rumour seriously.

Of further interest are the words, 'some gentlemen'. The word 'gentlemen' doesn't suggest a lynch mob, but it could suggest a group of men from the local district who perhaps used to work for Hopkins and were therefore keen to clear their names and consciences after Hopkins fell from favour, possibly at the instigation of Judge Godbolt.[3] I don't see this as a wild statement. Godbolt did not approve of the Swimming test employed by Hopkins, but he had successfully tried people for Hopkins after such tests, for example Vicar John Lowes. Surely Godbolt had a dilemma. He couldn't be seen to be trying Hopkins himself, but if he employed some 'gentlemen' to do it for him, thus discrediting Hopkins, then he was not associated with the incident at all and no finger could wag in his direction.

Hutchinson also wrote: 'Pity that they did not think of the experiment sooner.' Does this suggest that Judge Godbolt had or was conducting his own experiment by Swimming Hopkins? The document does not imply this, but it is certainly what I believe. All Godbolt had to do was assemble his priests, take them to a secret bathhouse and witness the human body float when placed in the water; and a pure body at that. It was after all simple mathematics and something of an experiment to discover whether Hopkins also floated. This being so, Hopkins could not be hanged but he could be discredited.

I find this theory a most credible solution, taking in aspects of the legend and documented evidence. Furthermore, in the second edition of Hutchinson's *Historical Essay Concerning Witchcraft* (1720), Lord Chief Justice of England, Lord Parker, stated, 'That if any [man] dare for the future to make use of that Experiment [Swimming], and the party lose her life by it, all they that are the cause of it are guilty of wilful murder.' What this tells us is that in the years directly after Hopkins's reign, and for the next eighty-odd years, the British judicial system became aware of the fraudulent misuse of the Witchcraft Act, primarily as a result of Hopkins's tyranny. Shame was cast across the land because of what he had legally been allowed to get away with. Montague Summers wrote what perhaps can be seen as a warning to the human race when he said of Hopkins: 'He desired not the glory of God but the fullness of Mammon.'

However, let us return to the first edition of Hutchinson's work, because it is here that the intrigue concerning the death of Matthew Hopkins really begins. Hutchinson wrote: 'that clear'd the country of him [Hopkins]' and 'it was time for Hopkins to leave the country'. Does this mean that Hopkins faked his own death and fled the country? What about the entry in the parish record? Could that have been faked? Could his mother have helped him escape to America?

I do not accept any of these things. I think that the entry of Hopkins's death in the parish record is genuine and that he was buried at Mistley Heath. But what is meant by 'clear'd the country' and 'leave the country'? I don't necessarily think that 'country' was a misspelling of 'county',[4] simply because the word 'country' is mentioned twice in paragraphs separated by several pages. I also suggest that *leaving the county* would probably imply the existence of documentation relating to Hopkins's body being returned to Mistley for burial or some local gossip appertaining to it.

When we look at John Stearne's reference to Hopkins's death, there seems to have been some rush over Hopkins's burial, some ambiguity, which I suggest was due to embarrassment. Hopkins was out of favour, a disgrace and perhaps had to be buried the day he died without ceremony. This story does hold weight when one recognises that certain legends state that Hopkins was buried at night without mourning.

Personally I believe the word 'country' meant 'countryside' and/or 'the country was rid of him', in other words his presence had been cleared away; or he had left this life having received a Christian burial and no more should be said of him. His name then went underground, and became a whispered piece of gossip, a threat, a myth, a legend, which is where the confusion stems from today. But the parish register is clear and there is much in Hutchinson's record to confirm it.

So Hopkins was swum and found guilty of Witchcraft, unofficially at least because the swimming test was illegal. Then he died and was buried? Well he was certainly swum and certainly buried; but how in fact did he die? If he wasn't hanged, how did this young man depart the earth? Let us now move on to John Stearne's description of Hopkins's death in his pamphlet *A Confirmation and Discovery of Witchcraft*: 'I am certain (notwithstanding whatsoever hath been said of him) he died peacefully at Manningtree, after a long sickness of a consumption, as many of his generation had done before him, without any trouble or conscience for what he had done, as was falsely reported of him.' Can we believe Stearne, who clearly needed to justify his own actions? I believe on this occasion we can. What I find most intriguing is Stearne's reference to Hopkins dying 'as many of his generation had done before him'. We know Stearne was an older man but I don't believe he was here referring to all young men and women of Hopkins's age, but rather to the Hopkins family; his 'generation' meaning his brothers.

If we return to Matthew's father's will, it states clearly that if the eldest son lived long enough he should go to America. What if he did not and died, or did make the trip but died out there? It may explain why no records of Hopkins's brothers exist in British parish records (that we can prove). Did a brother die of consumption or tuberculosis in America? Was there a family weakness for this illness resulting in death at a young age? All of this, although interesting, is simply speculation. So let us now rationalise the death of Matthew Hopkins based upon what we have learned so far about his fall from grace, his 'trial' and finally, his death as outlined in the best source material we have to hand.

THE DEATH OF MATTHEW HOPKINS

After caution and criticism from Judge Godbolt in connection with the Swimming test and then general pressure from John Gaule criticising many aspects of his business, Matthew released a pamphlet that he assumed would answer his critics. The pamphlet fell very short of its aim and Judge Godbolt decided to move against Hopkins, although secretly. Godbolt could not be seen to be doing this openly, otherwise he would leave himself open to criticism, since he had largely accepted or tolerated Hopkins's whims and straying from that path now would endanger his position. Why did he not stop Hopkins earlier? Because Hopkins was carrying out vital work for the Parliamentary forces. Also, Godbolt had tried and found guilty the vicar John Lowes, and many influential people, including John Gaule, were still angry about that. Godbolt was in a sensitive position and he had to be as cunning as Hopkins if he wanted to successfully dethrone him.

Hopkins had been a prolific worker. He had travelled much on horseback over the winter months, but the ice and snow of the winter of 1646–7 was too much for him. Perhaps he got stuck in some remote location, and with his susceptibility to chest infection he became gravely ill. By mid-1647, Hopkins's health had deteriorated so much that he parted company with John Stearne. He went back to Mistley and took to his bed.

Then a group of 'gentlemen' came to town and carried out an experiment for Judge Godbolt. These men were probably known to Hopkins, local men experienced at carrying out such tasks; perhaps former members of his Company. The gentlemen took Hopkins and swam him at the Hopping Bridge, Mistley Pond, a stone's throw from his house at The Green, Mistley. Perhaps these gentlemen dragged Hopkins from his sick bed and bound him hand to foot and threw him in the freezing water. Already extremely ill, the test was the final torture. But behold, Hopkins swam!

Having been almost drowned, already unwell, Hopkins did not have the energy to try and defend himself. He was a proven Witch by his own methods – and in the eyes of the gentlemen who swam him – but the law dictated that he could not be hanged following such a trial. Certainly the gentlemen wanted to hang him, because they felt 'very angry at his discoveries'. They now knew those discoveries to be false and that all he had wanted was the money he modestly mentioned at the end of *The Discovery of Witches*. John Stearne had other, more God-fearing and plausible arguments to support his work (and his diary of people and events), and continued to do so in a less greedy manner for approximately one more year, until the Witch-hunt became too unpopular and convictions much too difficult to obtain.

So Hopkins lay gasping for breath on the banks of the river. He had swallowed much water because he was too weak to struggle. He lay beside the Hopping Bridge, adjacent to the mouth of the Stour, where a merciless chill-breeze froze him to the bone. He was mortally ill, his breathing becoming a deep gasping. The gentlemen stood motionless around him, but someone pushed through the crowd and tended to the former Witchfinder, cradled his head in her God-fearing arms until his eventual passing. There was mercy, even for Matthew Hopkins. His long illness had come to an end, albeit with some help. He was dead.

Provision had already been made for a Christian burial under cover of night and without much ceremony. Only a mother's love could arrange such a thing – a mother with strong ties to the Church. And although local people did not see the burial of Matthew Hopkins, they knew his presence had gone for ever.

Guilt hung heavy over the parish of Mistley and Manningtree. A guilt that would decay and create a legendary figure who would not be boasted of for 400 years. The Witchfinder was dead but so many innocent people had died because of his greed; and so many people were taken in by his scheming ways. The shame was heavy. People tried not to talk about the Witchfinder, apart from as a terrible bedtime threat to children: 'If you don't go to sleep Matthew Hopkins will get you.' And a disturbed slumber has continued for his spirit ever since.

Was this the end of Matthew Hopkins? I believe it was. However, let us examine a few other records of his death in the historical documentation.

To begin with, Deacon's alleged *Tendring Witchcraft Revelations* states: 'Nobody in the locality was present at his burial and if buried he was at Mistley it may have been outside the precincts of the church in the dark of night when no one else was about his business.' This statement supports my version of Hopkins's death, because the burial outside church grounds suggests that he had fallen from favour for some reason. I would also suggest an unmarked grave – perhaps a pauper's grave – to avoid desecration, and possibly inside the church grounds (at his mother's insistence).

The text also states it was 'in the dark of night', suggesting a secret burial place and perhaps the birth of the rumours that he might have escaped to America to be with a brother. What complicates this theory is mention in the *Tendring Witchcraft Revelations* that Hopkins had 'disappeared to New England to join a brother'. We are fairly certain that Hopkins had a brother living in New England at the time of his death, but in the face of the evidence offered in this book it is a leap of faith to suggest he went there. Furthermore, the Tendring document seems undecided as to Hopkins's fate, eventually favouring the burial at Mistley after being 'swam as a Witch'!

This is an interesting point, because although the Tendring document was allegedly published in 1725, it originates from 'diverse informers' from 1645–50, and ambiguity concerning Hopkins's demise is present even then. This may suggest that Hopkins's mother started the rumour that he went abroad, to steer those seeking a final revenge upon the Witchfinder's remains away from the local church – unmarked grave or not.

If Bishop Hutchinson used the same source material as the writer of the Tendring document (let us not lose sight of the fact that this document may be a forgery), then his ambiguous use of the word 'country' was deliberate, providing a scapegoat if it was later found that Hopkins had fled to America. A contradiction to my earlier statement? No, simply an observation as to how a bishop can avoid literary/scholarly embarrassment.

There is one last point, which could, if proved, be the authenticity needed to endorse my version of Hopkins's death, and the reason why Hopkins based himself in Manningtree to begin with: Thomas Witham was Rector of St Mary at Mistley. His first wife Mistress Free-Gift Witham was buried on 19 December 1633. However, in the burial records can be seen an entry for 1641: Dec 24 John son of Mary Hopkins (wife of Mr Thos Witham, Parson). Is this a remarried Marie Hopkins – Matthew's mother? Indeed, her first husband (Matthew's father) died in 1634, a year after Witham's first wife. Not only do the dates tally, but so do the profession, her son's name and the name of the church. I can't prove that Mary Hopkins is Marie Hopkins, but if she is, it explains the covert burial of Matthew, quite possibly in the dead of night in an unmarked grave, without an impartial witness or service of any kind; but with a note in the parish records.

The right church, in the right town, at the right time.[5] So Hopkins came to Mistley in the 1640s, possibly with his mother or to be near his mother who married the vicar of the church that sat not far from The Green where he lived. He set up his own house with his inheritance and took a job in line with his training. It then took him no more than three years to get bored with that and start to plot Witch-hunting (after Dowsings' work at his father's former church in 1644). It is a plausible argument and, when you consider that Hopkins settled in Mistley for no apparent reason, it can now be argued that he settled there to be near his mother. Furthermore, it could also be argued that if Marie Hopkins was in a privileged enough position to record parish business, then she could destroy certain key documents appertaining to her son's tyranny. A convincing conspiracy theory? Perhaps not. We know enough about Matthew Hopkins in order to pass severe enough judgement. But it is strange that so many records are missing concerning Hopkins's blood lust.

Matthew Hopkins's story is an allegory, as he was accused and tried as a Witch himself and, although he wasn't hanged for Witchcraft, the 'swimming' hastened his death through an already developed case of consumption that was acquired by his greed to find more Witches. So the allegory endures: he died a long, uncomfortable and lonely death, as John Stearne intimated.

Matthew Hopkins was a slight man, of approximately average height, maybe just shorter, learned, cold, calculating and greedy. The country was indeed better off without him.

Thou wast provoked by thy bloody mind,
Which never dreamed on aught but butcheries.
William Shakespeare, *The Tragedy of King Richard the Third*

FIFTEEN

The Stigma of Matthew Hopkins

And the fame of him went out into every place of the country round about.

The Leaper Healed – St Luke, King James Bible

There *is* a stigma attached to Matthew Hopkins's story, as far as his home town is concerned. There is much history in Mistley and neighbouring Manningtree, but regarding Hopkins you have to look for it; it is not publicised. Ask the locals about their famous Witchfinder and they will mention the Hopping Bridge, The Green, Mistley Heath and of course the Thorn Inn (and post office, which was once part of the Thorn Inn). They may even mention The White Hart and the cargo cellars underneath Manningtree, where Hopkins reputedly tortured some of his victims.

Manningtree Library will present a box-file of research material on request, but my point is: you must *ask* for Matthew Hopkins. He hides in the shadows. He is part of the proud history of Tendring Hundred; but a hushed part of that history, and that is a telling factor in the Hopkins story.

If one walks from Manningtree station (incidentally in neighbouring Lawford not Manningtree itself), through the town, along The Walls, over the Hopping Bridge (a stone's throw from The Green), and then walk into Mistley High Street, past the Thorn Inn and post office, up the hill and around the winding road to Mistley

Heath, one can clearly see that, historically, Mistley was also an important shipping town; but today it is Manningtree that has more bustle and, ostensibly, importance (it is, as I am proudly told by locals, England's smallest town).

Mistley holds history like a corroding iron chain. Its dilapidated shipping depots are testament to the fact, but also something more: Mistley is haunted by its past. Time hasn't washed away the sins. Like a famous battlefield, Mistley cannot recover from the evil that has festered there. You may think I exaggerate but in their books concerning Matthew Hopkins, both Richard Deacon and Malcolm Gaskill admit something similar. Something lies slumbering under the surface. Something no one can quite put their finger on; well, with the possible exception of the King James Bible, 'For thus saith the Lord, Thy bruise *is* incurable, *and* thy wound *is* grievous.'[1]

It is important for any historian to soak up the atmosphere of their chosen battlefields and, when looking for the Witchfinder General, one does find some very stark, rural and grossly unsettling locations, which appear unchanged even over the course of 400 years. Conversely, one must accept that Matthew Hopkins's story has nothing to do with the occult. It is a story very much of its misguided time, where people were penniless and paranoid. It is a sad story, concerning the murder of defenceless people, in a time when the monarchy, Parliament and the Church were in disarray.

However, because the word Witch is used so frequently in the story, a natural, macabre, unseen aspect dusts our perception. Add to that various unanswered questions concerning Hopkins (his life and career), then we have a deeply intriguing as well as disturbing story, where the powers of darkness creep into open wounds as easily as fairy tale and legend.

While writing this book I was asked if I had any spooky stories to relate or if I had seen an evil spirit – maybe Hopkins himself! In truth the answer is no (how I wish it were otherwise), but there was a piece of synchronicity that may satisfy the reader's curiosity. After collating research for two and a half years, I decided to begin writing the book one Saturday morning and completed the preface and introduction before the household awoke. I then decided to do some shopping in the local high street. After visiting the bank, I walked into the local Save the Children charity shop and, incredibly, staring at me from the shelf was Richard Deacon's book *Witch Finder General*. I had wanted to read the book – out of print for thirty years – to ensure my approach was radically different from Mr Deacon's, so it was odd that I should find the rare volume the same day I decided to start writing. A coincidence surely, but because it is Witchcraft I was writing about, a whole new aspect is easily suggested.

The stigma of Matthew Hopkins is the fact that he is associated with horror and the macabre; but the truth is, his story is one of cold-blooded slaughter and despair. Hopkins was a criminal and no glorification or honour should be shown to his memory; just the shameful truth of his burial.

But there hath been an abominable, inhuman, and unmerciful trial of these poor creatures.

Matthew Hopkins, *The Discovery of Witches*

SIXTEEN

The Legacy of Matthew Hopkins

I must not only punish but punish with impunity. A wrong is
unredressed when retribution overtakes its redresser. It is equally
unredressed when the avenger fails to make himself felt as such to
him who has done the wrong.

Edgar Allan Poe, *The Cask of Amontillado*

During the writing of this book I have met and conversed with
many people from Manningtree and Mistley. They all have
their little stories concerning Matthew Hopkins. Some say that he
was buried by the Hopping Bridge, some say that he tortured people
underneath Manningtree in the long cargo cellars, some say that he
had an office upstairs in the Thorn Inn; and virtually all of these
places boast the ghost of Hopkins. But all those people, so
approachable, so likeable, can never tell me why there is no
landmark to Hopkins today, something that could be classed as a
legacy – or a tourist attraction – something that could provide the
basis of a moral tale for the young; and the tale of Matthew
Hopkins is an allegory as I have found.

  Should there be a memorial to the dead, a statue of Hopkins, an
excavation of his supposed burial places? There should be
something. Manningtree is the smallest town in England and
deserves to boast the history of its most revered inhabitant. A man
who insists on hiding in the shadows to this day, but a man we can

expose for the beast he was. Matthew Hopkins should not be glorified; but he should be an example for generations to come. His story is indeed something we can learn from.

There is a natural beauty to Manningtree and neighbouring Mistley, but also an underlining bruise. It is high time for that bruise to be healed and Hopkins's tyranny to be acknowledged and laid to rest by placing a statue (or some such confessional legacy) in the centre of the town.

And then, all at once, blotting it out, a swarm of leaves were swirling through him, a host of yellow leaves, coiling, diving, rising, as they swept forward across a treeless desert, while overhead, like a bonfire in the sky, the sun shone down on the rushing leaves. It was a yellow world: a restless, yellow world.

Mervyn Peake, Gormenghast

SEVENTEEN

Paranoia and the Witch-Hunt

He died [Hopkins] . . . after a long sickness of the consumption
. . . without any trouble of conscience for what he had done.
        John Stearne, *A Confirmation and Discovery of Witchcraft*

It is not surprising that Matthew Hopkins's crusade against
Witches was finally thwarted. People in authority (Judges and
even the clergy) could see the error in his ways and were concerned
by Hopkins's temerity.

The weight of authority and authenticity he brought into court to
convict so many people was overwhelming to begin with. Not only had
he a professional Company to draw from, he had powerful friends too.
Also, King James had decreed after writing his version of the Bible that
there had to be witnesses to the claims of Witchcraft. Hopkins had all
this in abundance and it must have stunned the Judges.

The people were paranoid when it came to Witchcraft. But Hopkins
was too vicious, too ruthless, because too many Witches were tried at
the first Assizes in Chelmsford in July 1645. It was the biggest trial of
its kind; and Witch trials had been on the decrease for years.

The charade continued like a badly written play: the fantastical
manifestations of the Familiars, also the physical rape of the alleged
Witch by the Devil, did not sit well with any man of the Church.
Satan was a spirit not a cloven-footed creature who took old ladies
to bed. And that was the next problem. The women who faced

execution in Chelmsford, Manningtree[1] and Bury St Edmunds in July and August 1645 were old wretches who could not defend themselves before the likes of Matthew Hopkins and his Company. The pleas of 'not guilty' from the Witches were probably as sad and stupid as the confessions of making love to the Devil. But despite a tiny handful of exceptions, the 'guilty' were hanged, from the one-legged widow Elizabeth Clarke (who had to be helped up the ladder to her noose) to John Lowes (loyal Vicar of Brandeston). There was an undercurrent of injustice. The biggest ever Assize for Witches was just a slaughterhouse perpetrated by one man.

The biggest problem with Hopkins's Witch-hunt was that it was aimed at the paranoia of the masses, the lower classes, the people who didn't truly understand the intricacies of their Bible and the manifestations of evil (the Devil) in their everyday lives. This was a flaw the gentry could see through, but Hopkins had much support: influential contacts, his Company, local Magistrates, various eye-witnesses. And there were the confessions of the Witches themselves.

It is my belief that concern about Hopkins's work was rife from the very first trial, but because of the strength of the case constructed by Hopkins and the belief of the people connected to it, the authorities were powerless, or at least chose to be. This is why a special commission of the Oyer and Terminer was set up, to look at Hopkins's work. But Hopkins was a slippery fish and manipulated Judge Godbolt – so it was Godbolt's job to get rid of Hopkins.

And though many of these things may seem very strange, and hardly to be believed, yet this is the very truth; and that he [Hopkins] was the son of a Godly minister, and therefore without doubt within the Covenant. Therefore let no man take upon him either to speak or write more than he knoweth to be truth.

John Stearne, *A Confirmation and Discovery of Witchcraft*

It is not fair to suggest that the naivety of the nation was responsible for the East Anglian Witchcraft Trials. The reason why Hopkins had so much success was because of the weight of backing he had. Because of the Civil War and the instability of government, it took officialdom some time to bring Hopkins down (they had to protect themselves at all times because superstition killed).

Let us be fair about this. There were three separate hangings in July and August 1645; the next was in December the same year. So the officials slowed down Hopkins's blood-lust, and then throughout 1646 and into 1647 made it increasingly difficult for both Hopkins and Stearne to gain convictions. The officials stopped Hopkins and destroyed his Company within two years of the first trial. Godbolt was the lynchpin in this exercise and his perception should be applauded, but strangely, it is not.

To say that Witchfinding is a thing of the past is not strictly true. Even in the twenty-first century the governments of the Western world conduct their own Witch-hunts. But surely these hunts are for truly wicked people: the world's most wanted terrorists. But let us suggest that if one unscrupulous security company stepped forward and took a heavy reward for finding fifty-odd terrorists of their own choosing, with confessions and witnesses, and then began to find many more, would they be the modern-day equivalent of Matthew Hopkins and his Company?

I believe they would. Although the story of the East Anglian Witchcraft Trials is a sad one, it came about because it echoed the paranoia of the day. We cannot accuse John Stearne (an extreme Puritan and family man) over his beliefs, for he was as wise as any working man of his day, and I do believe that Stearne 'wised up' towards the end. Do we, however, forgive Matthew Hopkins? Was he a victim of his day, or just an unscrupulous underachiever? Most probably the latter, but he did immortalise himself – for the next 400 years at least – through his exploits as a Witchfinder over the course of two solitary years. Not bad for a lowly shipping clerk who died in his mid- to late twenties.

And in truth, concerning him who is dead, who likewise was an agent in the business, for my part, I never knew that he either unjustly favoured any, or received bribes, or used such extremity as was reported of him.

John Stearne, *A Confirmation and Discovery of Witchcraft*

EIGHTEEN

Afterword

You will confess yourself or you will hang! . . . Do you know who
I am? I say you will hang if you do not open with me!'
Arthur Miller, *The Crucible*

If you travel to Manningtree to seek evidence of Matthew
Hopkins, you will probably be disappointed by what you find.
There is little cold, hard evidence of his life and work. True, the
surrounding countryside is rustic and untarnished, which helps with
a perception of Hopkins's world, but the town boasts its own
modest industrial estate nowadays and a person would find greater
benefit in servicing their car with new tyres and a quality MOT than
discovering Witchfinders of the seventeenth century.

The mile-wide Stour estuary, which the persistent historian will
follow en route to Mistley (approximately ½ mile outside
Manningtree), is a sanctuary for wildlife and is both charming and
mysterious, but again sheds no light on Witchfinders.

At Mistley, the nineteenth-century church of St Mary's and St
Michael's (unfortunately not the medieval church of Mistley Heath
which no longer stands approximately 1 mile away), is quiet and
unassuming. For a small fee, a booklet[1] about the churches of
Manningtree and Mistley can be purchased and explains the fate of
three of those churches and the reason for the scant documentation
concerning Matthew Hopkins (after the churches at Mistley Heath,

Mistley and Manningtree High Street fell to ruin, St Mary's and St Michael's Church served both Manningtree and Mistley).

Nowadays, parish registers over 100 years old are held in the Essex Record Office but mention is made of Hopkins's burial in the church booklet, although it is clear that the church and parish say little about their historical Witchfinder.

As I walked along the Stour estuary wall, a bitter wind and icy rain assaulting me, I wondered what it must have been like to be bound hand to foot and thrown into deep freezing water in the biting winters of the seventeenth century, with no central heating to warm your bones afterwards (if you survived being swum that is), just a painfully cold cell as you awaited trial. I again contemplated Matthew Hopkins's death, strongly believing that he was accosted and swum for his sins as Witchfinder; a fitting allegory for him. I do not believe that Hopkins was spirited away to New England to live in obscurity or take some part in the Salem Witch Trials in his old age.

Romantics will conjure up many images but the story of Matthew Hopkins is not for the romantic. His is a savage and bloody story that has no let up in its unceasing death march. His accomplices, at his orders, conspired and tortured innocent people for a hideous crime that in the modern-day world we know to be fiction. And I, for one, believe that Matthew Hopkins knew that too. He knew his Bible, he knew how Witches were tried in Europe, he knew that the Scots were more brutal than the English at trying Witches, so he capitalised on this and made his money at the expense of hundreds of innocent people. But like most criminals, he overstretched himself, went too far too quickly and that, essentially, became his downfall.

It could be viewed that Marie Hopkins was behind her son's downfall. That she knew what he was doing was wrong and that it was she who had had him swum, to teach him a lesson and discredit him once and for all. So a woman – Hopkins's mother – sealed his fate? No. Matthew Hopkins came from a loving, God-fearing family and was comfortably off. In fact he abused his position, taking advantage of the times he lived in, and his downfall was instigated by Judge Godbolt, who was opposed to Hopkins's methods although originally brought in to support him and manage lawfully the weight of the Witchcraft trials that Hopkins instigated and also the obligatory Royalist hanging.

Abate the edge of traitors, gracious Lord,
That would reduce these bloody days again
And make poor England weep in streams of blood.
      William Shakespeare, *The Tragedy of King Richard the Third*

PART TWO

The Character of a Witchfinder

Now, why it should be that women exceed men in this kind,
I will not say, that Satan's setting upon these
rather than man is, or like to be, because of his unhappy
onset and prevailing with Eve.

John Stearne,
A Confirmation and Discovery of Witchcraft

NINETEEN

'The Discovery of Witches' by Matthew Hopkins: The Text

That there is strong reason to suspect the existence of a most
extensive plot, conspiracy, or design, secretly contrived.
Charles Dickens, *To The Gentlemen of England*

AUTHOR'S NOTE

I have told Matthew Hopkins's life story as clearly as source
documentation allows me. However, I have made some
unfashionable claims concerning Hopkins's actions. Some would say
that I have assumed too much. I make no apology for this. I have
interpreted the story in my own way after reading source documents
and visiting original locations. I approached the story of Matthew
Hopkins because there were big issues that I felt had not been
properly investigated. I wanted to share my opinions.

The problem with analysing source documents is that a purely
scholarly interpretation of key works would take much for granted,
or contradict only where there is much conflicting evidence. But we
are dealing with shrewd, perceptive people here, especially Matthew
Hopkins and his own writing, and we should apply our own shrewd
judgement when reading such writing.

Individual interpretation does play its own part, and my
arguments are either convincing or not. I believe they hold together

well and have much more support from source documentation than much previously published about Matthew Hopkins and his Company. It can be argued that I could have quoted extensively from the source documents, including examples of confessions within the main body of the first part of this work, but I feel this approach is often frustrating, shrouding, or at least obscuring, the basic facts. If certain documents are hard to come by then there is little opportunity for the reader to examine them and form a clear picture for themselves. In short, I put my own interpretation on trial with the reader through these documents in their entirety, and ostensibly add more detail to Hopkins's story. The analysis of Hopkins's pamphlet and the essay on John Stearne's pamphlet give me the basis for a fuller exploration of the issues and so allow the reader to take part in a full research experience.

I have deliberately left the confessions and examples of searches and tests of Witchcraft to the people who made them. Their words cry out from the page without any interruption from me. Here is the full horror of what Matthew Hopkins did as Witchfinder General.

THE TEXT

The following text is a contemporary transcription of Matthew Hopkins's own pamphlet concerning Witchcraft, *The Discovery of Witches*, the single most important document concerning the Witchfinder's tyranny we have. Published in 1647, the year of his death, *The Discovery of Witches* is Hopkins's own justification for his work as Witchfinder General. It was a direct answer to Vicar John Gaule's pamphlet against him, but equally fascinating is the tone of the pamphlet. We know Hopkins to be a schemer of the highest order, but to hear his clear voice emanating from this pamphlet not only justifies a complete transcription of it here, but allows the reader a full and direct experience of the man himself. Also, when this pamphlet is read in conjunction with that of John Stearne's (see Chapter Twenty-one), the two most important, but radically different voices within Hopkins's Company become clear to the reader.

THE DISCOVERY OF WITCHES:

In Answer to Several Queries, Lately Delivered to the Judges of Assize for the County of Norfolk.

And now published
By Matthew Hopkins, Witchfinder.
For
The Benefit of the whole Kingdom.

EXOD. 22.18.
Thou shalt not suffer a Witch to live.

London,
Printed for R. Royston, at the Angel in Ivie Lane,
M. DC. XLVII.

CERTAIN QUERIES ANSWERED, which have been and are likely to be objected against Matthew Hopkins, in his way of finding out Witches.

Query 1. That he must need to be the greatest Witch, Sorcerer and Wizard himself, else he could not do it.

Answer. If Satan's kingdom be divided against itself, how shall it stand?

Query 2. If he never went so far as is before mentioned, yet for certain he met with the Devil, and cheated him of his Book, wherein were written all the Witches names in England, and if he looks on any Witch, he can tell by her countenance what she is; so by this, his help is from the Devil.

Answer. If he had been too hard for the Devil and got his Book, it had been to his great commendation and no disgrace at all: and

95

for judgement in physiognomy, he hath no more than any man else whatsoever.

Query 3. From whence then proceeded this his skill? Was it from his profound learning, or from much reading of learned Authors concerning that subject?

Answer. From neither of both, but from experience, which though it be meanly esteemed of, yet the surest and fastest way to judge by.

Query 4. I pray where was this experience gained? And why gained by him and not by others?

Answer. The Discoverer never travelled far for it, but in March 1644 he had some seven or eight of that horrible sect of Witches living in Town where he lived, a Town in Essex called Manningtree with divers[1] other adjacent Witches of other towns, who every six weeks in the night (being always on the Friday night) had their meeting close by his house, and had their several solemn sacrifices there offered to the Devil, one of which this Discoverer heard speaking to her Imps one night, and bid them go to another Witch, who was thereupon apprehended, and searched by women who had for many years known the Devil's marks, and found to have three teats about her, which honest women have not: so upon command from the Justice, they were to keep her from sleep two or three nights, expecting in that time to see her Familiars, which the fourth night she called in by their several names, and told them what shapes, a quarter of an hour before they came in, there being ten of us in the room, the first she called was,

1. Holt, who came in like a white kitten.
2. Jarmara, who came in like a fat spaniel without any legs at all, she said she kept him fat, for she clapped her hand on her belly and she said he sucked good blood from her body.
3. Vinegar Tom, who was like a long-legged Greyhound, with a head like an Ox, with a long tail and broad eyes, who when this Discoverer spoke to, and bade him go to the place provided for him and his Angels, immediately transformed

himself into the shape of a child of four years old without a head, and gave half a dozen turns about the house, and vanished at the door.

4. Sack and Sugar, like a black Rabbit.
5. Newes, like a Polecat.

All these vanished away in a little time immediately after this Witch confessed several other Witches, from whom she had her Imps, and named to divers women where their marks were, the number of their marks, and Imps, and Imps names as Elemanzer, Pyewacket, Peckin the Crown, Grizzel Greedigut, etc, which no mortal could invent; and upon their searches the same marks were found, the same number, and in the same place, and the like confessions from them of the same Imps, (though they knew not that we were told before) and so peached one another thereabouts that joined together in the like damnable practise, that in our Hundred in Essex, 29 were condemned at once, 4 brought 25 miles to be hanged, where this Discoverer lives, for sending the Devil like a bear to kill him in his garden, so by seeing divers of the men's paps,[3] and trying ways with hundreds of them, he gained this experience, and for ought he knows any man else may find them as well as he and his company, if they had the same skill and experience.

Query 5. Many poor people are condemned for having a Pap, or Teat about them, whereas many people (especially ancient people) are and have been a long time troubled with natural wretts on several parts of their bodies, and other natural excrescencies, as Haemorrhoids, Piles, Childbearing, etc, and these shall be judged on by one man alone, and a woman, and so accused or acquitted.

Answer. The parties so judging can justify their skill to any, and show good reasons why such marks are not merely natural, neither that they can happen by any such natural cause as is before expressed, and for further answer for their private judgements alone, it is most false and untrue, for never was any man tried by search of his body, but commonly a dozen of the ablest men in the parish or elsewhere, were present, and most commonly as many ancient skilled Matrons and Midwives present when the women are tried, which marks not only he, and his company attest to be very suspicious, but all beholders, the most skilled of them, do judgements proceed from any [of] the above mentioned causes.

Query 6. It is a thing impossible for any man or woman to judge rightly on such marks, they are so near to natural excrescencies, and they that find them, durst not presently give oath they were drawn to evil spirits, till they have used unlawful courses of torture to make them say anything for ease and quiet, as who would not do? But I would know the reasons he speaks of, how, and whereby to discover the one from the other and so be satisfied in that.

Answer. The reasons in brief are three, which for the present he judge to differ from natural marks; which are:

1. He judge by the unusualness of the place where he find the teats in or on their bodies, being fair distant from any usual place from whence such natural marks proceed, as if a Witch plead the marks found are haemorrhoids, if I find them on the bottom of the backbone, shall I also be with him, knowing they are not near that vein, and to others by child-bearing, when it may be they are in the contrary part?
2. They are most commonly insensible, and feel neither pin, needle, aule[2] etc, thrust through them.
3. The often variations and mutations of these marks into several forms, confirms the matter; as if a Witch hear a month or two before that the Witchfinder (as they call him) is coming, they will, and have put out their Imps to others to suckle them, even to their own young and tender children; these upon search are found to have dry skins and films only, and be close to the flesh, keep her 24 hours with a diligent eye, that none of her spirits come in any visible shape to suck her; the women have seen the next day after

her teats extended out to their former filling length, full of corruption ready to burst, and leaving her alone then one quarter of an hour, and let the women go up again, and she will have them drawn by her Imps close again:

Probatum est. Now for answer to their tortures in its due place.

Query 7. How can it possibly be that the Devil being a spirit, and wants no nutriment or sustentation, should desire to suck any blood? And indeed as he is a spirit he cannot draw any such excrescences, having neither flesh nor bone, nor can be felt etc.

Answer. He seeks not their blood, as if he could not subsist without that nourishment, but he often repairs to them, and gets it, the more to aggravate the Witches damnation, and to put her in mind of her Covenant: and as he is a spirit and prince of the air, he appears to them in any shape whatsoever, which shape is occasioned by him through joining of condensed thickened air together, and many times doth assume shapes of many creatures; but to create anything he cannot do it, it is only proper to God: but in this case of drawing out of these teats, he doth really enter into the body, real, corporeal, substantial creature, and force that creature (he working in it) to his desired ends, and unset the organs of that body to speak withal to make his compact up with the Witches, be the creature cat, rat, mouse, etc.

Query 8. When these paps are fully discovered, yet that will not serve sufficiently to convict them, but they must be tortured and kept from sleep two or three nights, to distract them, and make them say anything; which is a way to tame a wild colt, or hawk, etc.

Answer. In the infancy of this discovery it was not only thought fitting, but enjoyed in Essex and Suffolk by the magistrates, with this intention only, because they being kept awake would be more the active to call their Imps in open view the sooner to their help, which often times have so happened; and never or seldom did any Witch ever complain in the time of their keeping for want of rest, but after they had beat their heads together in the jail, and after this use was not allowed of by the Judges and other Magistrates, it was never since used, which is a year and a half since, neither were any kept from sleep by any order or direction since; but peradventure[4] their own stubborn wills did not let them sleep, though tendered and offered to them.

Query 9. Besides that unreasonable watching, they were extraordinarily walked, till their feet were blistered, and so forced through that cruelty to confess, etc.

Answer. It was in the same beginning of this discovery, and the meaning of walking of them at the highest extent of cruelty, was only they to walk about themselves the night they were watched, only to keep them awake and the reason was this, when they did lie or sit in a chair, if they did offer to couch down, then the watchers were only to desire them to sit up and walk about, for indeed when they be suffered so to couch, immediately comes their Familiars into the room and scare the watchers, and heartneth on the Witch, though contrary to the true meaning of the same instructions, diverse have been by rustically people (they hearing them confess to be Witches), misused, spoiled, and abused, diverse whereof have suffered for the same, but could never be proved against this Discoverer to have a hand in it, or consent to it; and hath likewise been unused by him and others, ever since the time they were kept from sleep.

Query 10. But there hath been an abominable, inhuman, and unmerciful trial of these poor creatures, by tying them, and heaving them into the water; a trial not allowable by law or conscience, and I would far know the reasons for that.

Answer. It is not denied but many were so served as had Papps, and floated, others that had none were tried with them and sunk, but mark the reasons.

> 1. For first the Devil's policy is great, in persuading many to come of their own accord to be tried, persuading them their marks are so close they shall not be found out, so as divers

100

have 10 or 12 miles to be searched of their own accord, and hanged for their labour (as one Meggs a baker did, who lived within 7 miles of Norwich, and was hanged at Norwich Assizes for Witchcraft), then when they find that the Devil tells them false they reflect on him, and he (as 40 have confessed) advised them to be sworn, and tells them they shall sink and be cleared that way, then when they betrayed that way and float, they see the Devil deceive them again, and have so laid open his treacheries.

2. It was never brought in against any of them at their trials as any evidence.

3. King James in his *Daemonologie* said, it is certain rule (said he) Witches deny their baptism when they Covenant with the Devil, water being the sole element thereof, and therefore said he, when they be heaved into the water, the water refuses to receive them into her bosom (they being such miscreants to deny their baptism), and suffers them to float, as the froth of the sea, which the water will not receive, but casts it up and down, till it comes to the earthy element the shore, and there leaves it to consume.

4. Observe these generation of Witches, if they be at any time abused by being called whore, thieve, etc, by any where they live, they are the readiest to cry and wring their hands, and shed tears in abundance, and run with the full and right sorrowful acclamations to some Justice of the Peace, and with many tears make their complaints: but now behold their stupidity; nature or the elements reflection from them, when they are accused for this horrible and damnable sin of Witchcraft; they never alter or change their countenances, nor let one tear fall. This by the way swimming (by able divines whom I reverence) is condemned for no way, and therefore of late hath, and for ever shall be left.

Query 11. Oh! But if this torturing Witchcatcher can by all or any of these means, wring out a word or two of confession from any of these stupefied, ignorant, unintelligible, poor silly creatures (though none hear it but himself), he will add and put her in fear to confess, telling her else she shall be hanged; but if she do, he will set her at liberty, and so put a word into her mouth, and make such a silly creature confess she knows not what.

Answer. He is of a better conscience, and for your better understanding of him, he doth thus uncase himself to all, and declares what confessions (though made by a Witch against herself) he allows not of, and doth altogether account of no validity, or worthy of credence to be given to it, and ever did so account it, and ever likewise shall.

1. He utterly denies that confession of a Witch to be of any validity, when it is drawn from her by any torture or violence whatsoever; although after watching, walking or swimming, diverse have suffered, yet peradventure Magistrates with much care and diligence did solely and fully examine them after sleep, and consideration sufficient.

2. He utterly denies that confession of a Witch, which is drawn from her by flattery, viz. if you will confess you shall go home, you shall not go to the jail, nor be hanged,

3. He utterly denies that confession of a Witch, when she confesseth any improbability, as flying in the air, riding on a broom,

4. He utterly denies a confession of a Witch, when it is interrogated to her, and words put into her mouth, to be of any force or effect: as to say to a silly (yet wicked enough). 'You have four Imps have you not?' She answers affirmatively, 'yes'. 'Did they not suck you?' 'Yes,' she said. 'Are not their names so, and so?' 'Yes,' saith she. 'Did not you send such an Imp to kill my child?' 'Yes,' saith she, this being all her confession, after this manner, it is by him accompted[5] nothing, and he earnestly doth desire that all Magistrates and Jurors would a little more than ever they did, examine witnesses, about the interrogated confessions.

Query 12. If all these confessions be denied, I wonder what he will make a confession, for sure it is, all these ways have been used and took for good confessions, and many have suffered for them and I know not what, he will then make a confession.

Answer. Yes, in brief he will declare what confession of a Witch is of validity and force in his judgement, to hang a Witch: when a Witch is first found with teats, then sequested from her house, which is only to keep her old associates from her, and so by good counsel brought into a sad condition, by understanding of the horribleness of her sin, and the judgements threatened against her; and knowing the Devil's malice and subtle circumventions, is brought to remorse and sorrow for complying with Satan so long, and disobeying God's sacred commands, doth then desire to unfold her mind with much bitterness, and then without any of the before-mentioned hard usages or questions put to her, doth of her own accord declare what was the occasion of the Devils appearing to her, whether ignorance, pride, anger, malice, etc, was predominant over her, she doth then declare what speech they had, what likeness he was in, what voice he had, what Familiars he sent her, what number of spirits, what names they had, what shape they were in, what employment she set them about to several persons in several places (unknown to the hearers), all which mischief being proven to be done, at the same time she confessed to the same parties for the same cause, and all effected, is testimony enough against her for all her denial.

Query 13. How can any possibly believe that the Devil and the Witch joining together, should have such power, as the Witches confess, to kill such and such a man, child, horse, cow, or the like; if we believe they can do what they will, then we derogate from God's power, who for certain limits the Devil and the Witch; and I cannot believe they have any power at all.

Answer. God suffers the Devil many times to do much hurt, and the Devil doth play many times the deluder and imposter with these Witches, in persuading them that they are the cause of such and such a murder wrought by him with their consents,

103

when and indeed neither he nor they had any hand in it, as thus: we must needs argue, he is of a long standing, about 6,000 years, then we must needs be the best scholar in all knowledge of arts and tongues, and so have the best skill in physique, judgement in physiognomy, and knowledge of what disease is reigning or predominant in this or that man's body (and so for cattle too), by reason of his long experience. This subtle tempter knowing such a man liable to some sudden disease (as by experience I have found), as pleurisy, imposthume, etc, he resorts to divers Witches, if they know the man, and seek to make a difference between the Witches and the party, it may be by telling them he hath threatened to have them very shortly searched, and so hanged for Witches, then they all consult with Satan to save themselves, and Satan stands ready prepared, with a 'What will you have me do for you, my dear and nearest children, Covenanted and compacted with me in hellish league, and sealed with your blood, my delicate firebrand-darlings.' 'Oh thou (they say) that at first did promise to save us thy servants from any of our deadly enemies discovery, and did promise to avenge and slay all those, we pleased, that did offend us; murder that wretch suddenly who threatens the downfall of your loyal subjects. He then promise to effect it.' Next news is heard the party is dead, he comes to the Witch, and gets a world of reverence, credence and respect for his power and activeness, when and indeed the disease kills the party, not the Witch, nor the Devil (only the Devil knew that such disease was predominant), and the Witch aggravates her damnation by her familiarity and consent to the Devil, and so comes likewise in compass of the laws. This is Satan's usual impostring and deluding, but not his constant course of proceeding, for he and the Witch do mischief too much. But I would that Magistrates and Jurats would a little examine witnesses when they hear Witches confess such and such a murder, whether the party had not long time before, or at the time when the Witch grew suspected, some disease or other predominant, which might cause that issue or effect of death.

Query 14. All that the Witchfinder does, is to fleece the country of their money, and therefore rides and goes to towns to have employment and promise them fair promises, and it may be doth nothing for it and possess many men that they have so many Wizards and so many Witches in their town, and so heartens them on to entertain him.

Answer. You do him a great deal of wrong in every of these particulars. For, first:

> He never went to any town or place, but they rode, writ, or sent often for him, and were (for ought he knew) glad of him.
>
> He is a man that does disclaim that ever he detected a Witch, or said, 'Thou art a Witch', only after her trial by search, and their own confessions, he as others may judge.
>
> Lastly, judge how he fleece the country, and enriches himself, by considering the vast sum he takes off every town, he demands but 20*s* a town, and does sometimes ride 20 miles for that and have no more for all his charges there and back again (and it maybe stays a week there) and find there 3 or 4 Witches, or if it be but one, cheap enough, and this is the great sum he takes to maintain his Company with three horses.
>
> Judicet Ullus

TWENTY

'The Discovery of Witches' by Matthew Hopkins: An Analysis

The following is an analysis of Matthew Hopkins's pamphlet *The Discovery of Witches*. It is a stand-alone piece that complements the book by offering 'food for thought' where the vigorous constraints of the individual chapters have left little opportunity for supposition. Although certain weight is added to some of my arguments by this essay, its main purpose is to explore aspects of Hopkins's life and career solely using Hopkins's own words, thus providing a logical self-contained analysis.

Another important reason for analysing the pamphlet is to explore fully how Hopkins conducted his work. This needs to be highlighted almost line by line because so much has not been appreciated by historians and 'biographers' in the past, and so much wrong information has been accepted as correct.

There is one piece of folklore concerning Matthew Hopkins's life story that nobody had been able to substantiate: that he was deemed too successful at his work and accused of Witchcraft himself; that he was then bound hand to foot and tried by his own methods (swum) in his home village and on floating[1] was left to die. It is the dream of any biographer of the Witchfinder to prove the truth of this, but unfortunately only flimsy evidence has surfaced to substantiate the claim. Or is there more?

When opinion about Hopkins and his work turned against him (primarily through John Gaule), he released a small pamphlet arguing his methods. Having possibly been privy to the ways of the legal profession before becoming a Witchfinder, his choice of wording in the pamphlet was very careful – methodical. However, by analysing these words we can ascertain what was happening at a very crucial time in his career as 'self-appointed' Witchfinder General. The first major point in the pamphlet is Query 1 itself: 'That he must need to be the greatest Witch, Sorcerer and Wizard himself, else he could not do it.' It is very telling that Hopkins started his pamphlet in such a way. There is no doubt that the tide *was* turning against him; but what were the people saying?

The statement that is Query 1 is also in fact the answer: it was exactly what the people were saying, so Hopkins had to release his pamphlet effectively to save his own skin. The beginning of the allegory is there, people were saying, 'Hopkins has found so many Witches he must be one himself.' In other words, a case of 'it takes one to know one'. This is a valid argument if you believe in Witchcraft to begin with.

So was Hopkins a victim of his own success? No, he was a victim of his own greed. Nobody was safe from the clutches of Matthew Hopkins and his accomplices, ordinary people feared his arrival in their home town or village, people spoke in fear-tinged whispers about 'the Witchfinder', and so began the folktale (or fairy tale) of Matthew Hopkins, that contemporary threat to children: 'If you don't go to sleep Matthew Hopkins will get you.'[2]

It must be understood that Hopkins's victims were not always people without friends or relations; some locals had known the victims for a number of years. So discussion about Hopkins and his work was rife, especially after the execution of Vicar John Lowes and Hopkins's track record of successfully catching Witches.

However, Hopkins's answer to Query 1 in the pamphlet is quite shocking in its brevity, 'If Satan's kingdom be divided against itself, how shall it stand?' It is clear that Hopkins chose his words carefully and said only what he needed to say to cover himself and, although brief, his answer is evocative of its day: the fear of 'The

Devil and All His Works'. Throwing the question back to the enquirer put that person on the spot. Nobody wanted to stand alone against the Witchfinder, because they themselves would then be accused of Witchcraft (however influential a person they were).[3] So Hopkins's one-sentence response to Query 1 is a confident and bold statement; tinged with arrogance, it certainly exposes a lot of the man's cold and calculating personality. It was his sharp perception that made him write the pamphlet and allowed him to answer his fiercest critics. And it is done coolly and eloquently. We are dealing with a shrewd man here. Intelligent? I would suggest more perceptive than intelligent. His upbringing is deemed to be comfortable, and reading his pamphlet leads to a fair assumption that he could read and write well – and also knew his scriptures, as any son of a man of the cloth should.

And there lies the rub. Hopkins's one-sentence answer holds another meaning too. If one refers to 'Blasphemy against the Holy Ghost' within St Mark in the King James Bible, verse 25 has 'And if a house be divided against itself, that house cannot stand.' Also, verse 26, 'And if Satan rise up against himself, and be divided, he cannot stand, but hath an end.'

We know Hopkins knew his Bible, and to use such a pertinent turn of phrase at the opening of his pamphlet sets the scene nicely. Hopkins was on a holy crusade. I am not being sensationalist here; the theme he sets is the Bible, because as we will see, when the queries in the pamphlet cover such harsh criticism as torture (aspects which Hopkins could not deny), he hides behind spiritual/religious explanations, simply because in the real world what he was doing was wrong.

Hopkins's shrewdness is continued with Query 2 and its answer. To suggest (in the query) that Hopkins was assisted by the Devil in his work, is Hopkins showing his mettle: a man of immense cunning, ready and prepared to cover his tracks. Again, I would not suggest intelligence over shrewdness. The evidence we have on Hopkins's career as a lawyer is circumstantial. If he was a lawyer he would surely have pulled more obvious strings within his profession when taking up Witchfinding; especially when things started to go wrong for him.[4]

It is suggested by Query 2 that Hopkins found Witches with relative ease, almost as though he had a ready-made list from the Devil himself. Again, the ease of locating Witches mixed with the way he forced confessions from his victims caused great concern, among the authorities as well as the general public.[5] But this does beggar the question: were his accomplices locating Witches – in the town or village prior to his arrival? It is logical to suggest that his accomplices worked as his personal agents, ferreting out information concerning people who were in disgrace, disfavour or dispute with their neighbours, therefore providing the opportunity for many witnesses to conspire against the victim and vindicate Hopkins's wild accusations of Witchcraft.

But how did these agents win over the suspicious locals so quickly and learn about the disputes? Simply by acting as a respectable Matron or Midwife. Hopkins's most powerful tool was women, and these women would carry out professional examinations of people of all ages and if they found a mark of Satan on them, that person would become Hopkins's next victim. If no mark was found, the 'local information' would soon lead to a potential victim. Malicious gossip was rife in the lower classes and this provided Hopkins and his assistants with many potential Witches. But how many assistants did Hopkins have?

In his answer to Query 5 he states: 'a dozen of the ablest men in the parish or elsewhere, were present, and most commonly as many ancient skilled Matrons and Midwives present when the women are tried'. These words suggest that Hopkins and Stearne could call upon the services of a number of people (such as Mary Phillips who performed Matron duties); not only that, he would also use the services of respected locals for their professional advice – note his words 'in the parish'.

So Hopkins covered himself with a local second opinion – it would add to the authenticity of the claims made and also provide him with eyewitnesses. One of Hopkins's favourite tricks was to win local support and isolate those people out of favour (the Witches themselves). When that was done, he would execute the Witches discovered. This was a cunning plan because who would complain? Not the accused as who would listen to them.

With Query 3, there comes a very telling question. Having sourced so many Witches and moving around a great deal, it is clear that the obvious question would soon be asked: from where did he acquire the skill of Witchfinding? The answer is extremely interesting and tells us much about Hopkins and his methods.

Hopkins rejects the idea that he discovered the act of Witchfinding from the books of scholars. This is a crafty answer because such books or scholars would have to be identified and what master (or masterpiece) could Hopkins take as providence for his level of wickedness? Could he base all his knowledge on *Daemonologie* alone? Of course not, there had to be an exclusive angle; that is, there had to be first-hand experience.

So Hopkins made himself the scholar – the trail blazer – whose work would be documented and used as an example to others. He states, 'from experience . . . the surest and safest way to judge by'. It is an accepted maxim in today's society that the best way to become an expert at a job is to do it oneself, and not simply learn it in the classroom. So Hopkins's answer is sensible but at the same time without a possible avenue for criticism; indeed, he states that his experience is 'meanly esteemed of', but that is just a learned man observing that he has critics and therefore giving his honest and watertight answer.

All of this supports the idea that Hopkins dreamed up the idea of Witchfinding – the extent to which he took it – himself, and he did not look for any scapegoat or role model. This meant he had to lie with reference to the next query: where did he gain the experience for Witch-hunting and why was the knowledge not open to others?

It is assumed that Hopkins learned about Witch-hunting while in Europe during his teenage years, mainly because some of his methods were almost exclusively European and not been used in England before. But his quite long answer begins with 'The Discoverer never travelled far for it.' I find this answer fascinating, because if he did gain experience in Holland during his teens (even indirectly while studying to be a shipping clerk) why does he not mention it? In fact, if we refer further back in the pamphlet, Hopkins said that experience was the only way to learn.

But that legal mind comes into play here. He could be criticised for using Dutch Witchcraft techniques, as surely they would not work in England or, more importantly, could not be adapted to the English Witch-hunt. So again, Hopkins pre-empts his critics. Hopkins gives a close-to-home story as the spur for his crusade.

He then gives a detailed account of his 'experiences' with Witches to back up his claims.

If Query 4 questioned Hopkins's experience, then Query 5 questions his accuracy, because if people were condemned for having paps or teats on their body how did one man make the judgement that these were not natural marks, especially in older people? Hopkins quickly dispels the idea that judgement is made by one man alone. He states that 'commonly a dozen of the ablest men in the parish or elsewhere, were present.' One gets the distinct impression of a 'press gang' of Witch-hunters searching for and hounding the victim. Interestingly, though, Hopkins states that the 'ablest men' don't just come from 'in the parish' but 'elsewhere'. The fact that he states 'men' and 'elsewhere' surely implies that he did have a posse of able men to call upon, probably when he felt he would encounter some resistance in a certain town or village. It is assumed that Hopkins would have had to pay these men, so to enlist (free of charge?) the local parish made for a more profitable trip for him.

Hopkins goes on to say that 'ancient skilled Matrons and Midwives [were] present when the women are tried'. This is a very carefully made point. By stating that skilled women looked for marks of Witchcraft on women dispels any accusation that Hopkins and his Company[6] bullied or ill-treated the opposite sex. The phrase 'ancient skilled Matrons and Midwives' does not imply that the Matrons and Midwives were ancient, but that they were skilled in their duty to older – 'ancient' – people.

So we can clearly see that Hopkins was covering himself legally, which of course was the whole point of the pamphlet in the first place. The title states that it serves to 'answer . . . several queries lately delivered to the Judges of Assize for the County of Norfolk'. Hopkins was in trouble. Questions were being asked about his practice (namely by John Gaule) and he had to call upon his legal skills – scant though they were – in order to pull off a convincing argument; and as Hopkins was more perceptive than skilled, he fell slightly short of success, as we will later observe.

Hopkins knew that his answer to Query 5 fell slightly short of a convincing argument. Obviously the Judges of the Assize would not let the matter rest after such a flimsy reply. So Query 6 became a supporting thread to Query 5 in order to make a more watertight case. The query itself makes two observations: first, that the 'marks' the Witch-hunters were looking for were 'so near to natural excrescencies' that mistakes could be made and, more importantly, that 'unlawful courses of torture' were employed to drag confessions from the accused.

Hopkins's answer, in three parts, is methodical and calculating. First, he argues the observation about the marks, stating that he judges by the 'unusualness' of the placing of the mark. He then goes on to state (with regard to haemorrhoids): 'if I find them on the bottom of the backbone . . . knowing that they are not near that vein.' I would be inclined to surmise that these words suggest Hopkins acquired some medical advice (Mary Phillips was the main woman identified as working with Hopkins and Stearne in the role of Matron at the time). I believe that by observing Phillip's examinations, and picking up pieces of professional diagnosis, Hopkins gathered enough professional knowledge to temper some critics or, at the very least, convince sound Puritan Magistrates. In order to get away with the Witchfinding for so long and to be so successful, Hopkins had to appear a convincing and respectable man. In short, he surrounded himself with the right people.

It is clear that the answer to Query 6 supported that of Query 5. It is perceptive, approaching the argument from another viewpoint, so all Hopkins had to do in part two of his answer to Query 6 is throw in the supernatural argument, because when the Devil's mark is pierced, the accused feels no pain. The fact that they have probably been stabbed repeatedly beforehand and are therefore 'senseless' is overlooked in Hopkins's response.

The final part of the answer addresses the suckling of a Witch's Imps. Hopkins stated that some paps or teats do not look like such things, because if a Witch found out that Hopkins was coming, she would put out her Imps to suckle on other people, even children. So it was deemed important to watch the Witch for a designated time to see if the Imps would return to her and suckle. At this juncture Hopkins uses an interesting turn of phrase: 'the next day after her teats extended out to their former filling length, full of corruption ready to burst.' By using these words, Hopkins is acknowledging the stereotypical definition of a Witch as laid down in the King James Bible and *Daemonologie*: the woman as the weaker sex, the correlation of Eve in the Garden of Eden giving herself to the serpent. The hidden teats are not described as breasts but they are used in a similar way and, where a breast would be used to nourish a human baby – a child of God – the hidden teats 'full of corruption' are there to nourish the Imps in their ungodly pursuit.

Hopkins had already mentioned *Daemonologie* in his pamphlet and for him to use a learned work only added to his arguments of justification. He was using fashionable text, he was exploiting the paranoia of the day and, ostensibly, the weak-mindedness, fear and naivety of the lower classes to achieve his results. But as a consequence, he was making it very difficult for anyone to argue against him. He had text and witnesses on his side; then he had professional Matrons and Midwives. Also, he had shown that he dealt with his Witches justly by allowing more people to judge them; women for women, men for men and, in the uncertain and paranoid times of the Civil War, did any Magistrates or Judges want to argue against Matthew Hopkins and his legion?

It is interesting to note that in the three parts of Hopkins's answer to Query 6, he does not address the main point of 'torture'. This implies that he was perhaps more concerned about the discovery of Witches than the treatment of them. As the pamphlet is entitled 'The Discovery of Witches' and as Hopkins concentrates on this aspect, admitting at the end of his answer to Query 6, 'Now for answer to their torture in its due place', the Witchfinder becomes exposed, because the 'due place' is too soft a cover.[7]

So what have we learned so far about Matthew Hopkins? That he travelled with, or employed the use of, a select band of accomplices to justify his Witchfinding, both professional people and like-minded people. He drew upon 'witnesses' in the local village or town to condemn Witches. He had some form of legal knowledge; let's call it legal perception. He had Matrons and Midwives (those professional people) planted in a town or village ahead of him to locate Witches by bodily marks or local gossip, so he had a modicum of local knowledge on arrival – enough to get the masses on his side. He was perceptive and convincing in front of local Judges and Magistrates. He was cunning and vindictive in his ways of extracting confessions. He wrote his pamphlet mainly in answer to John Gaule's pamphlet against him and also because his perceptiveness drove him to do it. He considered the King James Bible, *Daemonologie* and his own experiences, as important in the justification of his Witchfinding activities.

An observation: because he was a respected man, a son of a parson with influential friends, Hopkins did have some individual power, influence and presence about him.

As Hopkins begins to include the supernatural in his pamphlet, he introduces torture in 'its due place'. This is an interesting point because it makes the justification of torture subjective (i.e. through the supernatural). But Hopkins had another trick up his sleeve. Query 7 asks why the Devil needs to suck blood if he is a Spirit. The reply is shrewd: the Devil only suckles to aggravate and taunt his Witch, joining with her and reminding her of her coven. It is the appreciating of this answer's sub-text that exposes Hopkins at his most devious: the conclusion of the previous answer in the pamphlet implied a discussion of torture next, but Hopkins didn't do such as thing, or did he? Of course he did, by discussing the torture of a Witch by the Devil – not by him or his Company.

So Hopkins has shifted his stance within the pamphlet by his answer to Query 7. He is no longer justifying himself to 'the good' (Judges, Sticklers and the general public), but proving himself a crusader to a higher 'good' (God). This is done very subtly and quite mechanically. He genuinely believed that his pamphlet was saying enough, that it was answering his critics – since they were all learned men and could see the sub-text he did not need to spell it out. This clearly shows his arrogance.

With Query 8, Hopkins states quite clearly *again* that the discovery of paps was not enough to convict a Witch, but that they must be 'tortured and kept from sleep two or three nights' in order to be 'distracted' enough to be tamed like a wild animal in order to confess. Hopkins states this within the query itself, so an answer is easily built from there (another shrewd trick).

Hopkins had already brought in religious arguments before, but now he had to further highlight the supernatural elements, the endemic paranoia of his age, to justify the unjustifiable.

By having the 'questioner'[8] of Query 8 discuss a theme rather than ask an outright question, Hopkins doesn't have to justify himself, he can discuss the matter in academic terms with his equals, the Judges of the Assize being his target audience. Hopkins begins his answer with: 'In the infancy of this discovery it was not only thought fitting, but enjoyed in Essex and Suffolk by the Magistrates.' But what he then says is if it was enough for the Magistrates then it was *not* enough for him. He had to go one step further. We have a very dangerous man here, because he had turned the accused – in other words himself – into a marshal (above the Judges and Magistrates?) working directly to God, a higher order befitting his egotistical self-made stature within society.

Hopkins then states that it was the stubborn wills of the Witches that kept them from sleeping; so he is blaming the Witch herself for sleep deprivation. He doesn't need to enforce torture upon the Witches, it is self-inflicted. So to put it simply, the first torture is from the Devil and the second is self-inflicted. But was Hopkins being too shrewd for his own good? Was he becoming a little *too* clever? He is certainly egotistical.

With Query 9, Hopkins had to pull things back a little to address a major query directly but now with the voice of authority gained through answering the previous eight queries. I surmise that

Hopkins read all this aloud in order to build up his legal defence. It is done superbly but not, as we will later observe, successfully.

Unfortunately Query 9 must be written out in full in order to discuss its implications/subtleties in their entirety: 'Besides that unreasonable watching, they were extraordinarily walked, till their feet were blistered, and so forced through that cruelty to confess, etc.' To begin with, the query is out of context with the previous query and its answer. But it is the authority of his answer to Query 8 that keeps the momentum flowing into Query 9. His answer is measured and logical, within the now established criteria of the supernatural. Hopkins explained that constant walking of the accused was only carried out during the 'night' they were watched, so their Familiars (Imps) could enter the room and expose their guilt. Hopkins also mentions the use of 'divers' (diverse), a group of people who were used for Watching. He notes that he cannot prove any abuse perpetrated by the people (his Company surely) upon the accused.

If Hopkins failed to achieve his purpose in writing the pamphlet, then the reason must stem from the answer to Query 9. Although it is the answer the Judges are looking for, the problem comes from the fact that it is a tissue of lies. Hopkins and his Company would keep the accused awake for days not one 'night', and he knew that even if not instigated by himself, the accused were being tortured. It is an admission of the fact that he places this query in the section of his pamphlet concerned with torture without actually mentioning the word. Furthermore, it was well known that John Lowes, who along with John Gaule had initiated Hopkins's problems, had been walked for three nights. Hopkins's critics could pick big holes in his answer to Query 9 thus discrediting the pamphlet, or more importantly, exposing its lies and, ostensibly, its writer for the fraud he was. This would show Hopkins's methods, not necessarily his motives, to be unlawful, so therefore he would not be found guilty of any crime, simply discredited and dethroned as a Witchfinder. This would explain how John Stearne was allowed to continue Witchfinding after Hopkins stood down; his work wasn't in question. This is a very important point, as it gives us essential clues as to Hopkins's eventual punishment, which has always been shrouded in mystery.

It is for this fundamental reason that we need to analyse Hopkins's pamphlet; his story is a one-off that should not be placed in juxtaposition to any other analysis of Witchcraft in England or Europe. Hopkins was a self-motivating lateral thinker, cunning and cold, who exploited his own social standing and, consequently, contacts for his own devilish purposes.

The impression I get of Hopkins is akin to the legend of Robin Hood and his merry men. A character who has been touched by folklore but underneath was most certainly a criminal with a bunch of vagabond assistants. And eventually Hood was found out, too.

Hopkins's pamphlet moves on to the act of 'swimming', that is, being tied hand to foot and 'swum' in a river. Query 10 states that this act was 'a trial not allowed by law or conscience'. Hopkins quickly makes a confession. He admits in the very first sentence of his answer that some innocent people were tried and drowned, while a number who were guilty floated. This is something Hopkins could not cover up. He was guilty of executing innocent people, and those innocent people had been accused of Witchcraft, watched and walked along with the 'guilty'.[9] So, drawing towards the end of the pamphlet, Hopkins does have to admit the very obvious, that he did indeed kill innocent people, but what was important from his viewpoint was why this happened. His four-point justification had to make a strong case.

Point 1 is probably the most important answer in the whole pamphlet, because not only does Hopkins present details – facts – of executions but he exposes his guilt quite openly. He mentions a person called 'Meggs a baker' who was searched for paps at his own request and then walked 7 miles (to Norwich) to be hanged. Is this statement true or false? Probably an exaggeration. He then states that forty confessed at the Norwich Assizes. The name of the individual and number of confessions must be true because they could easily have been checked at the time. However, the most cunning justification Hopkins made was that for killing the innocent, because quite simply, according to Hopkins, they were not innocent at all (hence the reason for the earlier admission). He claims that the guilty are told by the Devil to sink in order to be saved, but when they float – because they mistrust him – they see that they have been betrayed and are hanged. This treachery by the Devil is typical of scholarly texts of the time, therefore certain learned Judges would accept Hopkins's argument, because it appeared to be sound judgement.

What else does all this tell us about Matthew Hopkins? That his beliefs were more mature than other people's? Whether mature as far as a total faith in God and the Devil is concerned, or mature in the sense of being in line with present-day beliefs, i.e. that there is little to the Devil than suspicion, is unclear. Because of Hopkins's cunning tricks it can be assumed that he did not take the popular view of the day. But I am reluctant to suggest that he was perceptive enough to have anything close to present-day thought. I would opt for a middle ground: I believe Hopkins was an atheist. To convict people so coldly, so ruthlessly, he must have had an agenda. When William Dowsing started to destroy holy relics in Hopkins's area in 1644, it was only one month later that Hopkins reputedly – according to his pamphlet – found a Coven of Witches in his home town. This is a very telling fact and, something I cannot pass off as simply coincidence.

Hopkins knew something of religion from a young age and, if there was religious disorder, may have refuted it (perhaps because of the lack of fatherly influence or simply teenage rebellion). With the Puritan influence so strong in Essex and Suffolk, perhaps Hopkins did not accept the Puritan way. We can dismiss this question in all honesty because if John Lowes had Anglican/Catholic leanings, and if Hopkins was a secret Catholic, surely he would not have had Lowes killed just to hide his true faith. It doesn't seem plausible.

Also, I am not alone in my belief in an atheist Hopkins, for the Reverend Montague Summers wrote in his own study of *The Discovery of Witches*: 'Matthew Hopkins was undoubtedly a man of no small energy and of considerable force of character, possessing indeed a personality to be reckoned with, as his career clearly shows, yet his religious proclivities are nowhere protruded or even emphasized in circumstances which might well have been thought to have been most favourable to the exhibition of an unusual pietism and sanctimoniousness, which it is quite certain his fellow enthusiasts of the same kidney would have deployed and exaggerated on every possible occasion.' Summers is suggesting that others within Hopkins's Company instigated the religious aspect of the Witch-hunt and, obviously, we learn by reading his own pamphlet that John Stearne was indeed – as Hopkins's main accomplice – the instigator of that aspect. Summers called Stearne Hopkins's 'Jackal', and although this has the correct connotation from Hopkins's viewpoint, it is not correct from Stearne's. Stearne was an extreme Puritan so, ostensibly, he thought he was doing a good job.

Returning to the pamphlet text and the second point of the four, there is a one-sentence answer: 'It [the Swimming test] was never brought in against any of them at their trials as any evidence.' A simple answer to the critics because if it was an issue why was it not mentioned before? A valid counterclaim and a very learned turn of phrase. I'm not suggesting here that Hopkins was a lawyer. I believe the 'lawyer' gambit has been vastly blown out of proportion in the past, simply because there has never been a shred of evidence to suggest that he was a lawyer. However, there is a tantalising hint of something in Hopkins's words. Although not possessing such a talent, I believe Hopkins did sometimes harness it by observing his elders and betters. I do subscribe to the idea that he was a clerk and sometimes was asked to countersign documents – but then he aspired to greater things and so found the best vehicle for that talent.

In the third point, Hopkins used King James's *Daemonologie* as a justification for his work. It mentions the use of swimming so Hopkins shows that therefore he was only employing tried and tested methods. So in answering three of the four points, he had used the traditional tricks of the Devil as justification that all the guilty were indeed guilty. But what of point four? Hopkins explained how cunning the Witch was, because if she was verbally abused she quickly ran crying to the Magistrate; but she sheds no tears when performing her Witchcraft, therefore no one should feel sorry for the Witch if she is swum for her crimes by just men in Hopkins's employ.

All four points take a different angle in justifying Hopkins's work through the teaching of noble books, the judicial system, or simply a moral stance as Hopkins saw it (as detailed in the fourth part of Query 10).

Query 11 is the crux of the whole pamphlet. The off-hand, almost political, way of assaulting the opposition is displayed in the question in such a way that this must have been the crux of the building rebellion against Hopkins. The words are flippant and deeply critical of the Witchfinder. The query suggests that Hopkins's critics were well aware of his tactics in bribing the foolish Witch and in stating that if she confessed to Witchcraft she would escape hanging. Hopkins had to deliver an answer of some depth and substance. Not only did he write a paragraph in response, he then followed it with a four-point answer, thus revealing his own fears relating to the query and acknowledging its importance. But was his answer any good? And if not, was this the beginning of the end for Matthew Hopkins?

The opening paragraph of his answer includes the words 'he [Hopkins] doth thus uncase himself to all, and declares what confessions . . . he allows not of.' This is Hopkins as a scared man. In fact, the whole pamphlet has been a build-up to this Achilles heel. Hopkins had been exposed so, clearly, he had to justify himself, and so ensued the four-point answer. Point 1 had to start with the obvious: 'He [Hopkins] utterly denies that confession of a Witch to be of any validity, when it is drawn from her by any torture or violence.' Hopkins goes on to say that the Watchers themselves are the ones who suffer because they have to remain vigilant night and day until a Witch's Imps make themselves known and, consequently, seal the fate of the Witch. Hopkins then concludes the first point by stating that Magistrates did examine the Witches after adequate sleep to ensure their guilt. So Hopkins covers much ground with this first point. He refutes the possibility that 'valid' confessions can be obtained through torture. He then declares that his Watchers suffer for their art and that after the Witch has had adequate sleep Judges make their own decisions; surely he can do little more? Well, there are three other points he wishes to make here.

Point 2 is a very succinct denial in direct answer to the question: he denies that a confession is drawn from the Witch by flattery. In Hopkins's words: 'if you confess you shall go home, you shall not go to jail, nor be hanged.'

The answers made so far are very astute, almost ready for the courtroom, so again the 'legal' side of Hopkins is on display, or trial.

Point 3, again succinct, denies the ridiculous, thus suggesting that no person is condemned because of mental imbalance: 'He [Hopkins] utterly denies that confession of a Witch, when she confesseth any improbability, as flying in the air, riding on a broom.'

Point 4 is the longest and here Hopkins denies that he puts words – confessions – into the mouth of the Witch (obviously after watching/torture); but the important part of the narrative is Hopkins's conclusion that he 'earnestly doth desire that all Magistrates and Jurors would be a little more than ever they did, examine a witness, about the interrogated confessions.' Is this Hopkins exposed, cowering and begging for more support from the official bodies? Possibly, but again in that shrewd and cunning manner that has been present throughout the whole pamphlet. He's not begging for forgiveness but for support.

Query 12 is any good lawyer's counter to Hopkins's answers to Query 11, stating that all confessions are good confessions. This is a cunning means of moving the debate back on-line, i.e. in agreement with Hopkins's methods. The answer begins with Hopkins agreeing that whatever confession a Witch gives has validity in his judgement to hang her. But he then states that the discovery of teats and other factors were used as evidence first before pressing for a confession. He then mentions the Devil and his tricks which, in themselves, have to be circumvented. Hopkins continues by describing how the Devil's influence lays heavy on the Witch and how she has to denounce him almost in a confessional way – this in itself is Hopkins writing for his time. The *Daemonologie* influence, which is based upon Catholic beliefs, works in juxtaposition to the Puritan way, particularly in the moral justification of the conviction of Witches.

With the benefit of hindsight we see how Hopkins's justification falls apart, because who today believes in a Devil who possesses people in order to achieve his satanic goals?

Hopkins was the trendsetter of his day, in fashion one day, hopelessly out of date the next. But did he believe in what he did? No, I do not think he was that naive. Reading and understanding the whole of Hopkins's pamphlet suggests he had an agenda. Hopkins knew what he wanted to achieve through his Witch trials. He wanted money, power and fame, and it was the collapse of the judicial system during the Civil War that furnished him with a mechanism to achieve such goals. Couple this with his well-placed contacts, mainly through his late father,[10] and you have a very bitter and dangerous man, a man exposed: Matthew Hopkins, Witchfinder General.

Query 13 is most provocative, because it questions the Bible. This is another reason why I believe Hopkins was an atheist. The provocative element of the query did not bother him at all, but he knew it would bother everybody else, and that was why he was so dangerous, so cunning, and so successful. Matthew Hopkins played to everybody's fears, no matter what their social standing and intelligence. He could take them all on and win, because everybody feared God and the Devil; they also feared the blasphemy of contradicting the Bible.

This is a major point in the Hopkins story because if his beliefs were different from everybody else's, then he was a loner inasmuch as he was a dangerous free-thinker. Yes, he did bring in other people to assist him, but only to assist him in his own quest for power, respect and money. When things began to turn against him he got cunning, but then his loyal rabble (his Company) saw the error in their ways and violently turned against him.

Query 13 is very much based upon the adage: good transcends evil. So it is a biblical query and, ostensibly, anyone who questions it leaves themselves open to criticism. The line 'I cannot believe that they [the Devil and the Witch] have any power at all' supports this tradition of good transcending evil.

At the beginning of his answer Hopkins states that the Devil tries to delude God in many ways. However, he goes on to say that because the Devil has infiltrated the lives of innocent people for years, certain people have looked to Witches for assistance with many ailments; and then denounced them for failing to carry out a cure, resorting to making their own pact with the Devil as they have no other recourse.

This is an interesting concept and not a total fabrication of the truth. The lower, more uneducated classes did just this, thus creating the endemic menace of Witches during the Civil War. Whether these people were in any way dangerous is a matter of conjecture but the important point concerning Hopkins's answer is that he identifies a true social problem among the lower classes – a *justifiable* problem. However, his way of solving the problem was criminal; a 'Witch' was a menace not a servant of the Devil.

Throughout his answer, Hopkins takes the line that Witches make a pact with the Devil; but he also asks a question: whether any disease or ailments were present in those people accused of Witchcraft before they made their pact with the Devil? He clearly shows sound reasoning in his answer and this provokes the question: did Hopkins believe in what he was doing? In his own way, yes. As an atheist, and the son of a parson, I believe he could see the corruption that the Bible instilled in people, and when William Dowsing started his attacks on churches he formed the idea of Witch-hunting because he knew to what extremes he could go. He conducted his business for his own pleasure and profit, but he also had to justify it. Hopkins achieved this by stating that there were people who used the dark arts to cause mischief within any given town or village. These menaces did not cure people of their ailments, but instead they created disputes. He then took this further (in a religious sense), accusing Witches of making milk sour and sinking ships at sea, and when he introduced the Witchcraft aspect, he would authenticate it through *Daemonologie* and the King James Bible. He began with a local Coven, to see whether his idea would work: it was a means of getting rid of the lower orders whom he personally saw as a menace.

All this makes great sport of Hopkins's work. The 'official' justification would bring Magistrates on his side and 'like-minded' people to his aid, working through a fear of God and the Devil, which he himself sneered at. One further point: the accusation of Witchcraft in Puritan East Anglia, Cromwell's stronghold, allowed Parliamentarians to use Hopkins to accuse Royalist agents of Witchcraft.

The final question is the grand finale, because if only one question was to be asked of Matthew Hopkins then it would be whether he conducted his work purely for pleasure and profit? Hopkins begins his answer by admitting that he felt quite damaged by such an accusation. He then goes on to give a three-point answer. First he declares that sometimes he was indeed sent for by a particular town or village (which was true), then that he only finds Witches by fair inspection and then fair trial (not so true). Finally, he states that he charged 20s for his services and did not always make a profit.

This last point seems to be a little too out of the ordinary, but there is a point there with regard to the Witch-hunt of 1647. With Hopkins's poor health and the increasing resentment against him, he was becoming less popular and less successful. However, I am sure that sometimes Hopkins was sent for. Some people did believe in the work he was doing. If there was a certain 'Witch' causing havoc then perhaps she and her Coven should be exposed and hanged before they poisoned the whole town. This goes back to the point I made earlier: whether Hopkins did actually believe that he was providing a goodly service. People must have believed he was providing a legitimate service in order for him to be accepted for what was over two years of intense work. If indeed he took people in, why was he criticised and why did his pamphlet fail to help him continue his work?

The answer to both questions is: John Lowes. Questions were asked, while Lowes was on trial, as to Hopkins's methods. Hopkins answered the questions concerning the methods but not the root cause: hanging a priest, a man of the cloth, who was not from the lower orders, a man with influential friends such as John Gaule – Hopkins had overstretched himself.

So should Hopkins have given more detailed and direct answers to the questions presented in the pamphlet? Yes, but he failed to do so, keeping everything generic, and certain big questions remained unanswered. In the end Hopkins was a little too clever for his own good and the publication of the pamphlet marked the beginning of the end for him.

Finally, if one looks at the cover of Hopkins's pamphlet (as used in Montague Summers' analysis of *The Discovery of Witches*), one can clearly see an antique annotation 'May'. This suggests that the pamphlet was printed in May 1647 and this seems the most plausible date of publication – one month before Hopkins died.

His words were finally unconvincing, and there was nothing to stop Hopkins from being questioned by a higher order. It would cost him his life, and his pamphlet was *too* little, *too* late.

TWENTY-ONE

'A Confirmation and Discovery of Witchcraft' by John Stearne: The Text

AUTHOR'S NOTE

What follows is a contemporary translation of John Stearne's pamphlet *A Confirmation and Discovery of Witchcraft*, which was first published in 1648. The pamphlet has not been published in its entirety before for several reasons: one, that there is deemed to be too much Puritan jargon, two, that the English used is very poor and three, just as much can be learned by using select quotes as by translating and analysing the whole pamphlet.

To all of the above, I could not agree less. Stearne's pamphlet is an important document, which is underestimated nowadays. Also, people do not seek to understand the document today and academic study will only furnish half-truths (through no fault of its own). The whole document needs to be read in as clear English as possible, without upsetting the flow of Stearne's words, the polemic. This is absolutely essential if we are to get anything tangible from the work. The whole thing must be absorbed and then discussed (see Chapter Twenty-two) in order to get under the skin of John Stearne and expose the man, and more of the personality of his good friend and colleague Matthew Hopkins.

A note on the text: The reader will find few full stops within the pamphlet. This is faithful to the original manuscript. However, I have altered some punctuation to help clarify certain points.

126

A CONFIRMATION AND DISCOVERY OF WITCHCRAFT

Containing these several particulars;
That there are Witches called Bad Witches, and Witches untruly called Good
or White Witches, and what manner of people
they be, and how they may be known, with many
particulars thereunto tending.

Together with the Confessions of many of those executed since May 1645, in
several counties hereafter mentioned.
And also some objections answered.

By John Stearne, now of Lawshall near Bury St. Edmunds in Suffolk,
sometimes of Manningtree in Essex.

PROV. 17.15. *He that justifieth the wicked, and he that condemneth the just,*
even they both are an abomination to
the Lord.
DEUT. 13.14. *Thou shall therefore inquire, and make search, and ask*
diligently, whether it be true, and the thing certain.

London,
Printed by William Wilson, dwelling in Little Saint Bartholomewes near Smithfield.
1648

COURTEOUS READER

TO THE END I might satisfy the opinions of such as desire to be further satisfied concerning the diabolical art, or crying sin, of Witchcraft (as I may so call it). For the sin of Witchcraft, and the diabolical practice thereof, is omnium scelerum atrocissimum, and in such as have the knowledge of God, the greatest apostacie from the faith; for they renounce God and Christ, and give themselves by a covenant to the Devil, the utter enemy to God and all mankind, for in *Deut. 18.10,11,12.* God gave command to all the children of

Israel that none amongst his should be such. For those abominations were the children of Canaan driven out from before them, and utterly destroyed and plagued. As also Manasseth, *2 Cron. 33.6.* which wickedness of his was so abhorred of God, as in his displeasure he mentions it many years after by Jeremy, as cause of removing the Jews from their land, and so leading them away captive into a strange land, *Ier. 15.4,5.* Idolaters ought to die, as in *Exod. 22.20.* and *32.28,29.* Nay inticers to idolatrie, *Deut. 13.9.* because they worship Devils, *Psal. 106.37. 1 Cor. 10.20. Revel. 9.20.* But Witches worship Devils, they invocate them, crave help of them, work by them, and do them homage, sacrifice to them, and they do it not to stocks and stones, and so immediately to the Devil, as other idolaters do, but immediately to the Devil himself, and therefore the greatest idolaters that can be, and are not they then more worthy of death? And to convince others who are of such an erroneous opinion as to say, notwithstanding God's law against them, and the holy scripture speaking of them, beside the laws of nations, both heathen and Christian, made to punish them, that there are no Witches, but that there are many poor silly ignorant people hanged wrongfully, and that those who have gone or been instruments in finding out or discovering those of late made known have done it for their own private ends, for gain and such like, favouring some where they thought good, and unjustly prosecuting others, I therefore (as my leisure hath permitted me) have given myself to the reading of some approved relations touching the arraignment and condemnation of Witches; as also treatises of learned men concerning the Devilish art of Witchcraft; adding withal some few things which otherwise I have learned and observed since the 25 March 1645 as being in part an agent in finding out of discovering some of those since that time, being about two hundred in number, in Essex, Suffolk, Northamptonshire, Huntingdonshire, Bedfordshire, Norfolk, Cambridgeshire, and the Isle of Ely in the county of Cambridge, besides other places, justly and deservedly executed upon their legal trials. Now the occasion being thus offered, and Master Hopkins dead, I desire to give some satisfaction to the world, that it may appear, what hath been done, hath been for the good of the commonwealth, and we free from those aspersions cast upon us, and that I never favoured any, or unjustly prosecuted others, but that all that be guilty of this ought to die; as well the Good or White Witches so called, as the other: and that there is, and hath been more favour showed, or at least less care taken for the discovery of such as be guilty, then by the word of God there ought. For how many are there now a day which could be contented to pass by many of them, as Magicians, Necromancers and such like? Of whom his late majesty of famous renown in his *Demonologie* giveth a dreadful censure, who saith they are to be dealt with all, as with Sorcerers, and especially the curing Witch, commonly called the Good Witch. Nay these rather get credit and estimation, love and liking, as did the Magicians and Sorcerers with Pharaoh, *Exod. 7.8.* with Nabuchadnezer and Belshazzar, *Isa. 47.12 Ezek. 22.* As did also Simon Magnus with the Samaritans, who was held to be the great power of God, *Acts 8.* Likewise Elimas with Sergius Paulus, *Acts 13.* And the Pythonesse with her master, *Acts 16.* And will not many say, surely they work by God, because they use good prayers and good words, and often name God? But let those remember that the Devil himself can use good words, *Mar. 1.24.* and *5.7. Acts 17.* that he can counterfeit the habit and words of a holy man, *Samuel. 1 Sam. 28.13,15,17.* that he can turn himself into an angel of light, *2 Cor. 11.* Therefore he not teach his servants to feign holiness and yet be these in many respects worse than the others, and the holy scripture exempts none, but utterly forbids any going to them, or asking council of them. I hope this my labour will excuse me, and give some better satisfaction to those who are not yet fully satisfied herein, for that I shall make it plainly appear, that I neither formerly, in any of my proceedings concerning this matter, or in penning of this, ayme[1] at mine own private ends rather than the public good, for that I shall discover, so far forth as I am able, or at least, as civility or modesty shall give way; yet I am not ignorant how dangerous it is for me to put myself so far forth into the sea of common opinion, and I cannot see that by reason of the shelves and rocks of injurious conceits which are ready to be found on every hand I am like to pass any adventure; having had experience already how forward many be in taking part with many of those who have been detected to promote them forward to take the least advantage by suit of law, thereby to acquit themselves, when as many times it hath fallen out otherwise, and been a means to bring to their deserved punishment, but let such remember, the Devil needs no provoker. And though Balack sent to Balaam to pursue the people, yet we find the contrary, for surely said Balaam, there is no enchantment in Jacob, nor divination against Israel. And yet nevertheless craving pardon if in anything herein I have taken too much upon me, I have once ventured to commit myself to thy sensure and doubt not prosperous acceptance, if but a charitable construction be had of my true intent and meaning therein, as from a plain country man, who intend not to pen anything but what I shall be able to make appear plainly to be truth, and then I shall reckon it as a sufficient recompense for my labour and pains. And so with due respects I take leave.

John Stearne

A CONFIRMATION AND DISCOVERY OF WITCHCRAFT

Man being born in sin, has since the fall of our first parents lost the Image of God in which he was created, through the temptation of Satan, and is naturally, wholly polluted with sin and corruption, whereby he is become of very near kin unto the Devil, even his own child, *1 John 3.10*. And that being his child, he will do the lusts of his father, *John 8.44*. and that no doubt in one thing as well as in another, for men love darkness more than light, *John 3.19*. Yes, and naturally are given to work all uncleanness even with greediness, so captivated are they to their lusts, *Ephes. 4.19*. For Satan has his wills, *Ephes. 11*. his devices, *2 Cor. 2.11*. his depths and policies. *Revel. 2.24*. his sinners to catch people unawares. *1 Tim. 3.7.2 Tim. 2.26*. And being thus furnished, he dare set upon any, yes upon our Saviour Christ himself, to solicit him, yes, and to a most execrable impiety, even to have Christ to fall down and to worship him a Devil, *Mat. 4*. for he watcheth opportunities, he seeketh occasions, and the least offer he espieth and quickly taketh the same, and so prevailed often . . . but with the greatest spirits and sharpest wits many times. For man being given over to his unruly passion, is violent, inconsiderate and vehemently greedy to have desired ends, by what means soever he can attain them; which maketh him seek means of the Devil to become injoyer of his inordinate desires, regarding more the having of his present will, than respecting his future state after death, and is more taken up to obtain what he liketh for the body and outward estate in the world, than with the care of his spiritual condition and estate before God in the world to come, which the natural man very little or nothing at all regarded. This being the condition of a natural man who remains still unregenerate and given over of God unto Satan's temptation in this kind, how can they resist? Man is weak, Satan is strong, and withal subtle to beguile, they may easily yield, for that he hath over mere natural men a ruling power, *Ephes. 2.2.* who are already in his snare, and at his own will are taken captive, *2 Tim. 2.26.*

Here some will say, you go about to make all subject to Witchcraft, or at least all unregenerate persons.

I answer, it said in *John 3.6.* That which is born of the flesh is flesh, and that which is born of the spirit is spirit: and therefore Witchcraft being [as] Saint Paul saith, amongst the fruits of the flesh, *Gal. 5.20.* one may fall into this sin as well as into any other, if God prevent it not. Wherefore it behoves man (if he would prevent the power of the Devil and whatsoever Witches can do) to labour to entertain and uphold the preaching of the gospel. For where it commeth, down goeth the power of Witchery, *Acts 8.* and *13.*

History likewise tells us, where the gospel came among the heathen, there the hellish power of Devils and spirits greatly diminished, and we hear now by travellers, that in other countries where the gospel is not preached, and where they still remain, (as I may say) according to be abominations of the Canaanites, I mean in such places where the heathens still remain, as in the Indies, where they by travellers relations, worship the sun, moon and stars, nay I have heard in some places, the Devil himself, and where popery and provenance is, with contempt of preaching or vile neglect thereof, there Witchcraft is most rife. Therefore it behoves men to labour to

131

bring forth fruits worthy [of] the gospel and amendment of life. For God hedgeth[2] the virtuous man about, *Jer 1.* so as Satan cannot come at him, without very special licence from God, and that only for a trial. The Angels of God do also pitch their tents about such, *Psal. 34.* yea, and have charge over them to keep them in their ways, *Psal. 91.11,12.* And to have religious duties in our families: and as the apostle saith, to pray continually. *1 Thes. 5.* And as Saint James telleth us, *Jam. 5.16.* that the prayer of a righteous man availeth much if it be servant, David did not only serve God openly in the Tabernacle, but returned home to bless his house, *2 Sam. 6.20.* And Job every day sacrificed to God, and Sacrificed his children and family. *Job 1.5.* And God gave to Israel a law to sacrifice their houses. And so going ever well armed against these rulers of darkness, devils and evil spirits, furnished with the heavenly furniture and spiritual weapons of which the apostle speaketh, *Eph. 6.14.18.* and being thus qualified, and armed, to trust in God only, who will keep thee under the shadow of his wings, *Psal. 91.* No man shall need to fear Witches or Devils; knowing ever this, that they cannot do the very least harm unto any of the least creatures of God without leave from him: no, not to enter into the heard of swine of the very Gardarens, for surely there is no enchantment in Jacob, nor any divination against Israel. It is the Lord, let him do what seemeth him good, *2 Sam.15.26.* It is the Lord that giveth, it is the Lord that taketh away, blessed be the name of the Lord, *Job 1.21.* And therefore many yeald thus far as that Satan needs no provoker to set him forward, as the scripture tells us. For the text saith, that he compasseth the world to, and fro, *Job 1.* going up and down like a roaring lyon seeking whom he may devour, *1 Pet. 5.8.* He is ready (if God give way) to be a lying spirit in the mouth of Ahabs prophets to seduce him, *1 King. 22.* and to beguile; and that the people which brought the possessed to our saviour, complained only of the Devil, *Mat. 15.2 Luk. 9.39.* They made no mention of Witches, nor (for ought we know) had any suspicion of them, for we find that God hath often sent the Devil, as an executioner of his displeasure without any means of a Witch, as amongst the Egyptians, he sent evil angels, *Psal. 78.49.* between Abimelch and the Sichites, *Judg.*

9.23. So upon *Saul, 1 Sam.16.15*. And so we read of a Legion sent by Christ into the heard of swine, *Mat. 5.12*. Thus we see Devils immediately sent from God without any instigation of Witches. And therefore conclude that all is from the Devil by Gods permission, and that there are no Witches at all. But whosoever thou best that art of this opinion, and although many have gone about to prove that there are no Witches: yet besides the former reason, the contrary tenet is undeniably true, that there are Witches.

First, from the laws that God himself hath made against them. First, in forbidding the practice of Witchcraft, and that none amongst his should be Witches, Wizards, Necromancers and such like, *Deut. 18.10,11,12*. Secondly in forbidding any of them to go to them, *Levit. 19.20. Isa 8.19*. Thirdly, his commandement to put Witches to death, *Exod. 22.18*. Fourthly, Gods judgements against them, *Deut 18.12*. which if there were no Witches what need these laws?

Secondly, from the history of the Bible, which nameth to us certain Witches, as the Sorcerers of Egypt, *Exod. 7*. Jannes and Jambres, *2 Tim. 3.8*. Those in Babylon and Persia, *Dan. 2.5.7. Isa. 47.12*. And amongst the nations driven out before the children of Israel, *Deut. 18.12.13*. So we read of other Witches which were, of Balaam *Numb. 22. Jos. 13.22*. Of Israel, *2 King. 9.22*. Of Manasses, *2 Chron. 33.6*. Of Simon Magus, *Acts 8.9*. And Elimas, *Acts 13.8*. Secondly, it maketh mention of the practices of Witches, *Exod. 7.2 Chron. 33.6. Isa. 47.9. Eze. 21.21*. Thirdly, it speaketh of some going to them, *I Sam. 28.7*. and sending to them, *Numb. 22.5. Ios. 24.9*. Fourthly, it relateth how some kings put them to death, *I Sam. 28.3,9*. And cut them off, *2 King. 23.24*. all this should be false if there were no Witches.

Thirdly, from some comparisons or similes fetched from Witchcraft, by Samuel, *I Sam. 15*. and by *Isa. 29.4*. Which were absurd if there were no Witches.

Fourthly, (as before) St Paul's mentioning of Witchcraft amongst the works of the flesh, *Gal. 5.20*.

Fifthly, God's threatening damnation upon Sorcerers, *Rev. 21.8*.

Sixthly, the laws of nations both heathen and Christian against them.

Seventhly, the truth of histories, and many relations of their Arraignment and conviction.

Eighthly, experience amongst ourselves, and in other countries, together with the confession of some of those Witches condemned and executed since May 1645 in the several counties aforementioned, hereafter, herein expressed, I hope will give all sufficient satisfaction that there are Witches.

Now here some may say, this is sufficient to prove that there are Witches in some counties, or at least have been in former times with us here in this country; but how will you make it appear that there have been any since the gospel preached amongst us? For many are of opinion that there are Witches in other countries where the gospel is not at all, or very little regarded, but where the gospel is faithfully preached as with us in England and Scotland, etc. that there are not any, no not since the coming of our saviour.

I answer that if any man can make it appear that the gospel frees us from sin, more than the law did our forefathers, that then it might be so. But the gospel frees us not, and therefore we are as like to have such miscreants amongst us as our forefathers. For we are as sinful as in the time of the law. And Satan still remains amongst us. And we are as impatient, profane, and unconscionable as ever, having distempered passions, violent in affection, given to ill company, and vain curiosities, not having respect of religion, by which occasions the Devil taketh advantage and works to have his will, for he goeth thither where he is either sure or hopeth well for entertainment, *Mat. 12.44.* He therefore watcheth the time when he may best offer his services to such as any way he finds the least kind of preparedness in, as when any fall into passionate sorrow, accompanied with solitariness for some loss, as husband, wife, children or such like, the Devil offers himself to comfort such in their sorrowful melancholy mood. So in time of death through extreme poverty it many times causeth many to be desperately impatient; or so impatient through poverty when they would need to be rich, even against God's providence, as that they be in such a distempered passion, as they would have their wants satisfied and their desires fulfilled, be it by what means it possibly can be, (as I may say) right or wrong; or when one is enraged with anger, plotting revenge, or is Familiar with such as be Witches; as likewise when any are addicted to the reading and studies of dangerous books, enticing to the practice of hidden mysteries, of magic and enchantments. Thus by these and such other like means as may be gathered from the confessions of Witches, they prepare themselves for Satan's temptations, to draw them to Witchcraft, as I could instance in those innumerable examples, as you shall read hereafter more at large when I come to speak of what sorts of people are most addicted to Witchcraft; and therefore do you not conceive that there are still such people remaining amongst us? Yes certainly there are, and Witches likewise.

But you will still say it doth not yet plainly appear to be so since the gospel, though all these sins still remain, for the Devil needs no provoker as before, for he can, if God permit, greatly trouble us, and can bereave one of his wits, and make one lunatic, deaf, dumb and blind, bow the body together, so that one shall not be able to lift up himself, he can even enter in and possess any really and make them invincibly strong, and work other effects. Of all which you may read in *Matth. 9.32.* and *15.22* and *17.15. Mark 1.23* and *5.5,7* and *72.6.* and *9.17,18,19,20,22,25,26* and in *Luke 4.35.* and *7.2.* and *8.29,39* and *11.14.* and *13.11,16.* and can enter into children, *Luke 13.16.* young folks, *Mark 7.26.* Men, *Mark 5.1,2,3.* women, *Luke 13.16 Matt.* the *15.22.* Yea through the permission of God, such as be the elect of God. *Job 1 and 2.* A daughter of Abraham, *Luke 13.11.* And Mary Magdalene, *Luke 7.2.* and can counterfeit the resemblance of an holy man, *I Sam. 28.12.14.19.* Yea and for a long time, *Luke 8.27.* from a child till one be grown up, *Mark 9.21.* even eighteen years, *Luke 13.16.* and so we read in *Luke 7.2.* of seven Devils in one at once, and more *Luke 11.26.* Yea a whole legion, *Mark 5.9,16,14.* and sometimes the Lord is pleased to send Devils as executioners of his displeasure, as is before expressed.

To this I answer, and grant it for truth, and not to be denied, but yet notwithstanding all this, there are Witches likewise, and yet the Devil doth all this, and more if God permit, for in *Gen. 3.* We may learn there that the Devil may enter into a dumb creature, and come out of the same, utter a voice intelligible, and so offer conference (if any will hearken) to deceive as our Witches now a days confess, and that he chooseth the subtlest creature to deceive by, and the weaker vessel to confer with, but by the confessions of Witches now lately detected, he chooseth such creatures as they themselves are most addicted to, as you shall hereafter find by their confessions, by the several shapes he appears in, but how ever we may read there, it was a powerful persuasion to overcome, and yet work by Witches, Wizards, Necromancers, Sorcerers, Soothsayers, and all kind of magic art, as we may read in *Exod. 7.1,12.* and *8.7.* Where we may see that pharaoh called the Wisemen, the Sorcerers, and the magicians of Egypt, who did with their enchantments in like manner as Moses and Aaron. But I pass by the proofs out of the Old Testament for this because I desire to give such satisfaction (as I am able) that it may appear that there be Witches now as in former ages. And if what hath been already spoken will not give satisfaction herein, you may read in the 2. *Tim 3.8* who they were, that were the opposers of the truth, but such as Jannes and Jambres, who withstood Moses, and then search who they were, and you shall find they were such as Pharaoh called to him, as in the before mentioned places, who with their enchantments did the like as Moses had done.

So you may read of Elimas the Sorcerer, *Act. 13.8.* who resisted the Apostles in the time of the Gospel.

So likewise in *Act. 8.9.* you shall read of Simon Magus a Sorcerer, to whom in the 10th verse it is said, they all gave heed from the least to the greatest, saying, this man is the great power of God, for in the 11th verse it is said, because that of long time he had bewitched them with Sorceries, and in the 13th verse we read he was baptised, but read the 20,21,22, and you shall read what Peter said to him, and so read no more of him in all the New Testament.

Also in the *Rev. 21.8.* you may read how Sorcerers shall with other sinners there reckoned up, have their part in the lake which burneth with fire and brimstone.

And so likewise we read in the Epistle of Jude the Apostle speaking there of false teachers, which were crept into the church to seduce them, for whose damnable doctrine and manners, horrible judgement was prepared, in the 11th verse pronounceth woe unto them, for they have gone in the way of Cain, and ran greedily after the error of Balaam, by which we may plainly see that there were Witches in the time of the Gospel, and after the coming and ascension of our Saviour, and do any doubt then whether there be any now? Do any think that we be free from such, where sin and ignorance besides so much abounds? Or do you desire to have proof of Witches since then, you shall have enough of their confessions to make this evident, besides the relations of learned writing concerning Witchcraft. But if you would but rightly observe that place in *2.Tim. 3.1* and so on to the 8th. You shall find that in the last days shall come perilous times, etc. And in the 8th verse it is said, And as Jannes and Jambres withstood Moses, so do those also resist the truth. There you may see plainly that there should be such to the latter end, besides in divers other places speaking expressively of Witchcraft; as *1. Tim. 4.1.* and *Jude 18.*

Likewise of the Pythonesse which brought her mistress much gain *Acts 16.16.* Also in *Rev. 21.8.* And so I might nominate divers other places, for those which remain doubtful either of being bewitched or of Witches themselves, but because their own confessions clear this evidently, besides the forenamed places, I proceed to distinguish between those called Bad Witches, and those called White or Good Witches, which is easily to be discerned and known.

But yet I say all Witches be bad, and ought to suffer alike, being both in league with the Devil: for so is the good, so untruly called, as well as the other, either open or implicit. And therefore I conclude, all that be in open league with the Devil ought to die. And the scripture maketh mention only of ten sorts, which speaks rather of those called the good, which the world so much runs after, then the other. As we may read: First in *Deut. 18.10. 2 Kings 17.1* of a Diviner foreshowing things to come, such the people delighted in and consulted with, *Jer. 27.9. Ezek. 21.22.* Such a one was Balaam, *Jos. 13.22.*

Secondly, we read in *Deut. 18.10.* of an observer of times, or Soothsayer, one which by gaping on the Heavens could also foretell something. To these likewise did the people give ear, *Jer. 27.9.* And such as one was Manasseh, 2 *Chron. 33.6.* And what was Elimas the Sorcerer spoken of in the *Acts?*

Thirdly, we read the *Deut. 18.10.* of an observer of times, or searcher out; one which observed times to know when it was best to begin a business: as Hamans Witches did by crafting of lots before him. Of this Manasseh also was guilty, 2 *Chro. 33.6.* To which might be added that in *Hester. 3.7.* and *9.24.*

Fourthly, we read in *Deut. 18.10. Isa. 47.12.* of a Magician, one that could deceive the Eye-fight by making something to appear otherwise then it is. Such Pharaoh called to him to oppose Moses. Herein, Jannes and Jambres, of whom Saint Paul speaketh of, were guilty, and so likewise was Manesseh, 2 *Chron. 33.6.*

Fifthly, we read in *Deut. 18.11.* of an enchanter, or Conjurer; one joined in league with another, as the Witch is with the Devil. Such a one used Charms to tame Serpents *Psal. 58.5.* Many such were in Babylon, *Isa. 47.9.* and *Eccl. 10.11.*

Sixthly, we read in *Deut. 18.11. Lev. 20.* of one which hath a spirit in him or her which doth give answer to such as come to enquire of them. Such a one was in the Witch of Endor, *Sam. 28.* Such a one was the Pythonesse which brought her Mistress much gain, *Acts 16.* In *Isa. 29.4* called a Whisperer. To such the people had regard, *Lev. 19.21.* and encouraged one another thereunto, *Isa. 8.19.*

Seventhly, we read in *Deut. 18.11.* of a Wizard, *1 Sam. 28.9.* One also which could foretell some things, and so called for his or her foreknowledge; as now we term them a wife man, or a wife woman. After this sort the people fought also, *Lev. 19.31:* and *20.6.*

Eighthly, we read in *Deut. 18.41.* of a Necromancer, one that consulted with the dead. *Isa. 8.9.*

Ninethly, we read in *Isa. 19.3.* of a Whisperer, with secret or soft words, as our White Witches do, endeavouring to help man or beast. To these the Egyptians sought after, as they did to their idols, as in the last tormentationed place is expressed. These are now (as I have read) translated Charmers.

Tenthly, we read in *Exod. 8.11.* of such a Pharaoh sought to, as we call them Jugglers, deceivers, beguiling the eye-fight. Some hold them to be crafters of Nataivities, which tell people their fortune by

The will of James Hopkins (Matthew's father and vicar of Great Wenham), which sheds some light on the early life of the Witchfinder.

In his pamphlet *The Discovery of Witches* (*above*), Hopkins claimed that the spirit of a bear had been sent to kill him. This was not a new superstition, as this early seventeenth-century pamphlet (*right*) clearly shows.

The Miracle, of Miracles. 44

As fearefull as euer was ſeene or heard of in the memorie of MAN.

Which lately happened at Dichet in Sommerſetſhire, and ſent by diuers credible witneſſes to be publiſhed in LONDON.

Alſo a Propheſie reuealed by a poore Countrey Maide, who being dead the firſt of October laſt, 24. houres, 1613. reuiued againe, and lay fiue dayes weeping, and continued propheſſing of ſtrange euents to come, and ſo died the 5. day following.

Witneſſed by M. Nicholas Faber, Parſon of the Towne, and diuers worthy Gentlemen of the ſame countrey. 1613,

With Lincolneſhire, Norfolke, Suffolke, and Kent their Teares For a great deluge, in which fiue Villages were lamentably drowned this preſent month.

T. I.

At London printed for IOHN TRVNDLE: and are to be ſold at

The earliest known likeness of Matthew Hopkins is this woodcut dating from the time of his career as Witchfinder. He is shown with two Witches and their Imps.

The only known copy of Matthew Hopkins's signature from a conveyance document of 1641, before his time as Witchfinder.

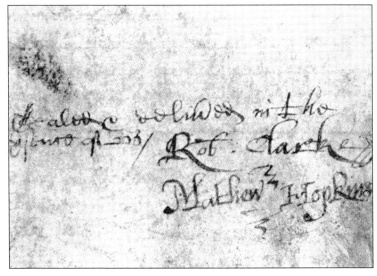

John Stearne's judgment of the marks found on Thomas Pye's body, signed boldly at the bottom.

Astrologer William Lilly, who possibly advised Hopkins on astrological matters at The Thorn Inn, 1645/6.

Matthew Hopkins's image still exerts a powerful effect today, as this contemporary cartoon shows. Note the obligatory burning in the background, something that only happened once. The rest of Hopkins's Witches were hanged.

The Thorn Inn today is a rather pleasant restaurant, but one can still spend a night in a room that boasts the ghost of Matthew Hopkins, if one dares.

The bank beside the Hopping Bridge (off picture, left), where Hopkins allegedly gasped his last breath and, according to some legends, was buried.

The Hopping Bridge at Mistley pond today. A rare view from the woodside. A road runs over the bridge adjacent to the Stour estuary.

The White Hart in Manningtree, where Hopkins may have held court with his Company of hand-picked accomplices.

Peter Cushing as the Puritan extremist hunting Witches in Hammer's *Twins of Evil*. The character was heavily based upon Matthew Hopkins, though the storyline was pure fantasy.

Legendary actor Vincent Price managed not to camp up his role as Matthew Hopkins in *Witchfinder General*, and consequently gave one of his finest screen performances.

the time of their birth. These are only expressed in the Old Testament: But the New speaketh, as I may say, only in general against Witchcraft, which comprehends all the ten aforementioned. And therefore it cannot be denied, besides their confessions hereafter herein expressed, but that there are such to this time, and that they all ought to suffer alike, which have made an express league with the Devil. An art so execrable, to renounce God, and to betake themselves to the Devil, as for this thing only they deserve death in the highest degree: for the Law of God faith without exception. Thou shalt not suffer a Witch to live, *Exod. 22.18.* If a Witch justly convicted, Death is due to such a one, *Levit. 20.27.* For, those abominations the Lord utterly destroyed the Canaanites, and plagued Manesseh, which wickedness of his so abhorred of God, as in his displeasure he mentioned it many years after, as a cause of removing the Jewes from their Land, and of leading them away captive into a strange Land, *Jer. 15.4.* And did not good King Josiah put such sorts to death that he might fulfil the Law? *2 Kings 23.24.* And so did Saul, *Sam. 28.* Nay, hath not the Lord threatened great judgements in the aforementioned places? Yea, and doth he not by the Prophet promise to cut off Witchcrafts and Soothsayers, when he intends to bless a Nation? *Mich. 5.12.*

Now, who they be that make this express or open league, are both sorts. But for the hurting and cursing Witch, there is but one sort. All of which makes this express or open league; and they do it only for mischief, though several ways: for they take their Familiars; some for the mischief, some for another. When as there be two sorts of the other; the one in express and open league, for so I term it, though made never so secret, because it is done by conference with the Devil; and the other is by implicit, or secret league, only be confidence in believing, that such or such a thing shall produce such, or such an effect. Now the first of these two have Familiars, as well as the other, or at least a brand, by which they may be known and discerned by, as well as the spirit. Some to set spells; some charms; some to cure diseases several ways, either by words, or washing clothes, or anointing the instruments which gave the wound to cure the wound, some only by laying on soft their hands, some by using and saying superstitious words, or some of prayers, using good words to bad ends, some by both, some by herbs, some to know where stolen goods be, either by raising the Devil, or Familiar Spirits, some only [by] words, and so likewise the same for lost goods, or man or beast, and to bring them again, and some by many such like ways and means do they work by. Yet many times they are, all of these, for the Devil cannot perform his promises at all times. So that it is not to be questioned, but all these sorts are in league with the Devil. For it is not to be doubted, but before any of them can have power to do anything, against, or for any party, or have any desired ends effected, the league express or implicit is first made; be it expressed then confirmed; but for confirmation hereof their confessions will make it plainly appear, and plain proofs and reasons for the other, that they confidently trust that their desires shall be effected accordingly to their belief, as the curing Witches do of them which come to them for help. All which I will make plainly appear, when I come to speak how they may be known. For here some may first demand of me what sorts of people they be of either sorts?

I answer, as for the first most women, and for the other most men. And albeit there be of both sorts of both: as Elimas the Sorcerer, and Simon Magus, and so likewise Balaam, and the Witch of Endor, and of these young, middle, and old age, of which instances may be given; yet of Witches in general, there be commonly more women than men. This is evident.

First, from Gods Law against Witches, *Exod. 22.* In the feminine gender, *prestigiatticem ne sinito vivere.*

Secondly, from Sauls speech, when he said, seek one out, a woman that hath a Familiar spirit, *Sam. 28 7.1 Chron. 10.13,14.* in naming a woman and not a man.

Thirdly, from experience it is found true here, and in all countries, especially of hurting Witches, that they are most in number, as appears by their own confessions, with the stories and relations even from these in our own kingdom. As of those of Burton-Old, where there met above fourscore at a time. And at Tilbrooke bushes in Bedfordshire, near adjacent to Catworth; in Huntingtonshire, where there met above twenty at one time, as John Wynick, and others confessed who suffered at Huntington last May was two years: as also by the confessions of some others which suffered at Northampton not long before. So likewise were those which met at Manningtree in Essex, as Elizabeth Clarke, and Anne Leech confessed, and those which were condemned, there being about twenty-eight, at Chelmsford, in the summer 1645 were (as I remember) all women. And those at Bury St Edmunds, where sixty-eight were (as I likewise remember) condemned, most women. All at one jail delivery, in the summer 1645. So I could nominate far more instances in other places, and of about two hundred executed since the said May, 1645. In the several counties aforementioned, the women far exceeded the men in number. And as I have read, those in Lancashire, where nineteen assembled, and but two men, and that those that bewitched the Earl of Rutland were women; and that those of Warboys were women, and but one man. Women therefore without question exceed men, especially of the hurting Witches; but for the other, I have known more men, and have heard such as have gone to them say, almost generally they be men, and so likewise find them to be in authors, which speak of such, and never knew any women questioned in that way but men, and of them as hitherto not many. For as before, men rather uphold them, and say, why should any man be questioned for doing good; but I am certain the word of God is contrary.

Now, why it should be that women exceed men in this kind, I will not say, that Satan's setting upon these rather than man is, or like to be, because of his unhappy onset and prevailing with Eve; or their more credulous nature, and apt to be misled, for that they be commonly impatient, and being displeased more malicious, and so more apt to revenge according to their power, and thereby more fit instruments for the Devil; or that, because they be more ready to be teachers of Witchcraft to others, and to leave it to children, servants, or to some others (but that you shall find to be a great inducement thereto by their confessions) or that, because, where they can command they are more fierce in their rule, and revengeful in setting such on work whom they can command, wherefore the Devil laboureth most to make them Witches: for Satan is subtle, and seeketh whom he may devour, and if false teachers.

141

But as Saint Paul saith, Witchcraft being amongst the fruits of the flesh, one may fall into this sin as well as into any other (if God prevent it not) and therefore whether men or women. These sorts following are the aptest, as by experience plainly appears amongst us nowadays.

I pass by infidels, and heathen people in former times (from whom these abominations mentioned in *Deut. 18.10,11* came into Israel, and savage nations now (amongst whom) by travellers relations, Witchcraft is most rise) and will speak only of such sorts as be called Christians, and these be:

First, ignorant people whose eyes are blinded by Satan, *2 Cor. 4.4.* and are led captive by him, as is said in another place.

This appeareth in those Witches commonly detected amongst us, silly ignorant persons many of them. Elizabeth Deekes of Ratlesden, in Sussex, a silly ignorant young woman being found with marks, confessed that she was guilty, and had two crop-eared Imps, as she said, which had sucked two or three times upon those marks found upon her, which Imps (she said) came from mice; the one white, which she called birds, being the least, the other gray, which she called Teates, which Imp asked her to deny God, and Christ, and told her if she would she should never want, but she said she then refuted. Whereupon (she said) her mother asked her to give her soul from God to the Devil, which (she said) she likewise refuted: but as she was going to bed, either upon a pair of stairs, or ladder, her mother pulled her back in much danger of her life, and confessed many other things then more at large. But for her ignorance she was saved at first, when her mother suffered, yet afterwards, notwithstanding this, and her refusing those temptations, she confessed, she did make a league and Covenant with the Devil, and sealed it with her blood, and employed those Imps, to the much prejudice of her neighbours and townsmen, as she confessed before the Justice of the Peace. Also Joan Wallis of Keyston, in Huntingtonshire, a very ignorant Scottish woman, confessed the Devil came to her in the likeness of a man, in black clothing, but had cloven feet, which she called Blackman, who used to lie with her, and have the use of her body, yet she confessed he was more uglier than man, and not as her husband, which speaks to her like a man, but he as he had been some distance from her when he was with her, who told her, if she would be ruled by him she should never want, but should have what she desired, and brought her two others the third time he came, which (she said) she called Grizzell and Greedigut, for so (she said) they called themselves, and that those, after she had consented to the other his demands, and confirmed the Covenant, she could and did employ as she then further confessed, both to the townsmen, and after to the Justice of the Peace, and some of the mischiefs she had done. Ennumerable of these instances I could nominate in many of their confessions, as you shall find in some of those following. But I desire to answer one objection before I proceed further (that is) some say, and many will and do say: but you watched them, and kept them from meat, drink, or rest, and so made them say what you would. A very unnatural part so to use Christians. I answer so it were. But I never knew any deprived of meat, drink or rest, but had what was fitting till they were carried before some Justice of the Peace to be examined, and had provision to rest upon, as bolsters, pillows, or cushions, and such like, if they were kept where no beds were; yet I do not deny but at first, some were kept two, three, or four days, perchance somewhat baser, but then it hath been, either when no Justice of the Peace was near, or when the witness against them could not go sooner, but then they had beds, and for other provision, I never knew any kept, of what rank or quality soever, but that they had better provision, either meat or drink, then at their own houses. For the watching, it is not to use violence, or extremity to force them to confess, but only the keeping is, first, to see whether any of their spirits, or Familiars come to or near them; for I have found, that if the time be come, the spirit of Imp so called should come, it will be either visible or invisible, if visible, then it may be discerned by those in the room, if invisible, then by the party. Secondly, it is for this end also, that if the parties which watch them, be so careful that none come visible, nor invisible but may be discerned, if they follow their directions, then the party presently after the time their Familiars should have come, if they fail, will presently confess, for then they think they will either come . . . or at least have forsaken them.

Thirdly, it is also to the end, that Godly Divines and others might discourse with them, and idle persons be kept from them, for if any of their society come to them to discourse with them, they will never confess. This was observed at Bury St Edmunds in Suffolk, as I remember, when there were eighteen to be executed; most of them kept in a barn together, they made a Covenant amongst themselves, not to be confess a word next day at the gallows, when they were to be hanged, notwithstanding they had formally confessed, and some of them after they came into the jail, and some before the Bench and Country, but most of them (if not all) before the Justices of the Peace, and so died next day accordingly very desperately, except one penitent woman which refused their Covenant or agreement: so she made it known, and how they made a singing of the psalme after they had done it. But if honest godly people discourse with them, laying the hainousness of their sins to them, and in what condition they are in without repentance, and telling them the subtleties of the Devil, and the mercies of God, these ways will bring them to confession without extremity, it will make them break into confession hoping for mercy.

Now that the Imps come visible, it is true and apparent, and so watching hath produced true and strange effects, and is a great means (under God) to bring them to confession, as for example, Elizabeth Clarke of Manningtree in Essex, being kept three days and three nights, she confessed many things, but how she was kept I know not well, for I came not at her during that time, notwithstanding I lived then in town, and was one which caused her to be questioned, who did accuse some others which lived in their several parishes, the townsmen desired me to go with her confession taken in writing by another, to the Justices of the Peace for a warrant for those she accused, the warrant was made for the searching of such persons as I should nominate, whereupon, I would first go to her before the warrant should be served, to know of her who she did accuse; Mr Hopkin being with me went together, and when I had asked her who she had accused, we were agoing away; but she said to us, if you will stay, I will show you my Imps, for they be ready to come. Then said Mr Hopkins, Bess, will they do us no harm? No said she, What? Did you think I am afraid of my children? You shall sit down. So we did, where she appointed us. Then one of the company which was appointed to be with her that night, said to her, Bess, I asked you a question of late, but you answered not, then she said, what is it? Then he [this is Hopkins] replied and said, tell the truth, if it be the truth, say so, but if not true, then say so, hath not the Devil had the use of your body? she said, why should you ask such a question? He answered, I desire to know the truth . . . then said Mr Hopkin, in what manner and likeness came he to you? She said, like a tall, proper, black haired gentleman, a properer man than yourself, and being asked which she had rather lie withal, she said the Devil, and so particularised every thing, and how he came in, and his habit, and how he lay with her, and spoke to her, as she then affirmed to be truth, and so presently fell a smacking with her lips and called Lought [name of one of her Imps] two or three times, which presently appeared to us eight (for there were six which were appointed to be with her that night before we went) in the likeness of a cat, as she had formerly told us; for she told us before what shapes they should come in, and so that presently vanished; then she called again as before, Jermarah, then appeared another, like a red or sandy spotted dog, with legs not so long as a finger (to our perceivance) but his back as broad as two dogs, or broader, of that bigness, and vanished, and so after that called more, as before, by their several names, which came in several shapes, one like a greyhound, with legs as long as a stag, another like a ferret, and one like a rabbit, and so in several shapes they appeared to us, till there were some seven or eight seen. Some by some of us, and others by other some of us; then I asked her if they were not all come, for there were more come then she spoke of, she answered that they came double in several shapes, but said, one was still to come, which was to tear me in pieces, then I asked her why, she said, because I would have swam her, and told me that now she would be even with me, and so told in what manner it should come, black, and like a toad, and so afterwards did come, as the rest averred that saw it, and so she confessed their meetings, and the manner how they worshipped the Devil at their meetings, and said

145

to us, that they be found with these marks that I am found withal, are without question Witches, yet said, that there might be some Witches which had not those marks; but affirmed it over and over again, that all those that had those marks were Witches, and had Familiar spirits which sucked of them, and so confessed what mischief she had done with her Imps, in a very large manner, and so did next day, after she had slept; for the Justice gave me order that she should sleep before he examined her, lest she had not slept before, and so I did accordingly, and yet she then confessed at large before two Justices of the Peace, and how she would have been my death; this was the first accused, and her marks and confession, the beginning of our knowledge: yet I confess, the marks be difficult to find from natural marks, as I shall hereafter declare. Rebecca West of Lamford [Lawford], in Essex, who was (as she confessed) married to the Devil, and the manner, had an Imp came to her in the time she was kept, but of her confession more at large hereafter. Also Elizabeth Finch of Watson in Suffolk, confessed, that about twenty years before she was found with the marks, the Devil appeared to her in the likeness of a smoky coloured dog, which asked her to deny God and Christ, which she said, upon his promises she did, and let him have blood to seal, or confirm the Covenant or agreement; and that soon after that, there came two more, black on the backs and reddish in the bellies, which sucked her two or three times a week, upon those marks that were found on her, and that sometimes she fetched blood in other places for them, and gave it to them; she also had her Imps came visible. For she confessed in the time she was kept, one which was with her to look to her, saw one of them, and flung it into the fire, which she affirmed was one of her Imps, and that whilst they were busy about that, thinking to burn it, she confessed the other came, and threw her out of the chair she sat in, which hurt her forehead and wrist, which was done accordingly, and so further confessed. Of these I could bring diverse instances, but I will proceed. They come likewise invisible; as one Binkes of Haverhill, had a Imp sucking of her whilst she was talking with others, and presently confessed it. Another whilst I was in the room with her, at Huntington, I perceived by her carriage that she was sucking her Imps, spirits, or Familiars so called; I layed it to her charge, but she denied it: yet presently after she confessed it was truth, when she was asked by the Justice of the Peace. And as I remember, it was the same woman; but I am sure of Keyston in Huntingtonshire, and so was she, that to the thinking of two which were with her, she sat still in her chair, when two more in the yard saw her go out into the yard, and her going in again. This woman confessed the Devil sat in her likeness, and she went out, and sucked her Imps in the yard, as the other two affirmed. So in the same town, one Clarke's wife skipped out at a hole in a stone wall, above half a foot thick, which was some nine inches long, and some four and a half broad, all the one side head and all, and but little to be seen of her but one leg; and the hole was near a yard and a half from the ground, and yet one pulled her back again, and afterwards went away, nobody knew how, yet I say, if those which look to them be careful, it is to be discerned; this is apparent by that I nominated at Huntington. And so at Codman in Suffolk, being told how a woman there carried herself, I caused her to be searched again, and there was alteration of the marks, and the woman presently confessed it, and made a large confession; and so it hath been common in all our proceedings, and a great cause for keeping them; for the blood hath sometimes been found on the end of the mark, or to stroked out when they be taken on a sudden. As I could instance the one half of their confessions; but because it is so apparent, I instance no further. But now to manifest that good council will do it, and so likewise without keeping; for I hold they two depend most upon one. Then say I, that upon good exhortations after the marks found, they may be brought to confession, either by keeping, though everything necessary be afforded them, as I never did otherwise, but now lately keep none, or not above one night till we go thence, and yet have their confessions. Witness those executed at Ely, a little before Michaelmas last, who made large confessions. Also one at Chatterish there. One at March there. And another at Wimblington there now lately found, still to be tried, who made very large confessions, especially the first two. Nicholas Hempstead of Creeting in Suffolk, being found, upon exhortations, and laying the

147

hainousness of the sin, and God's judgements, and God's mercy, and
the like, notwithstanding he at first railed on me in very approbious
terms, yet presently sent for me, and would have asked me
forgiveness, he presently confessed that he had made a league and
Covenant with the Devil, and how he had made a league and
Covenant with the Devil, and how he had confirmed it with his
blood; and the shape of his Imps, and of the Devil when they
Covenanted, and how he killed a horse of one of the constables,
because he pressed him for a soldier, and five of the best horses on
Colonel Rositer's troop; and divers other things he had done,
making a very large confession, with a great deal of penitency and
sorrow, which he so continued in (as I since heard) to his very
execution without alteration. To this I might add, Henry Carrs
hereafter mentioned, and the boys next, after the objections
answered, and diverse others which you shall here find; because it
falleth out better, when I shall speak how to discover them, I leave
here, hoping this is sufficient for that objection, if not, I will answer
more fully, as occasion shall serve. But then some will say, you swam
some of them, especially at the first, was that not extremity? I
answer, that hath been used, and I durst not go about to clear myself
of it, because formerly I used it, but it was at such time of the year
as when none took any harm by it, neither did I ever do it but upon
their own request; and were to such as first were found with the
marks; but now lately, there hath been no such course taken that I
know of. For I am of opinion, that it is one way of distrusting of
God's providence, putting confidence that that shall bring such or
such an effect, or event, neither was it ever given in or taken, that I
know, as evidence against any, nor used by any of us but the first
summer, from March, or May 1645 to about the middle of August
next following; when Judge Godbolt that now is, forewarned it.
When Divines gave their opinion of the unlawfulness thereof, it hath
ever since been left, and not many before so used: notwithstanding,
it was then the desire of such persons themselves, thinking thereby
to clear themselves, whereas it fell out otherwise. Yet under favour,
let me speak one thing that I have found in that way, that it is a true
rule in one respect, that the water entered not into any of them,

when it will into a free person, though they swim both alike, for so they will, if the water be enchanted, but the free person will presently be choaked, when the other lay on top of the water, striving to get their heads, or themselves under the water, but cannot, neither can they bring out water in their mouths, though they be foretold of it, not spit clear water; for the water enters them not when it will the other thus far I have observed, or further: but because it is held unlawful, I should be sorry to speak anything, either to give offence to any, or to be a means to animate any in such courses. For if any did confess, rather then go into the water, or to come out of the water, or presently after, except they had been shifted, and refreshed every way, and known to be in perfect memory, it hath been taken as no evidence, and so hath all other forcement been. But there is one, a very remarkable thing concerning this, that was done at St Neotts, in Huntingtonshire, of a woman that had been searched two or three times, and not found, for they can hide their marks sometimes, as you shall hear after herein, yet was still in great suspicion of many of the townsmen to be guilty (the brand is difficult to find if she had notice) and the rather, for that she fled, or went away after she was searched twice, for some are not found at first, yet be in the end. So at her return some would swim her, and did, she swam apparently, where they had formerly cast a freeman in, tied after the same manner, she was not further medled with then. But as I have heard, and in part from the man himself, where the act should be done, a dog was seen in his yard, which a Mastif dog would not seize on, but his son stroke at the dog, and [gave] him two or three blows over the back, up to the shoulders, presently a bitch seized on him, and bit him on the neck . . . and then the dog got away: so it remained, but this woman not being seen in the street as formerly, was caused to be viewed; and found bitten on the neck, or bruised on the other parts in a most fearful manner. There are some similitudes, that there is something in swimming (if lawful) but to proceed. This one more, that ignorant people are most apt to be Witches, as aforesaid. Of a boy in Ratlesdon aforesaid, who was accused, when he was under nine years of age, when all know he could not be of such capacity, he

149

without watching, or keeping, voluntarily confessed, that he suckled an Imp, and had it at command to do mischief, and nominated some, as the killing of some chickens, and some other mischiefs he had then done, as he confessed, together with the reasons he caused his Imp to kill the chickens, which was, because the man which owed them had chided him for spoiling his grass, when, as he said, they did it, for the next time he saw them there, he did it. This boy being young, (suppose the Jury had hopes of his amendment, as I confess I then had) he was released, and went to the town again, where he continued some time, and was suspected again for further mischief, and so apprehended again, and put into prison, where he then voluntarily confessed likewise his renewing of the league and Covenant with the Devil, and the sealing of it with his blood, after his mother was hanged; for she suffered for Witchcraft, about the Michaelmas 1645 and then was he first questioned, and that he had more Familiar spirits, or Imps, as they call them, and that the Devil appeared to him, in the likeness of a black-brown mare, and would carry him whither he desired, and confessed abundance of mischiefs he had done, between the time he was released, and committed again. But after he was in Bury jail, not long before the Assizes, the first since these wars, the Jailer missing a prisoner in the morning, which he had over night, a notorious offender, whom he kept double shackled, the Jailer questioned this boy, and upon some threatening speeches, the boy confessed, that he was gone home on his mare over the walls, and showed where, and told him he should find him with his wife; whereupon, the Jailer sent forthwith to the prisoners house, being at least twelve miles, and there found him at his house, as the boy had said, having shackles on as he went out. Will this with the other give you satisfaction? But I might add to this, superstitious and idolatrous persons. But I pass, intending only to take the heads, agreeing with the confessions of Witches.

Secondly, malicious people, full of revenge, having hearts swollen with rancour, upon the least displeasure, with bitter . . . curses, threatening revenge, or requitals; this is manifest by the nature, quality, words, and deeds of Witches convicted, who have showed themselves to be such, as ever found so to be, as the said John

Wynnick confessed, that when he lived at Thrapston in Northamptonshire, he having lost his purse with some seven shillings in it, as he was in a barn, where he lived, there in an inn, as he was making up of bottles of hay, he was in a passion for his purse of money, and in such a rage of banning and cursing, that he was saying to himself, would he knew where he might go to a cunning man for it, for have it he would, though he went to the Devil for it; (here was a paradeness for the Devil) for he confessed, the Devil appeared to him immediately, in the likeness of a bear, but not above the bigness of a rabbit, which told him, if he would fall down and worship him, he would help him to his purse, and money again, and that he should have it where he stood, next day about the same time; so he did fall down and worship him. And the next day he came again, to see for his purse and money, and found it accordingly, but confessed, that before he could tell it, the Devil in the same shape appeared to him again, and told him, he must fall down and worship him again, and then he fell down, and said, Oh my Lord my God, I thank thee, and then he asked him to deny God, and Christ, and to serve him as Lord, and then he should never want, which he confessed he consented to, then he demanded blood, and he bade him take it, so he skipped on his shoulder, and fetched blood with his claw, on the side of his head, which mark was seen at his Trial. Then he confessed, there appeared two more, which the first told him he must worship also, and take them for his Gods, and they should be at his command, and so he said, he did, then that like a bear turned like a rat, and so those sucked on the three marks I found on him, after to the time he was taken, at their times appointed, and were at his command, as he then confessed more at large, before the Justices of the Peace, and confessed at the gallows likewise, the last words he spoke. Also one Moores wife of Sutton, in the isle of Ely, in the county of Cambridge, after she had confessed the league and Covenant made, and sealed with her blood, confessed, that she sent one of her Imps to kill a man, or at least to hurt to him; for that she had bought a pig off him, for two shillings and two pence, and paid him two shilling, and afterward he coming by her door, asked he for it, which man, was soon after taken sick, and in his sickness, cried out for her, saying he could not depart this life, until he had spoken with her, so she was sent for, but she refused, whereupon (he lying in such extremity) she was by some of his friends, at his request, being so desirous to speak with her in such extremity, forced to go to him, and then soon after he died, according as he formerly said. So this woman confessed divers other things, and seemed to be very penitent, and sorry for it, for she wept at her trial, and confessed herself guilty before the Judge, Bench, and Country. But what she did after, or at her execution, I know not. Thomazine Ratcliffe of Shellie, in Suffolk, confessed, that it was malice that had brought her to that she was come to, meaning Witchcraft, for she confessed, that soon after her husband's decease, above twenty years before her confession, there came one in the likeness of a man, into bed to her, which spoke with a hollow, shrill voice, and told her, he would be a loving husband to her, if she would confess to him, which she said, she did, and then he told her, he would revenge her of all her enemies, and that she should never miss anything, in which she said, she found him a liar, but said, that Satan often tempted her to banning, swearing, and cursing, which she confessed she did use a long time, and that many times it fell out accordingly, and that she, falling out with one Martin's wife, who had a child drowned, for that she called her Witch, saying, she was the cause of the childs drowning, she bad her go home and look to the rest, lest she lost more, and one died suddenly after. Also Anne Randall of Lauenbam in Suffolk, after she had confessed the Covenant, for still you must remember, that is first done, before the Devil, or their Familiars, or Imps etc, or do anything, confessed that she had two Imps, which were heavy and soft, but came in the likeness of cats, or kittens, of a blue colour, called Hangman, and Jacob, and that those sucked on the marks were found upon her body, some thirty years together, sometimes once a week, sometimes once a fortnight, and that she sent her Imp Hangman to kill a horse of one William Baldwin's of Thorpe, some two miles from Lauenbam, for that she asked him to bring her in some wood, and he bad her pay for that she had first; and the Imp returned, and told her he had done, he had killed two, for they were [tied] together, so he killed them both, which horses were killed (but in such a tempest) as was supposed by a Devil in thunder, until she confessed it of herself. Also she confessed, that being at Stephen Humfries in Thorpe aforesaid, and a begging for Almes,³ he came home well, and she being at the door, he chided her, or gave her such words as she liked not of. As she went over the way from the house, her Imp Hangman appeared to her, and asked her what he should do, and she bad him go and kill one of his hogs, which she saw, which she said he did before she was out of sight, which hog died accordingly. Likewise she further confessed, that she being angry with one Mr Coppinger of Lavenham, she sent her Imp Jacob to carry away bushes, which he had caused to be laid to fence his fences, above one load, here some, and there some, all along by the hedge side, as they were to be hedged out, and in one night they were gone, no man knew what way, until such time as she confessed her Imp did it. But as I have since heard, they were known to be in another man's ground, who confessed, they came the same night, but how, he knew not till then. Also a young man in Denford, in Northamptonshire, who suffered for Witchery since the said time, at Northampton, confessed, that he sent one of his Imps, to one Cocke's Cattle of Denford, because he would not let him keep them, and the cattle ran so violently away foaming, that the owner had much ado to catch them with a horse, and more to get them home into his yard again, and so many other things he confessed, as I could particularly instance. And so for this, I hope it is sufficient, to give all satisfaction, for all confessions, or most of them at least, tend to prove this in some part. Those that are given to over much curiosity, to seek after vain knowledge, in pride of heart to go beyond others, to understand secret and hidden things, to know things to come. Such are those, as not bounding themselves within the limits of reason, nor of God's revealed will, fall foul unawares upon the Devil, and are in great danger to be intrapped by him, and made his slaves by his inticements. Thus was Parson Lowes taken, who had been minister (as I have heard), in one parish above forty years, in Suffolk, before he was condemned, but had been indited for a common imbarriter, and for Witchcraft, above thirty years before,

153

and the grand jury (as I have heard) found the bill for a common imbarriter, who now, after he was found with the marks, in his confession, he confessed, that in pride of heart, to be equal, or rather above God, the Devil took advantage of him, and he Covenanted with the Devil, and sealed it with blood, and had three Familiars or spirits, which sucked on the marks found upon his body, and did much harm, both by sea and land, especially by sea, for he confessed, that he being at Langarfort, in Suffolk, where he preached, as he walked upon the wall, or worked there, he saw a great sail of ships pass by, and that as they were sailing by, one of his three Imps, namely his yellow one, forthwith appeared to him, and asked him what he should do, and he bade it go and sink such a ship, and showed his Imp a new ship, amongst the middle of the rest (as I remember) one that belonged to Ipswich, so he confessed the Imp went forthwith away, and he stood still, and viewed the ships on the sea as they were a sailing, and perceived that ship immediately, to be in more trouble and danger than the rest, for he said, the water was more boisterous near that than the rest, tumbling up and down with the waves, as if water had been boiled in a pot and soon after (he said) in a short time it sank directly down into the sea, as he stood and viewed it, when all the rest sailed away in safety, there he confessed, he made fourteen widows in one quarter of an hour. Then Mr Hopkin, as he told me (for he took his confession) asked him, if it did not grieve him to see so [many] men cast away, in a short time, and that he should be the cause of so many poor widows on a sudden; but he swore by his maker, no, he was joyful to see what power his Imps had, and so likewise confessed many other mischiefs, and had a charm to keep him out of jail, and hanging, as he paraphrased it himself, but therein the Devil deceived him; for he was hanged, that Michaelmas time 1645 at Bury St Edmunds, but he made a very fair large confession, which I have heard hath been printed; but if it were so, it was neither of Mr Hopkins doing, nor mine own; for we never printed anything until now. I do this (he being dead) but make no use of any confessions taken by him, but only this, for that it falleth out so fit for this purpose, yet I heard, that other confessions have been printed, and

154

some other things besides, as if it had been of ours, or one of our doings, or at least, by one of our consents; when as I know, he never had any hand in any, and for my own part I utterly renounce all for me. Also I may add to this, one Henry Carre of Ratlesden, in Suffolk, who I have heard was a scholler fit for Cambridge (if not for Cambridge scholler), and was well educated; yet fell into this grievous sin, and confessed, that he had two Imps, which sucked on those marks I found upon him, two years together, and came in the likeness of mice, which he felt oft, and said, they were hairy and heavy, and so seeming to bewail his condition, said, that he had forsaken God, and God him, and therefore would confess no more, he said, until he came on the Gallows to be hanged, for he had confessed enough for that, and then he would confess all, and make all other known he knew of, but in the meantime, he would confess no more, nor did; yet he was much importuned to it, but that was always his answer, and was arraigned at the Barre, three or four times, and yet by reason of an Alarm at Cambridge, the jail delivery at Bury St Edmunds was adjourned, for about three weeks, and he died in the jail in that time: so it was conceived to be pride of heart, which was the first original cause, by reason of his knowledge; yet I confess, he fell into poverty before his death, but as for that, I think it is seldom or never known, that any get estates, or thrive, that thus give themselves over to Satan, but rather consume their estates, if they have any, yet the word of God says, the wicked man thriveth as well as the Godly in this world, but for Witches, I never knew any. To these likewise might be added, those observers of times, *Deut. 18.* And such as profess to cure diseases, by such means as have no reason, or work of nature to do the cure, nor have by any ordinance of God, from his word, any such operation to heal the infirmity. And therefore such remedies must be diabolical, and the practicers either Witches already, or their implicit faith, the next door to Witchcraft. Such be they that use spells, charms and such like; and what be Juglers and legerdemain[4] companions? For that they sport with such resemblances, and utter words, as the invocating of a spirit, the reality whereof, is called an abomination before God, and as Saint Paul speaketh, children of disobedience. What be the fortune tellers, and such like? But apt to be Satan's slaves in Witchery, as they be his otherwise in impiety. For through curiosity of knowledge, if reason and art fail, will it not move men to seek help of a spirit, who is ready at hand to attend, to draw them into the pit of Magic, and Sorcery and Witchcraft? As one Mr Cooper speaketh of, in his book, called, *The Mystery of Witchcraft*, whom himself was delivered from, by Gods preventing grace; but because as yet, these have not been so commonly found out nowadays, I forbare further, though I might instance diverse examples more. Those who with greediness gape after worldly wealth or fear poverty. As Meribell Bedford of Ratlesden aforesaid confessed, that above six years before she was found with the marks, which Witches usually have. There came a black thing to her, and called Meribell, which asked her to deny God, and Christ, and told her, if she would, she should never want, but should be avenged of all her enemies, which she confessed to; then she said, he had blood of one of her little fingers, to seal the Covenant, which being done, she said, four more came, one like a cow, called Tib; one like a miller called Tom; one like a spider, or a spinner called Joane; and the other like a Wasp called Nann. These she confessed were at her command, to perform the Covenant, and did suck upon those marks found upon her body, two or three times a week, during the said six years, and did much harm, as she freely confessed with much penitency. To this I may add, one Elizabeth Hubbard, widow, of Stow Market in Suffolk, who confessed, that above thirty years, she had three things came to her in the likeness of children, which asked her whispering to deny God, Christ, and all his works, and to cleave[5] to them, and she should want nothing. These she said, as they named themselves, were called, Thomas, Richard, and Hobb, and that they scratched her back, and fetched blood to seal the Covenant, and that they used to suck on those marks which were found upon her, two or three times a week, about break of the day, and that she did say, I pray to God to do to him as he dealt by me (meaning a man of the same town) and he languished and died, and many other things she said she did, but was ashamed to tell them. Alice the wife of Edmund Wright of Hitcham, in Suffolk, confessed that she had four Imps above threescore years; two like little boys, one like a lamb, and the fourth like a grey buzzard, and that the biggest boy spoke to her with a great horse voice, as if he had been grieved, and asked her to go into the field, and she should have money, and should never miss or want anything, and asked her to deny God, and Christ, and to curse God two or three times, and that she took her elder brother with her, and went into the field, but when they came to the place where they appointed her to go, they found none, and that she used often to be in pain and trouble, after they had nipped or sucked her, where her marks were found, sometimes once a week, sometimes once a fortnight, and that she felt on them, and that they were soft, and that they came sometimes severally, sometimes altogether, and that they often asked her to go and do mischief, which she confessed, to some cattle of her neighbours, and said, that she was much troubled and tormented, and in extreme pain, which they have put her to for denying their demands. Furthermore, Joan Ruce Ulver of Powstead in Suffolk, confessed, that in the field called Horsecroft of Hog-Marsh, there appeared in a bush things like chickens, about five or six, and that she catched three of them and the rest ran away, and that she carried three home, which soon after turned to the likeness of mice, whose names she called Touch, Pluck, and Take, which spoke to her with a great hollow voice, and asked her to deny God, and Christ, and told her, if she would, she should never want meat, drink, or clothes, or money, but she said she told them, that if she denied God and Christ, she should lose her soul, but she said, they told her again, they were more able to save her soul than God, and that they would do more for her than she thought for, if she would consent to them, which then she confessed she did, and then they demanded blood, and she nipped her forefinger, and they pricked her finger with a pin, and there dropped six drops of blood which they catched, and so had it again after the same manner thrice, and that she did agree to give them her soul. Then I asked her whether they brought her any money or no, and she said, sometimes four shillings at a time, and sometimes six shillings at a time, but that is but seldom, for I never knew any that had any money before, except of Clarke's wife of Manningtree, who confessed the same, and showed some which she said her Imp brought her, which was perfect money: but this Ruce, further confessed to sucking of her marks, and how she sent her Imp Touch to kill a bullock, and that he came back again, and told her he had stuck it on the right side, and it died accordingly, and so many other things, and said she was stopped and could not confess when she would, but after had ease. Here you may observe, that if he cannot prevail for want, then he promises to free them of hell torments, and so delude them that way. As he did Ellen the wife of Nicholas Greenliese of Barton, in Suffolk, who confessed that three things came to her; one like a rat, cold and ragged as she felt on him; the next like a mole, soft and cold; the third like a louse; and that the mole spoke to her with a great hollow voice, and asked her to give her soul and body to him, for he could save her, and bade her not to be afraid of him, for he could perform what he promised, whereupon she consented, then he told her she should never want, but be avenged of all her enemies, and so should continue her life time, if she did not be wary [of] him, for if she did he would have the upper hand of her, and confessed that her wishes came to pass, as for example: she wished one Goodman Garneham might be lame, and so he was, and that master Lockweed might have lice, because he formerly accused her for sending, or causing him to have some when she did it not, and so he had, and that her Imps used to suck her two or three times a week, for nineteen years together; and that the mole said she should be questioned in some short time, but advised her to stand out and not to confess, for if she did he would cause her to drown herself, or put herself to death, and then he should have her soul, and after when she was kept, before she went to the Justice of the Peace, her Imp in the shape of a mole came to her, when those which were with her saw it not, and tore her as she confessed, as if he would have torn her in pieces, because she had confessed. This woman also confessed, that when she prayed she prayed to the Devil and not to God, and that she had her Imps from her mother-in-law, who she said spoiled her; and further confessed that the Devil had the use of her body, and used to come to bed to her, but was soft, cold, and heavier, so heavy as she could not speak, and that her Imp like a rat went upon her, wishing to lame Ralph Roggards horse or mare, because he said he would go for the searchers, and so it was. Besides the former marks know this, that it is more easier to find them on the breast then in any other place, for that the breast is all shrunk up, and the teat thereof extended longer than any woman's that gives suck, be it on man or woman, with a circle round about it as if it were sucked, and insensible as aforesaid, and if on a woman that gives suck, that breast is dry, for where the Imps suck there will come no milk, but the teat will stick out longer there than the other, and is nothing but skin, and will be much extended as aforesaid, and easily to be discerned by feeling of it. I should think this should give all satisfaction; that gain, revenge, fear of want, or poverty, or fearfulness of hell torments, or ill parents, or company, yea and lust also, or any one may be a means to draw one to Witchcraft.

As for ill company, bad and wicked parents, and such as are over-much given to lust, I will put them together, and instance some few more examples; as one Bush of Barton aforesaid widow, confessed that about three weeks after her husband's decease, being above fifteen years before she was questioned, the Devil appeared to her in the shape of a young black man, standing by her bedside, which spoke to her with a hollow voice, and came into bed to her, and had the use of her body, and asked her to deny God and Christ, and serve him, and then she should never want, but should be avenged of all her enemies, which she consented to, then she said he kissed her and asked her for blood, which he drew out of her mouth, and it dropped on a paper, and that he used to have the use of her body two or three times a week, and then used to kiss her, and at no other time but as beforesaid, but she said he was colder than man, and heavier, and could not perform nature as man, and that soon after she had consented to the Covenant and given her blood, there came two things more like mice, which used to suck her about twice a week during that time, and confessed how she sent an Imp to torment a maiden, who she thought was against her having relief at her masters, which was done, but afterward this maiden went to her and scratched her till she got blood of her, and then she confessed she had no further power over her (but this is not always true, nor to be observed, though it took effect there); but she confessed the killing of three and twenty turkeys at one time, and cowes, and how her Imps returned and told her it was done, and other things then at large. One more which I should think should be a warning to others, to have a care to bring their children up in the nurture and fear of God. Of one Ann Crick of Hitcham aforesaid widow, that she had three Imps about seven years together; the one in the likeness of a sparrow called Harrie; the other two in the likeness of reddish dunne mice, called Jack and Will, and they sucked her twice a week severally, all in one night, and the Devil fetched blood on her left arm to seal the Covenant, which was to deny God and Christ, and to serve him, which she said she promised faintly, but confessed the promise was first made by her, before the Devil had her blood; then I asked her if she did grieve for it after she had done it, she answered, when it was done it was too late to repent; then I asked her why she did it, she said she was left weak, and the Devil got the upper hand of her for want of faith, through want and otherwise, she also confessed the Devil had the use of her body, but she said she could not tell whether he performed nature or not, and said she could not confess before much company, but said the Devil spoke in a hollow voice, and confessed the employment of her Imps, as the sending of her Imp Harry to John Leverishes of the same town, to kill him a hog, because she was denied eggs and such like things, and they burnt his ears, and she could not keep from going; it being asked her why she went, she said they must needs go the Devil drives, and so many such like things. Also Susan Scot of Lavenham aforesaid, complained of one [person] coming to her with one Golding, who confessed the Devil used to have the use of her body, and spoke to her with a great easy voice, and that she had two Imps like cats and dogs, which sucked on those marks found upon her, and how she was the death of Thomazine, the daughter of one Mr Coppinger there, and diverse other things. Also one Richmond, a woman which lived at Brampford, confessed the Devil appeared to her in the likeness of a man, called Daniel the prophet, who bade her not be afraid of him, for he was so, and took her by the hand, and bade her trust in him and he would avenge her of all her enemies, and he should miss nothing, for he would curse her enemies, and that she after falling out with her neighbour, cursed her and bade the Devil take her, and she died after she had lain for some eight weeks, as she said, by her means, because the Devil promised her revenge; she confessed her Covenant was to deny God, Christ and his ministers, and to serve him, she said the Devil, for she said so he was that she called Daniel the Prophet, none shall need question it; and she confessed she had three more, one like a rugged red dog with cloven feet, one like a hog called Jack, and another like a dog called James, and confessed the Devil desired her to use cursing, and whatsoever she desired should come to her, and so confessed many things she did. Also Anne Goodfellow of Woodford, in Northamptonshire, widow, confessed that soon after her aunt's decease, about three years before she was questioned, the Devil in the shape of a white cat appeared to her, and spoke to her with a low voice, and bade her not be afraid of it, for he was her aunt's spirit, and asked her to deny God, Christ and her baptism, which she said she did, for he promised her that she should be saved, and would do for her what she desired, and then asked her for blood to seal the Covenant, and she further confessed that he bit her on the second finger, and got blood into his mouth, but what he did with all she knew not, but said amongst other things that she found him a liar, for she often wanted after. Also, Elizabeth Gurrey of Risden, in Bedfordshire, widow, confessed that the Devil had the use of her body, and lay heavy upon her, and that through her wilfulness, and poverty, with desire of revenge, she denied God, and Christ, and sealed it with her blood, about five or seven years before she was found with the marks, and confessed what she had done to one William Dickens, and another there, and the manner how, but afterward I heard she made a very large confession. Anne Hammer near Needham in Suffolk, of Creeting there (as I remember) confessed that soon after her mother's decease, which was above twenty years before she was questioned, there came two Imps to her, which she called Tom, Robbin, and Tom like a mole, and Robbin like a Dorr, which she sent to kill Mr Campe a child, which she said (very like to be true) for master Campe averred that a mole to their

161

thinking was seen in the house, going towards the room where the child lay, and that they had much ado to keep it out, nor could tell what became of it in the end, and that they used to suck her twice a fortnight on those marks found upon her, during that time, and that the Devil in the likeness of a calf asked her to deny God, and Christ, and to serve him as Lord, and told her that if she would he would free her of hell torments, and that she should never want anything but be saved, and she consented, then he told her he would avenge her of her enemies, but she said the Devil never performed anything but revenge, and that the Devil in the likeness of a black man used to come in at the key hole, and to bed to her, and have the use of her body, but was heavier and colder, and lay all over her as man, and used not to speak but only to ask to lie with her, and as she thought performed nature: but if I should go to pen all of these sorts, then I should have no end, or at least too big a volume, and therefore but this one more, that Anne Boreham of Sudbury, in the county of Suffolk, widow, confessed that as she awoke out of a dream she saw ugly men (as she thought) a fighting, and asked them why they fought, who answered that they would fight for all her, and then one vanished away, and then came to her into bed and had use of her body, but said he was heavier and asked her to deny God and Christ, and to serve him, but she said she told him she was a poor widow, and then he said if she would serve him she should never want, but to have her desire, and then she consented, for he promised her to free her of hell torments, yet she said he told her she must go to hell, but should not be tormented (a fearful and subtle delusion) for I have been with some who have confessed the same, and that he promised them that they should only walk to and fro the earth as their Imps did, and never suffer or feel torments. Now some may say, if all these sorts be Witches, then most part of the world be so. I answer no; so honest persons may be given to these, and yet free from Witchcraft; but this is only to show when any are given to the extreme in any of these, then is the Devil busy to work upon them, for he doth not upon all that be given to these ways, but upon such as he finds some kind of preparedness in, as for example, was there not a preparedness in Boneham, and Mr Parson Lowes, and so if you do but truly observe little or more in all their confessions, as take but this last when she saw that fighting (as she thought) would not a good Christian have had her thoughts upon God, rather than to have suffered one to come to bed to her, which she knew could be no less but the Devil, and no man, for then he could not have come into the room, for Satan appeareth not to them in any shape until he find some preparedness, and then as you have heard by these confessions past he appears in several shapes, and then maketh the league, and confirms it with blood, and then sends them Familiars more or less, and so proceeds by degrees: so you may find as I said before, extreme poverty, passionate sorrow accompanied with solitariness, too much enraged with anger and desire of revenge, those of such parents, and all that I have formerly reckoned; you see by their confessions, that the extreme makes a preparedness, and I have heard of some schollers for want of learning, to be learned have grown to it, and some through overmuch, as is instanced before. Likewise John Scarfe of Ratlesden aforesaid, confessed that about three years before he was accused to be searched, there came a thing into his house of a grey colour, of the bigness of a great rat, of about a quarter of an ell[6] long, which he took up and put into a box, and kept it some certain time there, and then took it out, and laid it down on his belly, and put it to the place where the marks were found, where he said it sucked half an hour (did he prepare himself, or was he desirous to be one?); I conceive he did desire to be one, for he was a heathenish man, and so the agreement past; but to show his willingness to put it to the place, for in his confession more at large, he confessed that within a fortnight after there came two more, of a whitish dunne colour, and less than the other, which he called Tom, and Will; but the first he called Harrie, and so proceeded. Now I will proceed to prove that Witches may be found out.

First, from Godin the giving of his Law against Witches. *Exod. 21.18.* Thou shalt not suffer a Witch to live, which implyeth a discovery of them, else it could never be put in execution, and so should be a Law to no purpose.

Secondly from the history, First Divine. For it is said Saul found out Witches, and executed the Law upon them, or put them to death, and so good King Josiah, *2. King. 3.14.*

Secondly [*sic*], we have chronicles, and many relations made of the evident discourse of Witches.

Thirdly, the many trials in our own country at many Assizes: so it is clear that Witches may be discovered, though it cannot be denied but that there is some difficulty therein, because the secrecy of the grounds of Witchcraft is so close and hidden, as being one of the greatest works of darkness committed this day under the sun; for that natural causes may arise very strong, and many may cunningly counterfeit outward appearances, and Witnesses may feign their accusations out of malice, being transported with rage and uncharitableness, and desire of revenge, because of the strange imagination they have through many seeming probabilities; some for words, or deeds, taken in the worst sense; some upon some sudden fight of some creature, and so likewise upon burning anything of the party suspected to be bewitched, if any shall come (through peradventure accidently) and so sometimes something else, as thatch over the door or such like of the parties suspected to be a Witch, and so I could reckon divers instances of several ways, which many times have produced strange and sometimes true effects, which means have partly been the cause of the questioning of many, who have been found no less than Witches, and have suffered since the aforementioned time: but I forebare to speak any further of those ways, for I conceive them to be unlawful altogether, and not to be used, for it cannot be conceived any less than a distrust in God's providence, in putting confidence that such means will make the Witch known, and effect their desires: yet to proceed as I have said, I cannot deny but those may be just grounds of suspicion, and cause of questioning them, but not always certain, besides the unlawfulness held by divines. But these cannot be denied to be just grounds as aforesaid. As when one shall be given to cursing and banning, with imprecations upon slight occasion, and withal use threatenings to be revenged, and thereupon evil to happen. As Cherrie of Thrapston, in Northamptonshire, a very aged man, who upon a small occasion, of falling out with one of his neighbours in the field, where they kept cattle, one of the two (I do not now remember which) I scared some cattle off the ground, where the cattle the other kept was to go, with a dog, the said Cherrie and the other fell at odds and [argued], whereupon Cherrie wished that his tongue might rot out of his head, the man was soon after strangely taken, and his tongue did come out of his mouth, hanging only by the roots thereof within his mouth, but could not be kept all in his mouth, and so continued to his death, and died in a miserable condition. This Cherrie confessed himself, and that he was his death, only upon that occasion. After which confession, that it came to be known, many of the townsmen of Thrapstone aforesaid averred that he died with his tongue out, and that in a manner it rotted. A fearful thing to be thought of, what a miserable condition the poor man died in.

Cherrie likewise confessed the death of two more which by his confession, and those that knew their deaths, died in a strange and miserable condition, through his wicked cursing (as he confessed) and so confessed many other notorious facts he had done. And being asked whether he did not do Sir John Washington, a knight which lived in the same town, any harm in his cattle or otherwise, for that he had suffered strange losses; he confessed he did, and particularised the death of much cattle, saying, when he had reckoned up as many as he could well remember, that he had been the death of so many of his, that he could not reckon them all.

Then it was demanded of him, why he would offer it to Sir John, who had been so loving to him in affording him relief constantly. He answered: the more he gave him, the more power he had over him to do him mischief, for he said his Imp must be employed, else they would not let him be quiet, but torment him.

This Cherrie also confessed divers other things and harms he had done, and the feeling of the Covenant with the Devil with his blood, to deny God and Christ, and to serve him the Devil for revenge, with promise of freedom from hell-torments, and that his Imps, the last time they sucked him, not long before he was searched, told him they would not suck him any more but that time, because he was an old man, and had but little blood.

This Cherrie confessed presently after he was searched, who died at Northampton in the jail there, the same day he should have been tried, much about the time the grand jury had found the bill of indictment against him, *Billa vera*, as it was reported, miserably. A just judgement of God, for it was reported, that a night or two before, his coat was all rent right down on the back, and his mouth stopped full, and when it was pulled out, he confessed that he had been at a bridge going into Thrapston town, and had a cord found about his neck.

To this I might add the aforementioned Thomazine Ratcliffe, who upon the falling out with another woman about the death of a child, bade her go home and look to the rest, lest she lost more. And one died suddenly after, as before is expressed.

Of these kinds I could nominate divers more, as you may observe in many of their confessions, and might add implicite confessions. As, when a question is asked the suspected party, if he or she were not the cause of such or such a thing, answer is made: he or she might have let me alone, or not done so and so, or such like. As for example, you may observe in most of their confessions, they did it because they had not, such things as they desired, or used to have. As Anne Leech of Hawford in Essex confessed in her confession, besides the death of two or three, the laming of a child of one Turners. It being asked her why she did it, she answered, her mother might have paid her for work she had done. Likewise one Anne Parker, being asked why she did one Pryer mischief, she answered, he might have given her money upon a Thanksgiving day, as well as he gave to others, but would not give her any, because she was not at church, whereupon she sent her spirit to him, who did accordingly. And so confessed how the Devil in the likeness of a . . . dog, had three drops of blood under her tongue, to seal the Covenant, and had a piece of paper in his hand, and wrote her name thereon with her consent, and so promised her money, and that she should never want, but should be avenged of her enemies, according as is expressed in others.

Hereto I might add such as said they have such things as Familiars suck on them, but cannot help it. Alexander Sussums of Melford in Suffolk, confessed that he had things which did draw those marks I found upon him, but said he could not help it, for that all his kindred were naught. Then I asked him how it was possible they could suck without his consent. He said he did not consent to that. Then I asked him again why he should do it, when as God was so merciful towards him, as I then told him of, being a man whom I had been formerly acquainted withal, as having lived in town. He answered again, he could not help it, for that all his generation was naught, and so told me his mother and aunt were hanged, his grandmother burnt for Witchcraft, and so others of them questioned and hanged. This man is yet living, notwithstanding he confessed the sucking of such things above sixteen years altogether, but was suspected for doing mischief, yet never questioned, but as he came into a house accidently where I was, and so proffered himself to be searched, and presently confessed these particulars, and so by that means brought to trial, but freed, and living, as aforesaid.

Likewise I may add, when the party suspected makes enquiry after the party taken sick, or desires to visit the party, or the party suspected: for many have confessed that after they have done a thing, they are sorry for it, but cannot help it, as King of Acton in Suffolk confessed to a woman whom he had bewitched, in the time she was in her extremity, long before he was questioned; but this woman desired him to undo what he had done; and he told her he could not undo what he had done, but told her he was sorry for it, and told her of another that could, as he said, and as she affirmed, that was one, as we untruly call them, White or Good Witches, and one that was then suspected, who accordingly did it.

To confirm this, I can tell you of a very remarkable example much tending to this particular, of one at Heddenham in the Isle of Ely in the County of Cambridge, where a child suspected to be bewitched was carried to the Justice of the Peace his house, where the party suspected was to be carried to be examined. This child being very sick, was sat in a chair, and held in it; but as soon as the party who was suspected came in, on a sudden it arose of itself, and got hold of her face to scratch her, as its strength would afford, she not stirring. Here you may observe the former confessions, where the Witch confessed, that after she was scratched, she had no further power over that party; for this woman stood still and so you may perceive that many of them, after they have done mischiefs, are sorry for it, and cannot help it (this it is to renounce God and Christ); for this woman presently confessed that it was she that had hurt the child, through her diabolical practice, and told him what Imp she had sent to hurt the child, and the occasion why she did it; and how she had sent one of her Imps a little before she was accused (for she had been searched and found with the marks) to destroy or spoil a whole field of corn in that Parish; and so made a very large confession, with the sucking of her Imps upon those marks found upon her, and the Covenant sealed with her blood (as aforesaid in other confessions) besides other mischiefs which she did. May not Spell-Setters and Charmers be also added? For I cannot conceive any less, when they shall say that by words they can charm, set spells and help or cure mad dogs, or anything bitten by them, and such like; though it be by their implicit league (as some of them do) yet it is a distrust of God's providence, putting their confidence in their words, rather then in the living God, who saith it is an abomination to him. And I have heard some of these, not long since, boast of their doings therein, saying they had it from their parents, and were not their parents good Christians? And they do but use the words for good ends. So likewise of those born of ill parents, if their carriage be not otherwise; as I have instanced enough of those, else I could instance more, as the aforenamed Rebecca West, who was drawn to it by her mother (as she confessed) after a strange manner, as she said; for her mother asked her to go to Manningtree with her, which was about a mile, and bade her work hard that she might go, and as they went, she told her she must not say anything whatsoever she saw, but consent to them, and do as they did, and then she should be a happier woman; or suchlike enticements. But when she came there, at the house where her mother went, there were her confederates met; then, before she could be entertained, her mother was asked whether her daughter was acquainted with the matter in hand; who answered she was. Then she was entertained, and as she confessed, the Devil appeared and first kissed the woman of the house, and so one after another, and at last herself and so she was asked then if she were willing to be entered into their society; who said, she was. Then appeared Familiars, which she confessed, also the sucking of her body on the marks, and the sealing of the Covenant with her blood. This young woman confessed the naming of their Imps, and the manner, which I am ashamed to express, and the initiation of a Witch, and every particular thing at large, especially, she confessed how the Devil took her by the hand, and the manner and words were used at her marriage, when she was married to the Devil (as she confessed) a fearful thing to declare. But one thing observed: that the Devil imitates God in all things as he can, much after the Book of Common Prayer, then in his outward worship. She likewise confessed that her mother prayed constantly (and, as the world thought, very seriously) but she said it was the Devil, using these words, *oh my God, my God*, meaning him, and not the LORD. This I put in the rather, because you may take notice, where such meetings be, there are just grounds of suspicion, for they cannot always do their mischiefs according to their desires, without their meetings, and the help one of another.

I might add the apparition of the party suspected to the party sick, and could nominate some instances thereof, as in Northamptonshire, and elsewhere, but because apparitions may proceed from the fantasy of such as the party use to fear, or at least suspect, I forbear, because I would not that any should be accused, but where there are just grounds of suspicion. But those called Wisemen, or Wisewomen, called your White Witches, which will show the other in glasses, or undo what the other have done (if proved) is it not sufficient?

But I hope there is none so ignorant or blind, as to think or believe it is lawful for any to go or send to such, much less to put any confidence or truth in them, who require faith to believe they can cure, before they will undertake it; seeing by the Law of God they ought to die, as well as the other. And the holy scripture utterly forbids any going to them, *Levit.* 2.6. where it is said, that he *will set his face against such as shall seek after those that have Familiar spirits, and will cut them off from amongst his people*; much more then such as should be guilty themselves.

Then some will say, How shall they be known one from another, or how shall they be found out, if these difficulties be? For it cannot be denied but that many of them have made great shows of religion.

I answer, it is truth: as the Devil can transform himself into an Angel of light, so have many of these Witches made outward shows, as if they had been Saints on earth, and so were taken by some; as one of Catsworth in Huntingtonshire, who made as large a confession, in a manner, as ever any did, and confessed at the gallows before her death, in my hearing. Likewise one Lendall of Cambridge, who suffered also, carried herself as if she had been no less; and so did the mother of the said Rebecca West, and many others, which by their carriage seemed to be very religious people, and would constantly repair to all sermons near them; yet notwithstanding all their shows of religion, there appeared some of these probabilities, whereby they were suspected, and so searched, and so by that means discovered and made known. For if you do but observe these and such-like other reasons as may be thereby gathered, together with the confessions, you shall find that they prepare themselves in some kind or other, and that by their outward carriage, either by ill company keeping, maliciousness, revengeful persons, or such as be born of such parents, or go under a general suspicion of Witchcraft, or one way or other as aforesaid, there will appear just grounds of suspicion, either by words or deeds, whereby they may be brought to be questioned, whereby it may appear there is a league made with the Devil, for notwithstanding all former reasons, to convict or prove one guilty of Witchcraft, is to prove a League made with the Devil, in this only act, standeth the very reality of a Witch, without which (notwithstanding great shows of possibilities) I know not, nor cannot conceive how any can be properly said to be Witches, for the Devil (through Gods permission) may hurt mens bodies, and kill their cattle, and ill haps may fall out upon his or her cursing, and but grounds to make enquiry and search, which must be for this League, which though never so secretly made, yet it is to be discerned, seeing it is that which maketh a Witch, and not to some of their own society, for besides the former reasons, it is not heathenish practice to seek such, *Isa. 19.3* and *65.4.2 King 17.17.* Now we should not be like the abominable heathen in any evil, much less in these abominations. And they which seek to them, are commonly wicked and evil people, haunted themselves by an evil spirit, who suggesteth this course into them, as he did into Saul, *1 Sam. 28.* Yea, such as esteem of these and think they work in God's name, and by his power, are bewitched in so thinking, *Acts 8.9, 11.* For it is found true by daily experience amongst ourselves, that those which most use them, most need them, as I might instance; but only I desire to prove the League, which is to be proved, for they that make this League, if express as before, have a Familiar or Spirit, more or less. For as soon as the League is made, the Spirit or Familiar, one or more, is Familiar, as was before sufficiently proved by Saul and Josiah in the forementioned places, when Witches were known to have Familiars, besides the confessions of Witches lately executed herein expressed, and so they have nowadays, by which, after their League made, they work their mischief, as is likewise proved by their confessions; as the said Elizabeth Clarke confessed, who averred that all were Witches who had such marks as she was found withal, and had Familiar spirits more or less, and that there were some which had none, which I have found true, for they have only the brand, or Devil's mark, as I may so call it, but for the other, you may observe it as a gentle rule in all their confessions, as John Bysack, alias Gleede, of Waldingfield Magna in the county of Suffolk, confessed that the Devil came in at his window in the shape of a rugged sandy-coloured dog, which asked him to deny God, Christ, and his Baptism, which he spoke with a great hollow voice, and he consented. Then he said Satan asked him for blood to seal and confirm the Covenant or agreement; and he bade him take it, and that Satan with his consent had, in the shape of such a coloured dog, [scratched] his leather doublet, with his claw. Then I asked him whereaway Satan had it, and he said, from his heart, and that Satan promised to free him of hell torments, and that he would send him other things which he must let suck his blood, and they should avenge him of all his enemies. All of which he said he consented to, and was willing withal; and then soon after those came, which he called his Imps, and sucked on those marks or teats which I found on his body, near twenty years together, sometimes once a week, sometimes once a fortnight, which he confessed came in the likeness

171

of snails, only they differed one from another in colour and bigness. Then I asked him how they could suck on that part of his body I found the marks on, and he said he used to lie down on his right side to let them suck, and was willing withal, for he confessed he oftentimes arose out of his bed and made a fire, and lay down by it to let them suck his blood, which rising out of his bed, and making, his wife averred to be truth, yet she said she never knew or thought him to be such a manner of person, for she said he used to tell her he was sick, and used to be troubled with a disease which he could not help himself better for to ease himself of his pain he used to be in, then by that means, and could not endure his bed, his pain was so troublesome. But to clear all suspicion which after might fall on her thereby, she was searched, and found clear, and no less thought to be by her neighbours before and since, as I have heard. He likewise confessed his Imps names were Sydrake, Leffry, Peter, Ayleward, Sacar, and Pyman; for he had six by his confession, and no less by the number of his marks. The first was to kill all manner of fowls, which was the first he confessed he employed. The second was to kill sheep and such like cattle. The third, hogs and such like. The fourth, cows and such like beasts. The fifth, all manner of horses. And the sixth, Christians, and so particularised many mischiefs he had done.

So they have their Familiars, some for one thing, and some for another, some to help them at their needs (though many times therein they fail them) and others to work their mischiefs and revenge, as the aforesaid John Wynnicke and many others have confessed. But I only instance their confessions in short, and but in part only, tending to that I quote them for as near as I can. For I could add divers more to this, but many of the other in effect tend to prove this, and so do most of the confessions little or more depend one upon another, so that I do but instance part of them, and of the effect of them, and not the third part of those I have, for if I should, I have many larger confessions, which perchance might give better satisfaction to some, but I only aim at the principle heads, and to clear and make it appear, that what hath done, hath been in a legal way, and not unjustly, as many have surmised, but for the good of the common-wealth, and I doubt not but agreeable to the word of God. And that all that be thus in league (as express or open league as aforesaid) are to be found out and known by these evidences, be they of either sort, Bad, or White or Good Witches so called; first, by Witches marks, which are most commonly upon those baser sorts called the Bad and cursing Witch, and so upon the other called the Good or White Witch, though not so easily found (if but only the brand, or Devil marks, as it may well be termed) but the other, which the spirits suck of, are easily to be distinguished and known from all the other marks, but yet have as before (if an express league).

This is not to be doubted of, it is the Devil's custom to mark his: God will have his mark for his, *Ezek. 9. Rev. 7.* the Beast will have his mark, *Rev. 13.* So the Devil himself will have his mark, as you may see as well by the relations and confessions of Witches, as also the witnesses of many learned men, writing of Witches and Witchcraft. Therefore, where this mark is, there is a league and Familiar spirits more or less, which marks are to be found by searching.

Now some will say, how shall they be discerned from natural marks?

I answer: first, as for that mark which comes by the sucking or by the drawing of the spirit or Familiar, more or less, which is most commonly upon the baser sort called the Bad Witch, and so many times upon the other so untruly called the Good or White Witch, for all Witches are bad indeed, though peradventure for the most part they have not commonly so many Familiars as the other, yet I say most of them work by Familiars as well as the other, and suckle them likewise, though not commonly above one. They are to be known by these tokens, as by the insensibleness of them, sometimes like a little teat or big, that is when it remains as the Imp or Familiar sucks thereof, if outward, then nothing to be discerned but as a little bit of skin, which may be extended and drawn out, and wrung, much like the finger of a glove, and is very limber, and hath no substance in it, except it be when their Imps have newly sucked them, and then it may be there may be a little watrith [waterish i.e. like water] blood perceived, but may be known from natural marks several ways, for it hath no fear, but at the very top a little hole, where the blood cometh out. But if it be inward, then it is beyond all natural marks, or where no such like (if natural) could possibly be, and remains but as a little red spot, much like, or little differing from a flea bite, only it is out of the flesh above it, when as the other is flat, but this as I say is out above it, with a whitish end at the top, and may be known both of them by a circle above them, much like the circle of a woman's breast which hath been sucked, and one may discern the place where the blood comes out, and many times it falleth out, if new sucked, the watrith blood may be stroaked out, especially in the time they be kept, if the Watchers be careful to discern when they be in the most trouble, though their Familiars come never so insensible, and therein (as before) Watching hath done good (though not deprived of anything necessary, as before). And the skin may be pulled one side from the other, and different from the other parts in colour, and remains as if it were a dead place, and so it is insensible of pricking and other usage, if it be done in a direct manner, and so may be easily discerned from any natural mark otherwise, if this were not sufficient to give satisfaction, which I doubt not but it will, as I could otherwise express, if it were neither for giving offence to some, nor a means to give some of such persons insight so far, as thereby they might grow more experienced to make away their marks, for that hath been too common amongst them already, for which I could instance many examples, but you find by their confessions, that all of them tend to manifest that their Familiars suck upon those marks which we first find, which are before expressed, and therefore I forbear to instance any to that particular.

Sometimes they be like a blue spot, that is, when they make them away, and then no more to be discerned besides the insensibleness thereof, but will grow or be drawn again by the sucking of their Imps or Familiars more or less, for they cannot hide them away, as one Marsh a woman of Brampton confessed, who had been searched two or three times one after another, and no other marks could be found upon her, at length, she being accused by another of the same town, was forthwith before she had any knowledge thereof, or thoughts (as I suppose) of being searched again, taken by the constables there in the streets, as she was coming homeward to

174

her own house, and brought to be searched again, upon the others accusation, but as she came by her own house, she desired to go in (as she said) to shift herself, for that she was very unwilling (as she pretended) to go to the women to be searched with a foul shift on her back, but the Constable having had notice of it formerly, not to suffer her to go to do it, it being known she did it before her former searching, brought her forthwith away to the place where she was to be searched, and when she was a searching, she was presently found to have the marks very apparent, and had a clean shift on her back. But not long after, in her confession, amongst other things, she confessed that if she had been let go home to have shifted herself, she had not been found with the marks, for that she had a shift so dressed, that her marks could not have been found at present, and that she thereby so escaped by the same means [as] the former searches, yet she was searched by those which were the first that ever to my knowledge found any of those marks, and so confessed that she had made a Covenant with the Devil, and sealed it with her blood, and set a round 'O' to the paper the Devil brought her, and confessed her Familiars, with the sucking of them, and the mischief she had done by her Witchcraft, or at least part of them, as she then further confessed, and suffered for the same. Here you may observe, that the diligentness of searching is a great matter, and one of the chiefest points of their discovery. For I have observed this one thing in my proceedings herein, that if all their marks, though in several places, be not found, they will hardly confess, but when all are found, and the just number of them more or less laid to their charge, according as they have, it is a great inducement to bring them to confession, and that hath made me careful when apparent marks have not been seen at first, that a second or third search be made, for it is a matter of concernment of life and death, and therefore, as I conceive, it were fitting that those which search, and those with them, they having some intelligence of the marks first given them, were sworn before searching, that diligent search might be made in all places of such as be suspected in such a case of life and death, for the detection of so great a height of sin and impiety, that none that be guilty might escape the punishment due according to their deserts here, and so those likewise that wrongfully go under that aspersion, be freed thereof. To which end, it were fitting that such as did it might be such as know what belongs to an Oath, and who make conscience to perform the same likewise, and such as be at the searching, able people, of discretion and good carriage, for I fear that money hath swayed some, and want of knowledge others.

Sometimes the flesh is sunk in a hollow, that is, when they pull them off, and pull them out with their nails, or otherwise cause them to be pulled off, as one of Over in Cambridgeshire confessed, it being so found and laid to her charge, that she heard of our coming to town, and plucked her marks off the night before a Justice of the Peace of the same town at large, both of the Covenant and her Imps, and the harms she did both to him and others by her Imps.

But some will say, it is strange they should know when they would be searched, if it be kept private.

I answer, let it be kept never so private, it hath been common, and as common as any other thing, as they themselves have confessed, for so did they of Fenny-Drayton in Cambridgeshire, who made very large confessions, as, that the Devil told them of our coming to town, but withal told them they should be searched, but should not be found, wherein they said they found him a liar, and so they said they did in his promising them they should never want, which they did, and so likewise that is useful with others; but those made very large confessions.

Also sometimes there is nothing to be discerned but red spots, as if the skin were perished (and so it is) for that is when they only cut them off, and apply no medicine at all to it; yet the blood will appear all round within the circle, as afore is expressed. And of these I have found diverse; but for the most part, those have been left for a second to search, or a third, as occasion or ground sufficient required. And of these though I have found diverse, yet I have but one example by confession, and that is of one Clarke of Keyston in Huntingtonshire, a young man, who was so found, and set at liberty, expecting to have been searched another time, when he should not know of it; but he soon after confessed he had cut off his marks, saying they were fools that were found with the marks, for he had made sure he could not be found with them, for he had cut off his two or three days before I searched him. But I perceived the blood, and showed it to the townsmen, and told them that I thought he was naught, and guilty of that sin, and doubted not thereof, but would not take oath, unless the marks had been apparently seen upon him.

Now some will say, notwithstanding all this that is said, there may be and are natural marks like all these afore spoken of.

I answer: For natural marks, as I conceive, there be wens[7] of diverse sorts; but view these well, and next adjacent to the flesh they are very small, and hang like a thread. But from thence like a teat or big; but feel of it, and it is fleshie, and will not extend as the other will do.

But some will say: It may be a rent, and so a piece of skin may hang.

I answer: This, though it be nothing but as a skin, yet it cometh firmly out of the flesh, and sticks out like a big or teat, and not hang down, when I conceive rents will either hang, or lie flat; but if hang, then I believe a scar is to be seen, and feels fleshlike besides; but these have no scar, only as it were a little hole on the top, where the blood comes out, which is easily to be discerned, for I have nipped blood out. And then likewise they be insensible, when the other be not. But I confess, if these be not pricked the right way, they will feel it likewise. Some have warts, but I answer: They be out of the flesh as well as other, but they are flat and fleshie, and sensible, and will not any way extend; but so far unlike the other, as I will not further speak of them. Some have moles, it is truth, I believe most men have, though they be of several colours; but those be flat to the flesh always, which is nothing like the other, nor will extend, but is sensible.

But some will say, it may be like the brand.

I answer: No, for it is different as well in colour, as also it hath no circle about it, but is as the rest of the skin is on the other parts of the body, only differs sometimes in colour, but not like the other, and is sensible: neither for the most part have any of the marks of those which have suffered been found, where there were either warts, wens, or moles, or commonly rents, especially of the men.

But then some will say: There are emrod-marks [haemorrhoids], and piles. I answer: True, but the emrod-marks are upon the veins, though they issue out, and are to be discerned either by the colour, or by the lying up of the veins; but if the veins be down, still, the colour remains in part, and are to be known that way. But however, they will not extend to be drawn out and twisted, as the other will, if at all, I am sure not so much, and if a little, then it is pain, and the other none, so therein the insensibleness clears this expressly; for it cannot be conceived that any should be insensible upon their veins, and the other are merely out of the flesh; for I conceive if they were upon the veins, they would bleed after they were sucked, and would not easily be stenched again; neither be they so inward as the emrods-marks, except the inward marks, which are beyond them, and where no natural cause can be of that colour, and insensible. And as for the piles, I think this is sufficient answer for that likewise, for they be out of their veins, and are sensible without question, and be flat, and will not be extended as the other will.

And then some others will say: But women have rents and other miscarriages by child-bearing.

I answer partly as before, and grant it for truth; but yet if that way will neither scar appear, nor will it feel fleshie, but will it be extended as the other; admit all this were truth, I will affirm the colour differs, and that there will be no circle about it, nor twisted, nor have a hole as the other have, and be insensible likewise, and otherwise, as I could further explain more at large, if it were fitting: for, 'all things' (as the proverb is) 'ought not to be spoken at all time', much less printed.

But if any shall hereafter make any objections against me (as I expect they will) I will then explain myself (through permission) as far as by experience I have found, or by reading or otherwise my knowledge shall extend to. For I am confident, and my conscience tells me, that those who shall be found with these marks, are expressly guilty of that diabolical art of practice of Witchcraft, whether they have done mischief or not, but only for that they have renounced God and Christ, and betaken themselves to the Devil, the utter enemy of God and all the world. And I had rather be an instrument (if any such thing ought to be) to save one who should confess and humble himself, as Manasseh did, then any of those who, being found with the marks upon them, shall deny. But I shall forbear herein, where it [no one] concerns me, but those in authority, for I would not give offence to any, only desire to clear myself, in giving satisfaction to the world that my conscience is, that none of these sorts ought to live amongst us, for by the Laws of God and the Realm, they ought to die, as it is said in the 18 of Deuteronomy. And then remember this one place, which is in *Micab* 5, where it is said, that when God intends to bless a nation, he will cut off or root out all Witchcrafts and enchantments, which I should think should give all sufficient satisfaction, that those which have these marks, are in league and Covenant with the Devil, and that it is not to be doubted but that there are Witches, and that those which have the brand be also guilty as aforesaid, be they of either sort, and are to be found as well as the other, by searching also, yet I confess that is very difficult to be known, and very few ever attained to the discovery thereof; but it is to be known by the insensibleness thereof, and otherwise, being drawn or shrunk up so with a circle about it, as if the skin were stretched to that place, or shrunk up about it; but very little by the colour, for that is as if it were or had been some natural cause, or where some issue had been, when as the skin was never perished, as may be easily discerned, only it shows in the middle thereof, for the most part, as if a little hole had been, except it be such as the places where the blood is fetched to seal the Covenant, which is only like a natural mark, either long or otherwise, as natural marks be, only it seemeth to be deader and harder, and so it is, and not so tender as other places be, or where plaisters have been used, but the other is for the most part round, but however, it hath a little circle about it, just adjacent to it, as if it were sunk in all the circle about, and then within that, next adjacent to the circle, somewhat higher then the flesh, and harder, and in the middle thereof, a little hole or pit somewhat sunk. This brand or mark, if it come to be tried for the insensibleness, will soon be felt, if greater care be not had in pricking of it; for though it be insensible a little way, yet it is not so deep into the flesh as the others be, but shows deadlike, much like as if it had been seared with a hot iron, and is firmly upon the body, and in no secret place, as the other be, but differs a little in colour, as a seared place doth from another, as I might somewhat enlarge, but I will not presume too far, lest others should unadvisedly and rashly proceed in the discovery of such persons wrongfully, and then fault me for the insight, as hath been formerly done by some, who when they have done that they are not able to give an account of, or render a reason for, or perchance say those be guilty, where they find some other evidence may be given that they be guilty, or where money will be largely given that they are guilty, when as if they come to be further questioned, they can only say they be such marks as such a one told me, and so likewise can say, I have seen some have such marks in the jail, of his finding out, or some who have confessed, when as they themselves cannot distinguish between natural marks, and those, neither indeed know them asunder, but however, know but one sort of the marks, and so let many escape, and I fear wrongfully thereby, or for lucre, accuse, a fearful thing to be considered of, and therefore I conceive it was fitting, that when such come to their trials in this kind, it might be done by those of knowledge and discretion, and upon good grounds, and not by every light-carriaged housewife, who regards more her own ends then the life of a Christian, who can render no other reason, but that they do but what they have learned some insight in, and to go where they are sent for, or else they would not do it; indeed for money, and not for the common-wealths good, as may be seen by their want of knowledge therein. For, I said, it had need be done by able, discreet, honest persons, especially for these last mentioned, and upon good grounds, and other clear evidence concurring with them. Yet I affirm that all that have these, or any of these marks, are guilty of Witchcraft, if plainly made appear, for I could have spoken somewhat more, both of wrongfully accusing, and excusing, only I know it will then be judged that I do it to take off all others, and that none, or but such as I like of, were fitting to do it, and so thereby take all upon myself, which I know many in the world will be ready enough to censure of me.[8] But for my part, where one hath the least insight herein, I wish there were hundreds in all countries which had the whole, and more then any now have; but only that such as be idle, or unconscious of their ways, and

180

careless of men and women's lives, or at least unskilled in these ways, might not be suffered to meddle in such a business of concernment of life and death, as this is. As for this, and the lucre of money, I shall more fully clear in the last objection in the close hereof, to acquit myself thereof.

Now for the implicit or secret league, if it be asked what these be which thus work by Satan.

I answer, in some sort, by way of similitude, from the direction of that place in *Mark 9.38,40.* and *Luke 9.49.* For Satan will be God's ape in all things whatsoever he can, and therefore will also imitate Christ therein. They are such as invocate the Devil by certain superstitious forms of words, and prayers, believing that these means can effect what they have offered them for, and do withal earnestly desire to have them effectual. Now the Devil herein consenteth, and affordeth his power, at the utterance of the words, to bring the thing to pass which is desired. Here therefore is a Covenant and mutual consent on both sides, for if a man or woman be content to use superstitious forms of invocation for help in time of need, and in using them desireth in heart to have the thing effected, if the Devil work the feat, there is a secret compact, for they have desired, and he hath consented. They are such as do know, that neither by God's work in nature, nor by God's ordination from his word, the things they do are warrantable (but rather hear such things forbidden) and that they also are absurd to common reason, and yet will do them, because they find an effect answerable to their expectation.

Hereto I might add the healing of a wound by anointing the instrument which gave the wound, spell-setters, and Charmers, and such like, who many of them are in express league as aforesaid, for the Devil contenteth himself sometimes, to wit, there were he well perceiveth the party will not be brought to the other, and let them please themselves with hope of God's mercy, employing them only about seeming good things, for that in so doing they suppose they sin not, nor are in danger of the Devil, nor under God's wrath, as the others are, because they fall not so foully into the pit of destruction by an express league, as the others do, and make an outward show of religion as well as others.

181

For what can be said of those who only cure diseases by laying on their hands, and using certain words or forms of prayers? Is it not done by this secret compact, though ignorantly they think otherwise? For if the remedy be not natural, then it is supernatural; if supernatural, then either from God, and so hath warrant from his word, and is ordinary, not miraculous, for that work of God hath ceased long since, or else is from the Devil, as works wrought by spells and charms, and such like, forbidden by God. Yet these sorts of persons, finding their practices successful, are not against Satan, nor can lightly speak ill of his working power, because of their secret and implicit league they have with him, and especially because of the profit they find come to them thereby. And herein also doth the Devil imitate Christ, who allowed some, which openly as yet did not follow him, to have power to cast out Devils, *Mark 9.38,39.* who were not, as he said, against him, nor could lightly speak ill of him, nor of his power, by reason of their secret and implicit faith, and Covenant with Christ, yet did it, because they found success in it.

So likewise in the scripture is found the cutting off hair, and burning it, *Numb. 6.18.* the writing of words, and the blotting of them out again, and to give them unto one, *Numb. 5.23.* Also the giving of a portion, *Numb. 5.27.* So Satan teacheth his to cut off hair and burn it, as the White Witch will do such as come to them, advising them to cut hair, or such like, off the beast they suspect to be bewitched, and to write a charm, and to blot it out, and give it one, also to use portions, thus seeming, by these imitations, to have scripture for their warrant. And so after this manner I might reckon up several other ways: as, the Lord had some which by cursing and threatening procured evil upon others, *2 Kings 2.24. Acts 13.* so Satan hath such, which by cursing and threats procure mischiefs upon others, as you may plainly see by their confessions.

Also the Lord tied his to certain rules and ordinances in his service, and sometimes to a certain number, *Josh. 6.15.1. Kings 17.21.* So Satan teach his Witches to certain words and deeds in going about his service, and to observe numbers, and to do a thing so and so often, three times, seven times, or such like, as the White Witches do, and so imitate Christ in many things, as his assemblies and Sabbaths, baptism and Covenants, so Satan hath all his, after his manner, as Rebecca West and Elizabeth Clarke confessed, as well in these as in other particulars, as you may find as well by theirs and others confessions, as also by the writings of learned men who have writ concerning the same.

And further, as the Lord had such as cured diseases by words, by prayers, and did anoint the party infirm; as by something brought them from the sick, and carried to the sick again, *James 5. Mark 6.13. Acts 19.12.* So hath Satan such as seem by words to cure diseases, by forms of prayers, and by oils, and also by bringing something from the sick party, and carrying the same back again.

So the Lord by his servants raised some from the dead, *1 Sam. 28.*

And as the Lord maketh some to be his, either by his immediate inspiration, and speaking to them, or winneth them to him by his instruments, so Satan maketh some Witches by inward suggestions, and his speaking to them, or by using other Witches to gain them to him, as you may find also by their confessions. And that as the Lord spoke by a beast unto a Witch, *Numb. 22.28.* so Satan speaketh to Witches, sometimes in one shape, and sometimes in another.

So likewise, as the Lord ordained sacrifices to be offered to him, Satan hath taught his to do so too, *Numb. 23.*

And as the Lord promised earthly blessings, to stir up people to serve him, so Satan, as you may find, is very large in his promises to such as will serve him, *Matth. 4.*

And so it is in many other particulars, as might well be observed, if you do but rightly observe their confessions, with their carriages, and Satans doings.

But here some will say: Is there no other way to find them out, but only by searching?

I answer: That is both the most ready and certain way, and such a way, as that, if they which undertake it be careful, there can be no mistake, especially in those who shall be found to have the marks, and for the other, if the express league, then by the brand, if implicit, then by the aforesaid reasons, and by their carriages. Yet they may be found by Witches words also, as when he or she hath been heard to call upon their spirits, or to speak to them, or talk of them to any, inticing them to receive such Familiars. As some of those of Rattlesden confessed that they had their Familiars from old mother Orvis, so had Elizabeth Clarke from Anne West, and so had her daughter from her . . . As also, when they have been heard telling of killing of some man or beast, or of the hurting of them, or when they have not only threatened revenge upon any or their cattle, but have told particularly what shall happen to such a one, and the same found true, and their boasting afterward thereof. Furthermore, if they have been heard to speak of their transportation from home to certain places of their meetings with others there, as was at Manningtree, Burton, Old, Trilbrook-bushes, and other places.

These and such like, as you may find by their confessions, prove a league and familiarity also with the Devil.

So also by Witches deeds, as when any have seen them with their spirits, or seen to feed some creatures secretly, or where the Witch hath put such, which may be known by the smell of the place, for they will stink detestably, which we have often found true in the time they have been kept, if their Imps or Familiars came to suck in the mean time, as you may find they often have. Also when it can be found that they have made pictures, as I have credibly heard of one of Yarmouth, who since the aforementioned time suffered there, and confessed that she had made a picture of wax and clay, I do not well remember which, of the proportion of a child which she was intended to work her mischief against, and had thrust a nail in the head thereof, and so had buried it in a place, which she then confessed, and that as that consumed, so should the child, and did, a long time, as I was told by Matthew Hopkins, who was there, and took her confession, and went to look for the picture, and that the child (as I have heard) did soon after mend, and grew lusty again. A hellish invention.

And so many such Witchery-tricks, both of this kind and otherwise, have thus been lately found out, as, the giving anything to any man or other creature, which immediately caused either pains or death, as was at Brampford and other places, as you may also find by their confessions. So likewise by laying on their hands, or by some one or more fellow-Witches confessing their own Witchcraft, and bearing witness against others, so as they can make good the truth of their witness, and give sufficient proof thereof, as, that they have seen them with their spirits, or that they have received their spirits from them, as beforesaid, or that they can tell when they used their Witchery-tricks to do harm, or joined with them, as those of Manningtree and other places at their meetings used to do, or that they told them what harm they had done, or that they can show the mark upon them, or such like, or by the Witches confessing of giving their souls to the devil, and of the spirits which they have, and how they come by them, and the sucking of them, and such other like ways, as you may gather by their confessions.

All which, notwithstanding, principally depends upon searching, which is the readiest way to bring them to these confessions.

Also some witness of God himself happening upon the execrable curses of Witches upon themselves, praying God to show some token, if they be guilty, who by bitter curses upon themselves, think thereby to clear themselves, as one Binkes of Haverhill in Suffolk, who confessed to me that she was guilty, and amongst other things told me, that the fly which was seen to fly about the chamber, was one of her Imps, but desired to speak with one Master Fairclough, who lived not above two miles, or thereabouts, from the town, being an able Orthodox Divine, who was immediately sent for, and came. This woman, notwithstanding her confessing to me, denied all to him, wishing and desiring withal, that if she were such a manner of person, that the Lord would show an example upon her, and that if she had any Imps, that they would come whilst he was there, presently after, she cried out, a just judgement of God, they are come indeed, said she. This Imp, in the same shape it was seen formerly flying in the room, was seen fastened upon another place of her body, not far from the other marks, but not upon them, and so remained above half a quarter of an hour, till some women came near a quarter of a mile, who saw it fastened on her body, she only crying out to have it pulled off, which at first they were fearful to do, but at length they wiped it off, as they say, with a cloth, and what became of it after, they knew not, but it had drawn a new mark, like the other.

185

Was this woman fitting to live, this evidence, with others, being against her, by credible witnesses? I am sure she was living not long since, and acquitted upon her trial, for she never confessed any more, but denied what she had formerly confessed.

Here you may take notice, first, that if they have their Familiars come to them either before or after confession, they will not confess till another time, or deny, and therein watching is of some consequence, till they be examined by a Justice of the Peace, or else they must expect but few confessions. This was observed as well by those at Bury, as indeed for the most part of all those now lately detected. And secondly, the extreme pain they put them to, especially when they first draw their marks, as most of them generally confess.

And I have observed in the time they have been kept, that if their Imps be a sucking, it is easy to be discerned and known, for then they will either covet to ruck or sit down upon the ground, or will lie shrinking up all of a heap, making sour faces, as if they were in extreme pain, so that they may be easily discerned by their carriage and gestures, whether any thing come to them, or not, while they be kept.

Also I have read that a Witch, in some cases, hath been brought to a dead party, who hath been suspected to have been bewitched by that Witch, to touch the dead corpse, which was no sooner touched by the Witch, but the corpse bled fresh blood.

These and such-like evidences may sometimes, though peradventure not always be given from God, when he is pleased to detect such malefactors guilty of blood, as well as in other cases of murder.

And thus you may plainly see that Witches may be discovered, albeit there be some difficulty therein, and may likewise be brought to confess their Witchcraft, as also, that there be Witches in these our days, nay I rather think more frequent then formerly, for if Satan be such a powerful deceiver and seducer, who can make an Eve in paradise (being in the state of perfection) to believe him, the Devil, before God, can he not seduce now? Yes certainly, more desperately, to manifest his bloody malice in these later times against mankind, and therefore he hath nowadays stirred up such cruel

Witches as be wholly set upon revenge, tormenting men and women, and their cattle, and making a trade of killing and murdering, of which sort for the scripture hardly give an instance, except it be in Balaam, hired to curse God's people.

Let us therefore learn to follow the Lord, and hate Witches, Wizards, Magicians, Soothsayers, Fortune-tellers, Enchanters, juggling companions, and all others that deal in Sorcery and Witchcraft, beholding in them a spectacle of mans misery, as being left of God unto the power of the Devil, and so be moved with compassion towards them, and pray for their conversions. Yet consider, though they be left of God for a time, yet not all so left, nor so dreadfully cached by Satan, but that they may, through the mercy of God, be his servants, and converted, as none can deny but Manasseh was, and so put a difference between their fearful sin and their persons, hate the one, but not the other, hate the one in conscience to God's commandment, utterly forbidding to regard such, *Levit. 19.31* for it is spiritual whoredom and defilement, *Levit. 26.6.* because such as used them were heathens, as, the Egyptians, Canaanites, Philistines, and Caldeans. Such as in Israel followed the heathenish customs, were wicked and ungodly; as Saul, who was a murderer, *1 Sam. 22.* a profane neglecter of God's worship, *1 Chron. 13.3.* and one whom God had forsaken, and taken his spirit from, *1 Sam. 16.14.* an evil spirit likewise was upon him, neither did God vouchsafe him any answer by sacred means, *1 Sam. 18.16.* and therefore he fell to Witches.

And what was Manasseh, but an idolater, and an observer of times, and so fell to Witchery, and so such as had Familiars? And the people which delighted in these, were haters of true teachers, and believed false prophets, dreamers, and diviners, *Jerem. 27.9.* and with us, what are they, but vain loose livers, superstitious neutrals, and such-like? But let them remember, that it *will be* but *bitterness in the end.*

Let Saul and Manasseh be a warning to all of this kind, besides examples abroad, and into histories, with those amongst ourselves, which may serve to terrify all good Christians from seeking unto or regarding such, for it is plainly said, *The Lord setteth his face*

187

against such, to cut them off, Levit. 20.6. And if God be against them, what may they look for in the end, seeing the least of these do entice people from God, in requiring faith of them, and do cause the people to run a whoring after them? As Moses speaketh, *Levit. 20.6.*

Being therefore in league with Satan and abominable idolaters, enticing people from their faith in God, they are therein worthy to die, or at least to receive punishment according to the statutes, for many of them are hurting Witches, as well as curing, and certainly to be discovered and known, with far less difficulty then the other, for they are to be discerned by their practices here, working openly by their cures, etc. when as the other work only secretly and in darkness. And surely let no man doubt but that the finding out of such miscreants is an acceptable service before God, else why should the Lord have given such command to the children of Israel, and to have driven out the nations from before them for those abominations, and to cause his own people to be led into captivity from those sins, threatening judgements upon them, and likewise against those who should suffer any such abominations amongst them, as in divers places both in the prophecies of Jeremiah and Isaiah, besides many other places of scripture both in the Old and New Testament, aforementioned. Nay, there are threatenings against such as shall resort unto them, as in *Exod. 20.6.* and so in divers other places before mentioned.

And doth not the Lord by the Prophet Micah promise to cut off Witchcraft out of the land, and that they should have no more Soothsayers, in the time that he intended to bless a nation? *Micah 5.12.*

And in truth, was there no alteration in England at the beginning and continuance of the suppression of this sin, and in some counties more than others? And who are they that have been against the prosecution of, or been partakers with such, but only such as (without offence I may speak it) be enemies to the church of God? I dare not instance, not only for fear of offence, but also for suits of law.

For was there not above forty in Essex (as I take it), all in Tendring Hundred, there where some were discovered, illegally outlawed, contrary to the law of this realm, upon a writ of conspiracy (as I have been credibly informed) I being one of the number, as I was likewise informed by some which were my neighbours when I lived there, by the means of one who is reported to have been one of the greatest agents in Colchester business, within the town, when as there was never any notice given to any upon the proclamations, as ought, am I sure? This man, with another who is likewise reported to have been fellow agent with him in that business, and the two chiefest in it, was the cause that some were not questioned in that town, but for his part, I saw him labour and endeavour all he could to keep this woman, whom he so much held withal from her legal trial, and likewise heard him threaten both me and all that had given evidence against her, or informed what manner of woman she had been in her life and conversation, to their knowledge, or as they had heard. Yea, as I since have heard, she was condemned at that Assize, and by his procurement reprieved. Since which time, on her behalf, this hath been done.

Was not this an animation to all such people in those parts, when so many gentlemen and yeomen thereabouts should be thus questioned for testifying their knowledge? And was it not a fit object for the Devil, to work upon others? Let the world judge. For I have heard many of them say, that the Devil hath enticed them to Witchcraft by some sermons they have heard preached, as when ministers will preach of the power of the Devil, and his tormenting the wicked, and such-like, as I have heard some say (I will not say, in the place where I now live) that the Devil will sit and laugh at such and such offenders when he torments them, and will jeer at them in tormenting them, when he hath got them. A fearful thing! When as the Devil is tormented himself, and tormenteth none, for it is the wrath of God for sins committed, and the judgements of God for his mercies abused.

These and such-like speeches, I have heard them say, the Devil hath made use of to persuade them to Witchery, coming to them and asking them: how do you think to be saved? For your sins are so and so (as he can set them out large enough) and you heard the minister say that I will torment you. Give me your soul, and agree with me, and I will free you of hell-torments. Ignorant people have been thus seduced. Therefore it behoves all to be careful in giving the Devil the least advantage, and to put a difference between their fearful sin and their persons, hating the one, but not the other, for that by corrupt nature we are no less apt to be misled by him then they, walking in sins and trespasses, *Ephes. 2.1.*

But in obedience to the law of God, and accomplishment of all things in the scripture contained, such ought not to live amongst us, lest the Lord should deal with us as he did with others for the same abominations; much less should any harbour such thoughts, as that there are not any, for did not the Lord leave some of the nations, to try and prove Israel? *Judg. 2.3.* and doth not St John say, (*Matth. 3.7.*) *O generation of vipers, who hath warned you to flee from the wrath to come?* Do not they, when they Covenant with the Devil to free them of hell-torments, who cannot free himself of them, flee (as much as in them lieth) from the wrath to come?

As for you that are of such an opinion, surely, if neither all the threatenings and judgements of God's against such, besides their own confessions, will not prevail with you, methinks the mercies of God should, in that fifth of Micah; for it is undeniably true, that there was, is, and shall be Witches, till Christ's conquest there spoken of, agreeable with that in *Revel. 20.1,2,3.* which as yet cannot be, for without doubt the Devil is busy in deceiving of nations, and that not only such as know not Christ, but others also, which could not be, if he were bound, nor the Jews or other nations still to come, but other places of scripture would be contradicted. And therefore every one must conclude with me, that (as yet) of Witchcraft there is no end.

Now whosoever thou beest that thinkest I ever made such gain of the way, or favoured any, and persecuted others, or took bribes, I call God to witness, that considering the charge of going to several places, and Assizes, and jail-deliveries, and the time I expended thereabouts, I never, one time with another, got so much as I did by my calling and practice, towards the maintenance of my family. And as for taking any money, or other thing, by way of bribe or gift, I never did, to the value of one penny, neither one way nor other, but what I openly took in the view of the townsmen where I came, and that in many places I never received penny as yet, nor any am like, notwithstanding I have hands for satisfaction, except I should sue, but many rather fall upon me for what hath been received, but I hope such suits will be disannulled, and that where I have been out monies for towns in charges and otherwise, such course will be taken, that I may be satisfied and paid with reason. And forever accusing one wrongfully, my conscience is clear before the Almighty, and I ever desired equal punishment to all that were guilty, or at least, if any favour, that it might be to those who confessed, but those still suffered, and others, though never so guilty, escaped. The reason why I did thus, was, because I desired so to satisfy the world in this particular, that it must needs be a great error to have such, and not to question others at all, as before mentioned, they being all guilty alike.

And in truth, concerning him who is dead [Hopkins], who likewise was an agent in the business, for my part, I never knew that he either unjustly favoured any, or received bribes, or used such extremity as was reported of him, only at first, before he or I ever went, many towns used extremity of themselves, which after was laid on us. And I do not deny but at first he might watch some; but to my knowledge, he soon left it, or at least in such a way as not to make them uncapable, but if he ever did at first, evidence was not taken till after they rested. And for my part, I never watched any at first, so as any way at all to disturb them in their brains; but when some have been watched before I have come to them, I have caused them to take their rest, before I would ever question with them; but now lately, and ever since the Michaelmas after the first beginning, I never used any but as aforesaid, with consent of the Justices, and not otherwise, nor ever did. But to my knowledge, we have been both much injured in words, and he since his death; but I am certain (notwithstanding whatsoever hath been said of him) he died peaceably at Manningtree, after a long sickness of a consumption, as many of his generation had done before him, without any trouble of conscience for what he had done, as was falsely reported of him. And though many of these things may seem very strange, and hardly to be believed, yet this is the very truth, and that he was the son of a

191

Godly Minister, and therefore without doubt within the Covenant. Therefore let no man take upon him either to speak or write more than he knoweth to be truth, for this I am able to manifest and prove to be truth.

And so I leave myself to the censure of the world, yet desire it might be left to the Almighty, who knoweth the secrets of all hearts: For, *blessed are they that do his commandments,*[9] *Revel. 22.14.*

[*FINIS*]

TWENTY-TWO

'A Confirmation and Discovery of Witchcraft' by John Stearne: An Essay

And to convince others who are of . . . opinion . . . notwithstanding God's law against them, and the holy scripture speaking of them, besides the laws of nations, both heathen and Christian, made to punish them, that there are no Witches, but that there are many poor silly ignorant people hanged wrongly.

John Stearne, *A Confirmation and Discovery of Witchcraft*

If one wishes to learn much about Matthew Hopkins and his Company, one must analyse the key documents concerning him. Not just his own pamphlet, but that of his chief accomplice John Stearne. It is through the writing of Stearne that we gain further information regarding the Witchfinder's friendship and working relationship with him and learn more of Hopkins, his personality and his interests.

To begin with, Stearne's pamphlet is full of the fire and brimstone of staunch Puritanism. His many quotes from the Bible are typical of such fanaticism and add to the confusion of an already poorly written document. When we compare Hopkins's pamphlet to that of Stearne's, we see a more cunning and, quite possibly, better educated writer in Hopkins. While recognising that better educated doesn't necessarily mean more intelligent, it can be suggested that a basic

193

comparison of Hopkins's grasp of English (and economy with the truth) compared with that of Stearne, reveals Hopkins to be the better of the two. Stearne, on the face of it, comes over as the blood-thirsty 'muscle' in the relationship, something that was interpreted so incorrectly in the film *Matthew Hopkins, Witchfinder General* (aka *The Conquering Worm*).

Stearne was very much a religious product of his time. Hopkins, however (as we have seen in the analysis of his pamphlet), was a loner, coldly calculating and malicious. Interesting then, that Stearne, at the end of his pamphlet, defends his ex-colleague's memory, concluding: 'Therefore let no man take upon him either to speak or write more than he knoweth to be truth.' Stearne seems so assured of their innocence and, it must be said, he appeared to be unchallenged until the end of his days (20 January 1671). Also, it is interesting to note that in 1651 Stearne challenged a neighbour at Lawshall for working on the Sabbath, typical of the staunch Puritanism we label him with today.

On the title page of Stearne's pamphlet we find the following: 'PROV. 17.15 He that justifieth the wicked, and be that condemneth the just, even they both are abomination to the Lord.' One can interpret this quote in many ways. Firstly, Stearne could be insinuating that the Witchfinder's critics are those who 'condemn'. This would ring true when we note the words Stearne used above when his/Hopkins's work was discussed. However, if what I suspect to be true is indeed true, then Hopkins employed Stearne under false pretences and if Hopkins is 'wicked' then Stearne was 'just'. However, Stearne's extreme Puritan heart will still label himself as much an 'abomination' in the eyes of 'the Lord' as Hopkins.

Did Stearne write his pamphlet out of guilt? Was he concerned about his own fate (maybe his final judgement in the eyes of God) after working with a charlatan like Matthew Hopkins? Stearne clearly wanted to protect his family but aside from that there really appears to be little reason for writing the pamphlet at all. Unless, of course, he really wanted to bare his soul to God for the things he has done. I do believe this to be true, because Stearne's document reads like the statement of a condemned man in the dock pleading his innocence. Look at the second quote (below the first) on the title page: 'DEUT. 13.14 Thou shall therefore inquire, and make search, and ask diligently, whether it be true, and the things certain.' He is allowing 'God', 'the people' to decide his fate after presenting his case. The quote is the justification for the pamphlet; the reason why it was written. Stearne is confused himself, he doubts himself or, more importantly, Hopkins. But because the pamphlet is called A 'Confirmation' of witchcraft he is battling for his innocence through his learned reading, hence all the biblical quotes of justification (be they relevant or otherwise – some do not appear to make sense). Also, by studying the title we notice that Stearne uses Hopkins's title, 'Discovery of Witchcraft', within his own suggesting that his (Stearne's) pamphlet is a continuation of the justifications as laid down by Matthew Hopkins the preceding year. Furthermore, Stearne starts the very first page of his pamphlet with the words: 'To the end I might satisfy the opinions of such as desire to be further satisfied concerning the diabolical art, or crying sin, of Witchcraft.'

But Hopkins's pamphlet did not save him. Was Stearne worried about his own safety? It is unclear, because why would Stearne claim that Hopkins died peacefully at home if he knew – or others knew – that he did not? This is where Stearne appears economical with the truth. He knew Hopkins had fallen out of favour, he was the ringleader and had to be punished. He met his comeuppance after his long journeys brought about the onset of his final illness of consumption; the Swimming Hopkins appeared to undergo only speeded up his death. So Stearne's words are still true, the clear conscience he claims that Hopkins had at his time of death is only his opinion, but one based upon extensive travelling with Hopkins. So here lies a very important point: If Stearne is making claims that are against public (official?) opinion, how can he prove his argument as he so sweepingly claims at the end of the tract? Quite easily: like William Dowsing, he kept a diary.

To me, this is an obvious statement, but no evidence of a diary ever having been kept by Stearne exists. So what do I base my theory upon? The many examples of Witchery Stearne gives so fully: locations, names, details. Surely the memory of all this eventually would have faded. Yet Stearne states that he could give many more examples of evidence/confessions. Simply, he must have kept a diary and this was the evidence he referred to at the end of his pamphlet.

But what good would a diary do him? It was irrefutable evidence of Witchcraft. It would name many witnesses whose evidence convinced Judges of local Witchery and therefore condemned 'innocent' people to death. It was a naming and shaming document that Stearne kept as an insurance policy, because if he was lynched for his presumed crimes then all those Judges and witnesses did wrong too. And that message would be loud and clear to his enemies.[1]

But why did Hopkins never carry a diary? He didn't need to because Stearne had one. Just like Hopkins did not need to appear at every Witchcraft trial. However, Stearne was present at most. There are indeed cases where Stearne is evidently in attendance while Hopkins is searching for more Witches. This is suggested in Stearne's pamphlet and can be proved through trial documents.

So what can we conclude from this? That Stearne was methodical, took his work 'in the eyes of the Lord' seriously, and kept his diary like a loyal Puritan because one day he would be held accountable for the things he did.

There is a loophole in this. If Stearne kept a diary for both Hopkins and himself, why didn't Hopkins call for it when he was lynched? There are several answers to this: one, he did not have a chance, two, he had fallen out with Stearne and therefore did not have access to it or, quite simply, it didn't exist. I believe it did exist, but either of the other two conclusions could equally be true. Hopkins was deliberately set upon by somebody and I believe it was done with official backing, so Hopkins not having a chance seems to be the more plausible reason. I think that Hopkins showed his true colours to Stearne towards the end. Stearne was seeing the official business through to its rightful and lawful conclusion, while Hopkins was trying to get richer by finding more Witches. If Stearne really wanted to see justice done, he had to see the work through to a hanging; that was the only just way. This must have stood him in good stead with officials. There was a just side to Stearne's nature and, ostensibly, his Witchfinding methods. Again, at the end of the pamphlet he admits that they 'at first' Watched Witches; but both Hopkins and Stearne grew in their experience and, that is when many examples of Witchcraft and just confessions and witnesses sort. Then this followed through to Assize. On top of this laboured length of example after example in the biblical cross-referencing. Stearne adds justification outside that of the law upon his interpretation of the Bible, and it is the weight of all this combined evidence, backed by his diary that gives him personally a watertight justification to his antics as Witchfinder. After the publication of the justification, Stearne retired to live with his God-fearing family and raise five more children. At that time (1648) he was seen as a man who did what he thought was right, but when the tide turned against Witchfinding he gently slipped away into obscurity. This was something Hopkins should have done, but he was far too devious for his own good and also had too many enemies. This is the only logical answer to Stearne's escape from the turn-round of justice that Hopkins and his Company faced. Those who escaped, all escaped into obscurity, even Rebecca West.

So what else do we glean from Stearne's pamphlet, apart from all the important examples of Witchery and subsequent confessions? Again we come to Stearne's insecurities. I began this essay with the main argument against Witchcraft mentioned by Stearne in his pamphlet, but early on in the pamphlet he does acknowledge the other big criticism against them: 'those who have gone or been instruments in finding out or discovering those of late made known have done it for their own private ends, for gain and such like, *favouring some where they thought good, and justly prosecuting others* [my italics]'. Stearne cuts deep with these words. I believe that the phrase I have placed in italics has some element of truth and that it backs up my claim (and the claims of others who have analysed Hopkins's work) that he indeed took commissions (not bribes) to prosecute Royalists for the crime of Witchcraft and that was why he was cut a lot of slack by Parliament and their agents, certainly at the outset.

Stearne also mentions that he joined Hopkins's Company on 25 March 1645. This also adds weight to my conspiracy theory that

Stearne was duped (even seduced) into the Company by Rebecca West, working for Hopkins. The date is perfectly placed and Stearne would have come in cold to the story with Hopkins clearly leading – orchestrating – the proceedings. But did the passion for money, resulting in more outrageous accusations of Witchcraft (made by Hopkins) during 1647, make Stearne suspect Hopkins of corrupting what he thought was just in the eyes of the Lord? I believe so, because Stearne stated that he never took a bribe or favoured any Witches, but immediately before saying this he writes: 'Now the occasion [thus] being offered, and Master Hopkins dead . . .' Was Stearne scared of Hopkins? I can't quite accept this, but he probably wanted to avoid an awkward confrontation while Hopkins was alive, thus leaving himself open to direct criticism and, quite possibly, prosecution.

John Stearne comes across as a cautious man. A God-fearing man. A family man. There is evidence of all this in his writing, and is the complete opposite to what we see and believe of Matthew Hopkins. This is a case of opposites attracting. One filled the gaps the other had, thus making a very strong partnership, albeit resulting from misrepresentation since Stearne was duped into joining Hopkins.

So from Stearne's writing we can learn more about him personally, which allows us to deduce more about Matthew Hopkins. This is why it is so important to first analyse the source documentation and only use later documents such as Hutchinson's work in support.

[I am] a plain country man, who intend not to pen anything but what I shall be able to make appear plainly to be truth, and then I shall reckon it as sufficient recompence for my labour and pains.

John Stearne, *A Confirmation and Discovery of Witchcraft*

Appendix One
A True Relation of the Arraignment
of Eighteen Witches

AUTHOR'S NOTE

The following pamphlet is presented in its entirety for several reasons: one, that it is the source document of the noted confession of John Lowes; two, it details that Hopkins rode with one other man and two women and that their work was ordained by a greater – official – order. (This may be an exaggeration as, quite importantly, the last paragraph details the 'mistake' of trying to condemn a 'gentlewoman' of Witchcraft by the narrator of the pamphlet . . . quite possibly Matthew Hopkins himself.)

There is no signature or initial to the document (printed or otherwise), but it is assumed by the terms used that Hopkins may well have penned it himself in order to spell out the accusations and justify his trade, which was prolific following its conception in mid-April 1645. Note that it only took him the best part of four months to have well over 100 people accused and imprisoned for Witchcraft, which beggars the question: did he believe he had gone too far too soon?

The pamphlet is one of the earliest and most important documents concerning Matthew Hopkins and his work.[1]

A TRUE RELATION OF THE ARRAIGNMENT OF EIGHTEEN WITCHES

That were tried, convicted,
and condemned, at a Session holden at St. Edmunds-bury
in Suffolk, and there by the Judge and Justices of the said
Sessions condemned to die, and so were executed
the 27 day of August 1645

As also a List of the names of those that were executed, and their several
confessions before their executions.

With a True relation of the manner how they find them out.
The names of those that were executed:

Mr. Lowes	Rebecca Morris	Anne Wright
[Parson of Brandeston]	Mary Fuller	Mary Smith
Thomas Everard	Mary Clowes	Jane Rivert
[a Cooper with	Margery Sparham	Susan Manners
Mary his wife]	Katherine Tooley	Mary Skipper
Mary Bacon	Sarah Spinlow	Anne Leech
Anne Alderman	Jane Limstead	

Printed in London I.H. 1645

THIS ABOVE-NAMED Mr Lowes Parson of Brandeston in Suffolk (being arraigned there for Witchcraft) confessed that he bewitched a ship near Harwidge, so that with the extreme tempestuous seas raised by blusterous winds the said ship was cast away, wherein were many passengers, who were by this means swallowed up by the merciless waves, further he confessed that he had done many other most heinous, wicked, and accursed acts, by the help of six Imps which he had that frequented him daily. This Lowes preached about threescore sermons after he had made his Covenant with the Devil, and had a teat on the crown of his head, and two under his tongue: and there is none that make a Covenant with the Devil but hath from him a private mark.

Also Thomas Everard, a Cooper, and Mary his wife both being employed in a brewhouse at Halsworth in the County of Suffolk, freely confessed that they had bewitched beer in that brewhouse: and that the odiousness of the infectious stink of it was such and so intolerable that by the lothesomeness of the smell or taste many people died. And they further said that many other mischiefs they had perpetrated and acted by their Witchcrafts and damnable sorceries, and that they also had their Imps to whom they gave suck.

One old woman confessed that she had been a Witch the space of above fifty years, in which time she also confessed that she had done many very wicked things in bewitching cattle, corn etc, but above all that she had bewitched seven persons of one family to death, to wit, a man together with his wife and five children, and that also she had her Imps which came to her in several shapes.

Another of the women Witches confessed that she had bewitched a child to death, and that she had been a Witch above five and twenty years, in which time she had bewitched great store of cattle, so that the owners of them were much impoverished and hindered both by the death of them sometimes; and sometimes by the unserviceableness of them. And also she confessed that she usually bewitched standing corn, whereby there came great losses to the owners thereof, for that they could reap no profit, nor the benefit, nor the benefit of these long, hard, and by her made fruitless labours: besides she confessed that she had committed many other such like evil deeds to the hinderance of many.

These and all the rest confessed that cruel malice and ill bred envy was their chief delight, continually a long time before they made their Covenant with the Devil, who also did often and sundry times and in several shapes appear to them, before they entered into Covenant with him, that they might be made Witches.

Further also these with all the rest being searched as they were taken, were found by the searchers to have teats or dugs which their Imps used to suck so often as they came to them. And that some under their tongues, some in the roof of their mouth, some on the crown of the head, some amongst their toes, some in their underment, and divers other places: their teats were but little, some of them are shaped like a thunderbolt. There several teats or dugs their several Imps to suck who came to them often, sometimes in the shape of mice, sometimes in the shape of kittens, sometimes in the shape of snails, and otherwhile in the shapes of snakes, hornets, wasps, and divers other shapes.

Besides these are 120 more suspected Witches in prison at St. Edmunds-bury, who had all their trial now: but that the Judge and Justices were compelled to adjoin the said sessions till another time by reason of the near approaching of the Cavaliers.[2] And of those Witches some have confessed that they have a carnal copulation with the Devil, one of which said that she had (before her husband died) conceived twice by him, but as soon as she was delivered of them they run away in most horrid long and ugly shapes.

And these confessed that they have bewitched divers men, women, and children to death, as also horses, oxen, cows, sheep-swine, and other sort of cattle, as likewise corn, herbs, and plants etc, and have raised great and very tempestuous winds and storms, to the overthrowing and battering of houses, stables, barns, stacks of corn, and hay with trees etc.

Another of these Witches by her own confession affirmed that she owing a grudge to a gentleman and his wife in Suffolk, having no occasion (but that they seemed discontented at her coming often to the house and wishing her to forbear coming) and only for this cause she sent one of her Imps in the likeness of a little black dog to play with their boy being very young and their only child. But the child at first refused to play with it, but it coming often, at the length the child made much of it till at last the Imp brought the child to a waterside and there drowned the said child to the great grief of the parents.

Among those remaining yet in prison there is one Witch they say to be burned,[3] who seems to be penitent for her former lewd and abominable endeavours, and acts, and desires to have petitions put up to divers godly ministers that they would be pleased to pray in their several congregations that her said Imps may have no further power to do any more such like hurt, neither by sea nor land, as they have divers time formerly done, to the destruction, loss, or utter undoing of many sundry good and honest people.

Now for the manner how they usually find out their Witches.

There are in the county of Suffolk four searchers appointed for the finding of them out, two men searchers and two women searchers, the men are to search those men who are suspected to be Witches, and the women searchers likewise are to search those women that are supposed to be Witches.

And also their manner is, in what town soever in the said County of Suffolk, there be any person or persons suspected to bewitch or Witches, thither they send for two or all of the said searchers, who take the party or parties so suspected into a room and strip him, her, or them, stark naked, and on whom the searchers find any teats or dugs, that party or parties, the said searchers set upon a stool or stools, in the midst of the room, so that the feet of him, her, or them, may not touch the ground. Nevertheless the party or parties may sometimes walk up and down the said room, so that there be sure watch kept, that none of his, her, or their several Imps come at him, her, or them, to suck him, her, or anyone of them so suspected, during the space of four and twenty hours and in that time (if they be Witches) either their Imps will come to suck him, her, or them, or else the party or parties that is a Witch or Witches will be mightily perplexed and much tortured for want of his, her, or their sucking Imps, and will be strangely out of order, and some at mouth or else be in some other extraordinary seeming tormented posture, and many times they do apparently see their Imps come to them.

The Examination of Anne Leech of Mistley in the County aforesaid, widow, taken before the said Justices, April 14 1645.

This examinant saith; that she had a grey Imp sent to her, and that this examinant, together with the said Elizabeth Clarke, and Elizabeth, the wife of Edward Gooding, did about a year since, send their Imps to kill a black cow and a white cow of Mr Edwards which was done accordingly: And this examinant saith, that she sent her grey Imp, Elizabeth Clarke a black Imp, and Elizabeth Gooding a white Imp: And this examinant saith, that about thirty years since, she sent a grey Imp to kill two horses of one Mr. Bragge of Mistley, which were killed accordingly; and that the occasion of her malice was, because mistress Bragge had told this examinant, that she suspected her to be a naughty woman; this examinant confessed, that she and the said Elizabeth Gooding, sent either of them an Imp to destroy the child of the said Mr. Edwards; this examinants Imp being then a white one, and Elizabeth Gooding a black Imp, and that about thirty years since, this examinant had said white Imp, and two others, a grey, and a black Imp, of one Aune,[4] the wife of Robert Pearce of Steak in Suffolk, being her brother; and that these Imps went commingly from one to another, and did mischief wherever they went; and that when this examinant did not send and employ them abroad to do mischief, she had not the health, but when they were employed she was healthful and well, and that these Imps did usually suck those teats which were found about the private parts of her body; and that the said Imps did often speak to this examinant and told her, she should never feel hell torments and that they spoke to her in an hollow voice which she plainly understood. And this examinant also confessed, she sent her grey Imp to Elizabeth the daughter of Robert Kirk of Manningtree, about three years since, to destroy her; and upon the sending of the said Imp, the said Elizabeth languished by the space of one whole year, until she died and that occasion of offence this examinant took against her the said Elizabeth was, for that she asked a coife[5] of the said Elizabeth which she refused to give to this examinant. And further, this examinant saith that long since, but the exact time she cannot remember, she sent her grey Imp to kill the daughter of the widow Rawlyns of Mistley aforesaid; and the reason was, because this examinant was put out of her farm, and the said widow Rawlyns put in, where she dwelleth at this present. And moreover, this examinant confessed, that she was acquitted with the sending of an Imp by the aforesaid Elizabeth Gooding, to vex and torment Mary the wife of John Taylor of Manningtree aforesaid about three years since, and this examinant being asked why she discovered it to the said Mary, she saith, the Devil would not suffer her, and that the cause of the said Elizabeth Goodings malice against the said Mary was, because the said Mary refused to give the said Elizabeth some good beer. And lastly, this examinant saith, that about eight weeks since this examinant, the said Elizabeth Gooding, and one Anne West of Lawford widow, met together at the house of the said Elizabeth Clarke, where there was a book read, wherein she thinks there was no goodness.

Whereas there was a book (of the Essex Witches) came forth in print, wherein on Mrs. Wayt a minister's wife was nominated for one, but it was a palpable mistake, for it is very well known that she is a gentlewoman of a very godly and religious life, and a very good conversation, and this was set on purpose to vindicate her, and lay the fault on the Author, in whom it was a great mistake.

[*FINIS*]

Appendix Two
A True Relation of the Arraignment
of Thirty Witches

AUTHOR'S NOTE

The following document, *A True Relation of the Arraignment of Thirty Witches*, has been transcribed in its entirety because of its importance. It details Rebecca West's 'carnal copulation with the Devil', and clearly shows the endemic paranoia of Witchcraft in the mid-seventeenth century and, perhaps as importantly, the willingness of a certain 'Witch' (Goodwife Clarke) to accept her dealings with the Devil and thus confess freely her own guilt; or so we are led to believe.

A TRUE RELATION
OF THE ARRAIGNMENT OF THIRTY WITCHES

At Chelmesford in Essex, before Judge Coniers, fourteen
whereof were hanged on Friday last, July 25. 1645.
There being at this time a hundred more
in several prisons in Suffolk
and Essex.

Setting forth the Confessions of the
principal of them.

Also showing how the Devil had carnal copulation
with Rebecca West, a young maid, daughter to
Anne West.
And how they bewitched Men, Women, Children, and
Cattle to death: with many other strange things,
the like was never heard of before.

The names of those that were executed:

Mrs. Wayt [a Ministers wife]	Jane Browne	Jane Briggs
Mother Forman	Mother Miller	
Anne West	Rachel Flower	Mother Clarke
Mother Benefield	Mary Greene	Frances Jones
Mother Goodwin	Mary Foster	Mary Rhodes

Printed at London by I. H.

THE CONFESSION OF REBECCA WEST, DAUGHTER TO ANNE
WEST OF COLCHESTER IN ESSEX

THE SAID REBECCA confessed at the Bar, that about Shrovetide
last her mother bade her make haste of her work, for she must get
along with her before Sun-down: and as they were going over the
fields, her mother gave her a great charge never to speak of what she
should hear or see, and she faithfully promised to keep counsel.
When she came to the house of meeting there were five Witches
more; the two chiefs were Mother Benefield and Mother Goodwin:

this Mother Goodwin pulled out a Book, and after their manner they prayed out of it, and presently their several Imps appeared in several shapes: six whereof appeared in the shapes of Kittens about a week old in Mother Benefield's lap, and after she had kissed them, she said unto Rebecca that those were all her children which she had by as handsome a man as any was in England. Then they commanded their Spirits come to kill such a man's Horse, some a cow, some a Child, etc. then Mother Benefield called to mother West, and asked if she were sure that her daughter Rebecca would keep counsel, or else she might seek all their blood. She answered, Rebecca had promised. They all then replied, if she ever did speak of it that she should suffer more tortures and pains on earth, then the pains of hell. Presently Mother Benefield said, for more certainty let her take her Covenant and Oath as we have already done. Then they taught her what to say, the sum whereof was to deny God and her Saviour Jesus Christ, to renounce all promises of his blessings, and the merits of his bitter death and passion, to believe as they did, and to serve and obey as they did. And the said Rebecca confessed that so soon as she had done thus, the Devil in the shape of a little black dog leaped into her lap, and kissed her three times, but she felt them very cold. Shortly after, when she was going to bed, the Devil appeared unto her again in the shape of a handsome young man, saying that he came to marry her. The manner was thus: he took her by the hand, and leading her about the room said, I take thee Rebecca to be my wife, and do promise to be thy loving husband till death, defending, thee from all harms; then he told her what she must say, whereupon she took him by the hand and said, I Rebecca take thee to be my husband, and do promise to be an obedient wife till death, faithfully to perform and observe all thy commands; the first whereof was that she should deny and renounce as aforesaid. And being asked by the Judge whether she ever had carnal copulation with the Devil, she confessed that she had. And being asked divers questions by a Gentleman that did speak several times with her before and afterward (giving her godly and comfortable instructions) she affirmed that so soon as one of the said Witches was in prison, she was very desirous to confess all she knew, which accordingly she did, whereupon the rest were apprehended and sent unto the Jail. She further affirmed, that when she was going to the Grand Inquest with one Mother Miller (indicted for a Witch) she told Mother Miller that she would confess nothing, if they pulled her to pieces with pincers: and being asked the reason by the Gentleman, she said she found herself in such extremity of torture and amazement, that she would not endure it again for the world: and when she looked upon the ground she saw herself encompassed in flames of fire: and presently the Grand Inquest called for her, where they admit but one at a time, and so soon as she was thus separated from this Mother Miller, the tortures and the flames began to cease: whereupon she then confessed all she ever knew, and said that so soon as her confession was fully ended, she found her conscience so satisfied and disburdened of all her tortures, that she thought herself the happiest creature in the world: withal affirming that the Devil can take any shape, and speak plain English.

Another Witch sent her maid to a neighbour's house for a handful of herbs, who meeting with her sweetheart stayed an hour by the way, saying she should be half hanged for staying so long: whereupon he told her that in such a place in their own garden there grew the same herbs, so it was but going over the pale and her journey was ended; which she did, and pleased her mistress well for her long stay, by bringing those herbs. At night her mistress bade her go up to bed first, which made her mistrust something; whereupon she peeked between the boards, and observed her mistress to cut the herbs in small pieces, showing them about the room: the next morning her husband rising betimes found twelve or fourteen great Hogs, being all his own, dead in the yard, and so for his Sheep and all his other Cattle, and telling his wife how they were undone, she replied, Hath the queane[1] served me thus? she shall suffer for it. Then he examined the maid, and both gave evidence. This was at Ipswich in Suffolk.

THE EVIDENCE OF MR LONG A MINISTER NEAR COLCHESTER IN ESSEX

First, that as he was riding on the way, the shape of a red dog passed by him, at which his blood did rise: and being passed a small distance, turned his face, his eyes appearing not like the eyes of any creature, his horse presently started, and never left kicking and flinging until he threw him down, but had not hurt. An old woman in the Town called goodwife Clarke being mistrusted and examined before Sir Thomas Boes, confessed that she sent forth this spirit, with command to make the horse throw Mr. Long and break his neck: and being demanded by Sir Thomas Boes what was the reason the Spirit did not perform her commands, she answered because the power of God was above the power of the Devil. But the horse did pine to death for his punishment.

THE EVIDENCE OF THE SAID MR LONG

He said that one morning as he was walking abroad, a poor woman being of his own Parish spoke kindly to him, but his answer was that he had a long time a good opinion of her, although he ever accounted her sister, an ill liver, and little better then those that are accounted Witches, but now he strongly believed that her sister had made her as bad as herself; this much troubled the old woman, and she would not leave following and persuading of the said Mr. Long to be of his former good opinion, professing her own innocence in any ill of such nature, or any compact with such evil spirit whatsoever: but finding him not satisfied with anything she had said, she assured him she would give him an evidence undeniable, whereupon she lifted up both her hands towards heaven, calling God to witness, and desired that he would show a present judgement upon her if she were not innocent and clear: now Mr. Long affirmed upon his oath that these words were no sooner out of her mouth, but she was struck to the ground upon her back before his face, where she did lie in a most lamentable condition, trembling and crying; he took her up and carried her into an Alehouse hard by, where she did lie in this extremity two days, and that so soon as she came to herself he gave her the best comfort he could, showing how merciful God had been to her in sparing her life, giving her time of repentance, the first step whereof must be her confession and contrition, whereupon she confessed that she had done much mischief, and that she had compacted with the

Devil, that he usually sucked her and appeared unto her in the shape of a Squirrel.

These aforesaid Witches have confessed that they did raise the great winds in March last, and caused a Hoy[2] to be cast away, wherein were many passengers.

When these Witches came first into the Jail at Colchester, the Jailer lost his meat often, and mistrusting that the Witches had got it, upon a time bought a good shoulder of Mutton, and said he would look to the dressing of it himself, but when it was ready the Witches had got it, and all the while the Witches were at supper with it, the Jailer instead of Mutton was eating Hogs-wash.

After this the Jailer desirous to see more of their feats, entreated some of them to show him a little of their cunning, thinking to make himself many for the loss of his meat, whereupon one of the Witches bid him go fetch her four pewter dishes wherein never water came; straightway went the Jailer to a Pewterer and got four new dishes, and afore he brought them to the Witch he wet one of them, contrary to the Witches direction, nevertheless as soon as the Witch had them, she put her hands and feet into the four dishes, and upon an instant was lifted into the air with three dishes that were dry, the fourth falling off, and by good chance was found in a meadow about half a mile off, and brought back to Prison.

[*FINIS*]

Appendix Three
List of the Condemned

Over the years many people have accused Matthew Hopkins of condemning a varying number of people as Witches, from 100 to 3,000 in total. What is known is that a conservative estimate would take the figure to almost 200, and it is also known that there were certainly more undocumented Witches whose fates are unknown. So the official number of condemned should be stated as 'more than 200'. The most accurate lists of condemned can be pulled together from various source documents.

The following list of Hopkins's Witches and their fates if known originate from these documents. The list is presented in its most authentic state, which means certain details are missing. The first batch of entries are from Essex Assizes and are taken from the Jail Calendar, Indictments and Jail Delivery Roll, with referral to *A True and Exact Relation* (1648) and *A Confirmation and Discovery of Witchcraft* (1648), which add some clarity to the records.

Surname	Christian Name	Home	Fate
Bonds or Boones	Joyce (married)	St Osyth	Hanged
Borton	Sarah	Ramsey	?
Bretton	Helen	Kirby	Hanged
Bright	Sarah	Manningtree	Hanged
Brooke	Dorothy	?	Acquitted
Cate	Anne	Holland	Hanged
Clarke	Elizabeth	Manningtree	Hanged
Clarke	Helen	Manningtree	Hanged
Cock	Susan	St Osyth	Died in jail

Cook	Mary	St Osyth	?
Coopen	Mary	Kirby	Reprieved
Cooper	Anne (married)	Great Clacton	Hanged? (possibly died in jail)
Cooper	Joan (widow)	Much Holland	Died in jail
Dixon	Alice	Wivenhoe	Hanged
Gibson	Elizabeth	Thorpe-le-Soken	Died in jail
Gooding	Elizabeth	Manningtree	Hanged
Greenleife	Mary	Alresford	Acquitted? (possibly died in jail)
Grewe	Margery	Walton-in-Soken	Hanged
Hallybread	Rose	St Osyth	Died in jail
Hare	Elizabeth	?	(Condemned but said to be reprieved)
Harvie	Elizabeth	Ramsey	Reprieved
Hating	Sarah	Ramsey	Hanged
Hockett	Marian	Ramsey	Hanged
Johnson	Mary	Wivenhoe	Reprieved
Jones	Rebecca	St Osyth	Hanged
Landish	Margaret	St Osyth	Hanged
Leech	Anne	Mistley	Hanged
Mayors	Bridget	Holland	Reprieved
Moone	Margaret (widow)	Thorpe-le-Soken	(Died on way to execution)
Moone	Judith	Thorpe-le-Soken	(Daughter of Margaret, fate unknown)
Rowley	Joan	Lee	Acquitted
Starlinge	Mary	Langham	Reprieved
Thurston	Anne	Holland	Reprieved
Walters	Dorothy	Clacton	Reprieved

Surname	Christian Name	Home	Fate
Wente	Susan	Langham	Reprieved
West	Anne (widow)	Lawford	Hanged
West	Rebecca (Daughter of Anne from Lawford, whose fate was stated in *A True Relation* as 'acquitted')		
Wyles	Mary	Great Clacton	Hanged

The next batch of entries are from the Suffolk trials held at Bury St Edmunds (one was almost certainly held in Ipswich). The main source documents from which this list is compiled are *A True Relation of the Arraignment of Eighteen Witches . . . at St Edmundsbury* and notes from John Stearne's pamphlet *A Confirmation of Witchcraft*. One missing entry is that of an unknown boy whose mother was hanged for Witchcraft and who stated that the Devil came to him as a mare and carried him wherever he wanted; conversely an unknown woman was noted as being searched twice because of a change in her marks. It is believed that a number of other individuals, in addition to those listed below, were accused and suffered as Witches, but a complete list does not exist.

Surname	Christian Name	Home	Fate
Alderman	Anne	?	Hanged
Arnoll	Anne	?	?
Bacon	Mary (married)	Chattisham	Hanged
Bacon	Nathanial (husband of above)		?
Beales	Joan (married)	Wickham	?
Barker	Anne	Glemham	?
Bayts	Margaret (married)	Framlingham	?
Becket	Mary	Framlingham	?
Bedford	Meribell	Rattlesden	?
Bennett	Margaret	Bacton	Hanged
Bigsby	Bridget	Hintlesham	?
Binkes	?	Haverhill	Acquitted
Bishop	Ellen	Glemham	?

Blake	Margery	Glemham	?

(a second Margery Blake is listed. Not known if administrative error.)

Boreham	Anne (widow)	Sudbury	?
Bray	Bet	?	?
Bush	Mary (widow)	Bacton	?
Bysack	John	Great Waldringfield	?
Carre	Henry	Rattlesden	Died in jail
Chambers	John	Bramford	?
Clamfield	Rose	Glemham	?
Clarke	Thomas	Glemham	?
Clowes	Mary (married)	Yoxford	Hanged
Collit	Priscilla	Dunwitch	?
Cricke	Anne (widow)	Hitcham	?
Crispe	Ellen (married)	Swefling	?
Deacon	Mary	Playford	?
Denham	Alice	Ipswich	Hanged
Dexe	Susan	Westhorpe	?
Dickes	Elizabeth	Rattlesden	?
Driver	Ellen	Framlingham	?
Eccleston	Margaret	Linstead	?
Edwards	Mary	Framlingham	?
Ellis	Anne	Metingham	?
Emerson	James	Ipswich	Acquitted
Emerson	Mary (married)	Ipswich	Acquitted
Everard	Mary (married)	Halesworth	Hanged
Everard	Thomas (married)	Halesworth	Hanged
Everard	Mariana (daughter)	Halesworth	Possibly reprieved
Fillet	Elizabeth	Wetherden	Possibly acquitted
Finch	Elizabeth	Wattisham	?
Foreman	Richard	Stowmarket	?
Fuller	Mary	Stowmarket	Hanged
Glamfield	Alice (married)	?	?

Surname	Christian Name	Home	Fate
Godard	Mary	Belstead	?
Gortnoll		Chattisham	?
Green	Sybil (married)	Wickham	?
Greene	Elizabeth	Wingfield	?
Greenliefe	Ellen (married)	Bacton	?
Gunburgh	Grace (married)	Wetherden	?
Hammer	Anne	Creeting	?
Hempstead	Nicholas	Creeting	Hanged
Hubard	Elizabeth	Halesworth	?
Hubbard	Elizabeth	Stowmarket	Possibly hanged
Keeble	William	Stowmarket	?
Kettle	Judith	Flowton	?
King	(male)	Acton	?
Lakeland	Mary	Ipswich	Burned (petty treason)
Leech	Anne	?	Hanged
Legat	Margaret	Playford	?
Linstead	Jane	Halesford	Hanged
Low		Stowmarket	?
Lowes	John	Brandeston	Hanged
Man	Elizabeth (married)	Wickham	?
Manners	Susan	Copdock	Hanged
Marchant	Susan	Hintlesham	Hanged
Marsh	Alice (married)	Bramford	?
Marsh	Anne	Tattingstone	Possibly hanged
Mills	Faith (married)	Fressingfield	?
Mills		Stowmarket	?
Mixter	Margaret	Shotley	?
Moats	Anne (married)	?	?
More	James	Halesworth	?
Morris	Rebecca (married)	Chattisham	Hanged

Muntford	Alice	Copdock	?
Orvis		Rattlesden	?
Palmer	Anne	Framlingham	?
Parker	Rose	Ipswich	Acquitted
Payne	(male)	Bramford	?
Potter	Joan	Hintlesham	?
Powell	Margaret (married)	Stowmarket	?
Prick	Rebecca (married)	Belstead	?
Randall	Anne	Lavenham	?
Ratcliffe	Thomazine	Shelley	?
Richmond	Elizabeth (married)	Bramford	?
Rivett	Jane	Polstead	?
Ruce	Joane	Polstead	?
Scarfe	John	Rattlesden	?
Scot	Susan	Lavenham	?
Scrutton	Mary (married)	Framlingham	?
Sexton	Mary	Glemham	?
Sexton	Rachel	Glemham	?
Skipper	Mary	Copdock	Hanged
Smith	Anne	Glemham	?
Smith	Mary	Glemham	Hanged
Smith	?	Bramford	?
Smith	Susanna (married)	Rushmere	?
Southerne	Elizabeth	Dunwick	?
Sparham	Margery (married)	Mendham	Hanged
Spindler	Sarah	Halesworth	Hanged
Stetgold	Susan	Hintlesham	?
Sussums	Alexander	Long Melford	Discharged
Sutton	Margery	Ipswich	?
Taylor	Lydia	Bramford	?
Tooley	Katherine	Westleton	Hanged

Surname	Christian Name	Home	Fate
Usher	Anne	Framlingham	?
Warne	Elizabeth	Framlingham	?
Warner	Sarah	?	?
Watcham	Elizabeth	Bacton	?
Wildes	Francis	Blaxhall	?
Winter	Mary (married)	Wickham	?
With	Margery	Framlingham	?
Wright	Alice (married)	Framlingham	Hanged
Wyard	Margaret	Framlingham	?

Those charged in the Norfolk trials were as follows:

Surname	Christian Name	Home	Fate
Blackbourn	Mary	?	Hanged
Bradwell	Elizabeth	?	Hanged
Clipwell	Alice	?	Hanged
Dudgeon	Elizabeth	?	Hanged
Fasset	Nazareth	?	Acquitted
Howard	Bridget	?	Hanged
Lacey	Joan	?	?
Lee	Dorothy	King's Lynn	Hanged
Meggs	?		Hanged
Prince	Mark	?	Acquitted
Verdy	Mary	?	Acquitted
Wilkinson	Barbara	?	?
Wright	Grace	King's Lynn	Hanged

Of the Northamptonshire trials, little is known. This fragment is taken from John Stearne's writing:

Surname	Christian Name	Home	Fate
Cherrie	(man)	?	Died in jail
Goodfellow	Anne	Woodford	?
(unknown)	(man)	Denford	Hanged

The following is taken from John Davenport's *The Witches of Huntingdon*:

Surname	Christian Name	Home	Fate
Chandler	Elizabeth	Keyston	?
Churcher	Elizabeth	?	Hanged
Clarke	John	Keyston	Hanged
Desborough	Anne	?	Hanged
Moore	Frances	Little Catworth	Hanged
Shepherd	Ellen (married)	Molesworth	?
Wallis	Jane	Keyston	Hanged
Weed	Elizabeth	Great Catworth	Hanged
Winnick	John	Molesworth	Hanged

Of the later trials, Bedfordshire?, Cambridgeshire and the Isle of Ely, little is known, and my research has only recorded the following definite cases:

Surname	Christian Name	Home	Fate
Ellis	Dorothy	Stretham	?
Ellis	Robert	Stretham	?
Farnaby	Joanna	Ely	?
Moore	(married woman)	Sutton, Ely	Hanged
Pie	Thomas	Ely	?
Sabie	Adam	Haddenham	?

(Eight others unknown have been recorded, three of whom were hanged and one reprieved, others unknown.)

Because there are so many gaps in the records, and the records are incomplete, some would argue that it is pointless to include a list of the condemned. I disagree. To study a list of women and men (some married) from different locations who all suffered to different degrees at the hands of Matthew Hopkins is important. It brings the horror of what he did closer to home. And some kind of record is better than none at all.

Notes

Preface

1 Many people have speculated about the number of people hanged
for Witchcraft at the hands of Matthew Hopkins and John Stearne.
The list of Witches in Appendix Three is incomplete but it
approaches John Stearne's estimate (see his pamphlet in Part Two) of
just over 200. More were certainly accused and even imprisoned, but
the final total of hanged is thought to be, conservatively, more than
200.
2 Hopkins almost becomes a child's incubus: a creature in a nightmare,
not unlike the mutilated Freddie Krueger of the *Nightmare on Elm
Street* films of the 1980s.
3 With its spaghetti western-type music and horse riders the film is a
cross between *The Magnificent Seven* and *The Good, The Bad, and
The Ugly*; so the Puritan posse was probably included by luck rather
than judgement.

Dramatis Personae

1 I have opted to use contemporary spelling for the names of key people
in this book.
2 Could possibly be known as Mary Hopkins; as suggested by some
source documentation and quoted in its proper place in the text using
the contemporary spelling.

Prologue

1 Creatures of the Devil who attach themselves to a Witch and perform
her evil mischief.
2 Parish register for Brandeston, Suffolk Record Office, FC105/D1/1.

3 The accused would be thrown into deep water. If they sank, they were regarded as innocent, but if they floated or 'swam' they were guilty. The test fell out of favour in the early seventeenth century but was given a new lease of life by King James in his *Daemonologie*, a book Hopkins used in his justification of Witch-hunting. However, the methods would be frowned upon by Parliament.

4 See *A True Relation of the Arraignment of Eighteen Witches . . . 27 August 1645.*

Chapter One

1 Surname spelt 'Hopkings' in the register.

2 Only known signature is on a conveyance document from 1641 (Suffolk Record Office).

3 J. Venn and J.A. Venn, *Alumni Cantabrigienses: A Biographical List of all known Students, Graduates and Holders of Office at the University of Cambridge, from the Earliest Times to 1900*, pt 1, vol. 2, (Cambridge, Cambridge University Press, 1922), p. 405.

4 Farrow and Barton, Index of Wills Proved in the Consistory Court of Norwich 1604–1686.

5 The spelling of James Hopkins's wife's name is important to this narrative, so I have 'Marie' as used in the will and not the more favoured contemporary 'Mary'.

6 Suffolk Record Office, Ipswich (will of Daniel Wyles of Great Wenham, 1619).

7 Note that the eldest son took his father's name James (very common for that time), then the names of the apostles follow: Thomas and John. Reasonable to assume that the next boy born would be named Matthew.

8 See Framlingham reference in Chapter Twelve, p. 63.

9 Richard Deacon, *Matthew Hopkins – Witch Finder General*, Muller 1976.

10 See Part Two for contemporary transcript and analysis.

11 In Malcolm Gaskill's book *Witchfinders* (John Murray, 2005), he reads more deeply into the story of Matthew's father, although along the same lines as my research. Mr Gaskill concludes that James was still at Peterhouse in 1608 and was ordained at Ely Cathedral and his

marriage took place some time soon afterwards. This new evidence further substantiates my deduction.

12 The eldest son.

13 James's will didn't suggest a close relationship with his relations. It seems that they were not so well placed and, indeed, one was quite possibly his maid.

14 Unfortunately one cannot dispute that all Hopkins documentation was deliberately destroyed after the death of Matthew.

15 Note that Lady Day, 25 March, was, during the 1600s, the first day of the New Year and not 1 January.

Chapter Three

1 Deacon, *Matthew Hopkins*.

Chapter Four

1 Jonathan Barry, Marianne Hester and Gareth Roberts (eds), *Witchcraft in Early Modern Europe – Studies in Culture and Belief* (Cambridge).

2 Commissioned by Parliamentarians in Manchester.

3 Matthew Hopkins, *The Discovery of Witches* (London, 1647).

4 Hopkins, *Discovery of Witches*.

5 Dowsing damaged nothing at Great Wenham, but did however destroy some artefacts at Little Wenham.

6 Again, there is the suggestion that Hopkins had some knowledge of law.

7 National Archives.

8 Oyer and Terminer is the Anglo-French name used to mean 'hear and determine', for one of the commissions by which a Judge of Assize sits.

9 Also some local Magistrates were appointed to conduct the trials.

10 Godbolt's commission was primarily formed to deal with the backlog of Witchcraft trials; mainly instigated by Matthew Hopkins.

11 See Samuel Clarke's life of Samuel Fairclough.

12 Suffolk Record Office, Brandeston Parish Register.

13 Trevor Cooper (ed.), *The Journal of William Dowsing: Iconoclasm in East Anglia during the English Civil War*, Woodbridge, 2001.

14 There is a theory that Stearne was tricked into working with Hopkins, which will be discussed in its proper place in this book.

Chapter Five

1 In the Vincent Price film *Witchfinder General*, John Stearne is portrayed as a rapist and sadist, which is a far cry from the historical evidence in this book.

2 In *The Discovery of Witchcraft* Hopkins stated that the four sent the Devil like a bear to kill him in his garden. We know that whenever he wanted to hide a major incident he would do so by inventing a supernatural story (see essay in Part Two that analyses *The Discovery of Witches*). The bear-like spirit was a story in circulation in the first half of the seventeenth century through pamphlets, so it is not a new creation by Hopkins.

3 *A True and Exact Relation of Witchcraft*, 1645.

4 For a more complete transcript of Rebecca West's confession, see Appendix Two.

5 Simon Peters, *The Witchfinder and the Devil's Darlings* (Lucas Books, 2003). Although the book lacks details of source documentation, Mr Peters arrives at a similar conclusion to myself regarding the 'relationship' between Matthew Hopkins and Rebecca West. The book includes a Select Bibliography and a traditional transcript of Hopkins's pamphlet.

6 *The Discovery of Witches*: 'Vinegar Tom [Imp], who was like a long-legged Greyhound, with a head like an Ox, with a long tail and broad eyes.'

7 C.W. and P. Cunnington, *Handbook of English Costume in the Seventeenth Century*, 2nd edn (1966).

8 Stearne stated that 'we had for long been investigating the circumstances and family of Rebecca West for there seemed in her case to have been proved hereditary connection with the Devil' (see *A Confirmation and Discovery of Witchcraft* by John Stearne in Part Two). But Stearne doesn't necessarily mean him personally; he could imply his partner Hopkins, or official bodies who in 1641 had accused Anne West, Rebecca's mother, of bewitching a sow.

9 See *The Scottish Dove*, 29 August–6 September, 1645.

Chapter Six

1 Hopkins, *Discovery of Witches.*
2 It was believed that Hopkins received 'a commission to discover Witches', see Samuel Butler, *Hudibras*, Pts 1 and 2, ed. Wilders and de Quenhen (Oxford, 1973), 161; *The Victoria History of the County of Norfolk*, vol. 2,294. Conversely, once rumours of his methods reached Parliament a special Commission of Oyer and Terminer was appointed to observe him so perhaps not.
3 Mary Phillips was present at the very beginning of Hopkins's Witch-hunt but was not the prominent female inspector at that time. Other women did join the Company over time, such as Grace Norman, Mary Parsley and Abigail Briggs (the latter possibly a relation to Pricilla Briggs, but this cannot be proved). However, the inclusion of these other ladies shows how 'fluid' Hopkins's Company really was.

Chapter Seven

1 People with full legal powers within the villages visited.
2 In the Essex Record Office indexes there are no references to the Thorn Inn earlier than 1750.
3 Lilly would not be a known member of the 'company', just a (possibly) covert associate.
4 It is difficult to prove that Lilly and Thurlowe were involved. Richard Deacon believed it and my research certainly suggests that people with their skills and political leaning were *essential* to Hopkins's success.

Chapter Ten

1 G.R. Stirling Taylor, *Oliver Cromwell* (Jonathan Cape, 1978). The incidents within Cromwell's family before his birth would be impressionable stories he would grow up with and therefore be part of his early learning.
2 See *A True and Faithful Narrative of Oliver Cromwell's Compact With the Devil* (1720).
3 See also the pamphlet *A most Certain Strange and True Discovery of a Witch, Being taken by some of the Parliament Forces, as she was*

standing on a small plank-board and sailing on it over the River of Newbury.

Chapter Eleven

1 See *Confessions of Mother Lakeland at Ipswich, who was arraigned and condemned for a witch at Ipswich in Suffolk* (1645).
2 *Ibid.*

Chapter Twelve

1 *A True Relation of the Arraignment of Eighteen Witches*, London, 1645.
2 Reverend Montague Summers, *The Discovery of Witches – A Study of Matthew Hopkins commonly call'd Witchfinder General* (The Cayme Press, 1928). Interestingly, according to Dennis Wheatley, Montague Summers was an occultist.
3 John Lowes became Vicar of All Saints in 1596 before he was 30 years old.
4 In Wallace Notestein, *A History of Witchcraft in England from 1558*, tr. 1718 (Washington DC, 1911) Professor Notestein said that John Lowes was 'indicative of the hysteria of the times and the advantage taken of it by malicious people. It was his hostility to the ecclesiastical and political sympathies of his community which caused his fall.'
5 Bishop Hutchinson was Vicar of St James's at Bury St Edmunds at the turn of the eighteenth century. Francis (Bishop) Hutchinson, *An Historical Essay Concerning Witchcraft*, 2nd edn (with considerable additions), 1720, (first printed 1718).
6 *Witch Hunting and Witch Trials*, C. l'Estrange Ewen, Suffolk Record Office, Bury St Edmunds, pp 300–1.
7 Deponents: one who testifies under oath.
8 Hutchinson is a contemporary supporter.
9 Hutchinson, *Concerning Witchcraft* (1718). '1645–6, many hanged at Bury St Edmunds in Suffolk, I have been told near 40 at the several times of executions.'
10 Roland Parker, *The Common Stream* (London, Collins, 1975).
11 Speculative; as Lowes described as a 'painful preacher' and no concrete evidence to substantiate.

12 William Laud (1573–1644). Archbishop of Canterbury 1633–40. At a time of Puritan unrest, he tried to steer the Church of England back towards its Catholic heritage, with a form of worship based upon the sacraments.

13 Lowes was not the only priest to be accused of Witchcraft, other cases as early as 1617–19 have been documented. However, it was unusual.

14 He had recovered enough after his torture to plead his innocence in front of the Magistrate.

15 Note the word 'Countries' and how that word is misinterpreted when discussing Hopkins's disgrace in Chapter Fourteen.

16 The longer title of this work is: *The Certainty of the Worlds of Spirits, fully evinced, by unquestionable histories of Apparitions and Witch-crafts, Operations, Voices, etc,; . . . Written for the Conviction of Sadducees and Infidel*, 8vo, London, 1691.

Chapter Fourteen

1 Plausible enough when we note that respected Astrologer William Lilly (and adviser to Matthew Hopkins?) was himself accused of Witchcraft.

2 At the end of the seventeenth century, stories of Matthew Hopkins were only a generation old and should hold some elements of the truth.

3 In his study of Hopkins's work, the Reverend Montague Summers mentioned a story of an old French man being lynched by a mob at Castle Headingham in 1865 and thrown into a brook. The man died of exposure twenty-four hours later, an interesting comparison to my beliefs concerning Hopkins's death.

4 Summers, *The Discovery of Witches*.

5 According to *Alumni Cantabrigienses* John Witham was the new Rector of St Mary at Mistley Heath in August 1645, very probably the son of Thomas Witham, the former rector, who died in 1644. Interesting therefore that Hopkins announces Manningtree as his local town in 1644.

Chapter Fifteen

1 *The Jews' return shall be gracious*, Jeremiah.

Chapter Seventeen

1 The women were hanged in Manningtree adjacent to The White Hart, on a little green halfway up the hill on the right-hand side (a road up the hill still exists today).

Chapter Eighteen

1 *The Churches of St. Mary's & St. Michael, Mistley with Manningtree*, a guide book written by W.J.E. (Bill) Moore and expanded and updated by Monica Hollis Drake, with help and guidance of Norman Brunning and the illustrations of Jen Parker.

Chapter Nineteen

1 Divers: several, various, more than one (modern day usage used in plural)
2 Aule or ayle: sharp instrument for piercing leather.
3 Paps: something shaped liked a nipple.
4 Peradventure means perhaps, perchance.
5 Accompted: accepted.

Chapter Twenty

1 Not guilty of Witchcraft.
2 Fear of Hopkins and his accomplices at the time, like Chinese whispers, spread and became more outrageous, resulting in the 'children's fairy tale' character of Hopkins and the legend perpetrated by twentieth-century cinema.
3 This supports one version of the allegory that a *group* of villagers set about Hopkins on his return to Manningtree. They tied him hand to foot, ducked him and drove him out. Hopkins then died of consumption (or tuberculosis) shortly afterwards – so the allegory and plausible story that he died alone can be pieced together to form the true conclusion to Hopkins's story.
4 The contradiction is that he could have been advised to write the pamphlet by his 'former trade'.
5 Again through the preaching and writing of John Gaule.

6 He also stated 'and as many' Matrons/Midwives as able men assisted him; which adds weight to Hopkins's Company.

7 For the three-point answer to the first half of query 6, which in turn, is further support to query 5.

8 Not all the questions in the pamphlet were actually put to him. He must have planned some himself to help the flow of the pamphlet and say everything he wanted to say.

9 Now not only are the Judges seeing the flaws in Hopkins pamphlet, the Witchfinder himself is admitting his guilt.

10 See the names mentioned in James Hopkins's will.

Chapter Twenty-one

1 Ayme: I am.
2 Hedgeth: block or make difficult the onward path.
3 Almes: money or goods given as charity to the poor.
4 Legerdemain: those who use slight of hand or deceitful skill.
5 Cleave: be faithful.
6 Ell: length from elbow to middle finger.
7 Wens: a harmless cyst on scalp or face.
8 Censure: an expression of strong disapproval or harsh criticism.
9 Stearne believed he only acted upon instructions from the Bible and never broke the law – unlike Matthew Hopkins who did 'Watch'.

Chapter Twenty-two

1 The fact that Stearne could have been wrong for condemning so many people must have rattled him. He cleared his own conscious by writing his pamphlet.

Appendix One

1 This document is in Appendix Three. The execution of John Lowes was a pivotal moment in Hopkins's career as a Witchfinder and for that reason alone the pamphlet should be higher in priority than the details of Hopkins's first Witch-hunt that has more significance in its sub-text (as highlighted in Chapter Five).

2 The trial was postponed as the King's men were approaching Bury St Edmunds. Hence why some of the hangings took place at a later date.
3 This was Mary Lakeland – see Chapter Eleven.
4 Aune probably means the name Anne.
5 Coife or Coif meaning in this context: a way of arranging one's hair.

Appendix Two

1 A derogatory title for a meddling woman, see 'Cot-queane' in *Romeo and Juliet* or the reference to 'A Witch, a Queane . . .' from *The Merry Wives of Windsor*; the latter quote suggesting the term 'Queane' as a lesser threat than a Witch.
2 A small sloop-rigged coastal ship, also a heavy barge for bulky cargo.

Sources and Further Reading

Primary sources

An Historical Essay Concerning Witchcraft by Francis (Bishop) Hutchinson, 2nd edn, London, 1720 (first published 1718)

A True and Exact Relation of Witchcraft, 1648

A True and Faithful Narrative of Oliver Cromwell's Compact with the Devil, 1720

A True Relation of the Arraignment of Eighteen Witches that were Tried, Convicted, and Condemned, at a Session holden at St. Edmundsbury in Suffolk, and there by the Judge and Justices of the said Sessions condemned to die, and so were executed the 27 day of August 1645, London, 1645. Transcribed by C. Cabell, 2006

A True Relation of the Arraignment of Thirty Witches at Chelmsford in Essex, before Judge Coniers, fourteen whereof were hanged on Friday last, July 25. 1645, London, 1645. Transcribed by C. Cabell, 2006

Confessions of Mother Lakeland of Ipswich, who was arraigned and condemned for a Witch at Ipswich in Suffolk, 1645

Daemonologie, King James I

Select Cases of Conscience, Touching Witches and Witchcraft by John Gaule, 1646

ThecMaq-Astro-mancer by John Gaul, Joshua Kirton, 1652

The Discovery of Witches: in Answer to Several Queries Lately Delivered to the Judges of the Assize for the County of Norfolk and now published by Matthew Hopkins, Witchfinder for the Benefit of the Whole Kingdom, London, R. Royston, 1647. Transcribed by C. Cabell, 2006

British Library, *A Confirmation and Discovery of Witchcraft* by John Stearne, London, 1648

Suffolk Record Office, FC105/D1/1, parish register for Brandeston

——, Will of Daniel Wyles of Great Wenham, 1619

——, *Witch Hunting and Witch Trials* by C. L'Estrange Ewen

The National Archives (TNA: PRO), *Calendars of State Papers Domestic 1625–1649*

Secondary sources

Barry, Jonathan, Hester, Marianne and Roberts, Gareth (eds). *Witchcraft in Early Modern Europe – Studies in Culture and Belief*, Cambridge, 1998

Bassett, Ronald. *Witchfinder General*, Herbert Jenkins Limited, 1966

Butler, Samuel. *Hudibras*, ed. John Wilders and Hugh Quenhen (Oxford, 1973)

Cooper, Trevor (ed). *The Journal of William Dowsing: Iconoclasms in East Anglia during the English Civil War*, Woodbridge, 2001

Cunnington, C.W. and Cunnington, P. *Handbook of English Costume in the Seventeenth Century*, 2nd edn, 1966

Dalton, Michael. *Countrey Justice*, 1618

Davenport, John. *The Witches of Huntingdon*

Davies, Godfrey. *The Early Stuarts 1603–1660*, 2nd edn, Oxford, 1959

Deacon, Richard. *Matthew Hopkins – Witch Finder General*, Muller, 1976

Farrow and Barton. *Index of Wills Proved in the Consistory Court of Norwich 1604–1686*

Gaskill, Malcolm. *Witchfinders – A Seventeenth-Century English Tragedy*, John Murray, 2005

Moore, W.J.E., with Drake, Monica Hollis. *The Churches of St Mary & St Michael, Mistley with Manningtree – with a Short History of the Parishes and Former Churches*, 1999

Notestein, Professor Wallace. *A History of Witchcraft in England*, 1909

Page, William. *The Victoria History of the County of Norfolk*, vol. 2, 294, Victoria County History of the Counties of England, 1975

Parker, Roland. *The Common Stream*, London, Collins, 1975

Perkins, William. *Discourse*, Cambridge, 1608

Peters, Simon. *The Witchfinder and the Devil's Darlings*, Lucas Books, 2003

Scott, Walter. *Letters of Demonology and Witchcraft*

Stephen, Leslie and Lee, Sidney (eds). *Dictionary of National Biography*, vol. 9, Smith, Elder and Co, 1908

Stirling Taylor, G.R. *Oliver Cromwell*, Jonathan Cape, 1978

Summers, Montague. *The Discovery of Witches – A Study of Master Matthew Hopkins,* The Cayme Press, 1928

Tompkins, Herbert W. *Companion into Essex,* Methuen

Venn, J. and Venn, J.A. *Alumni Cantabrigiensis: a Biographical List of all known Students, Graduate and Holders of Office at the University of Cambridge, from the Earliest Times to 1900,* Cambridge, Cambridge University Press, 1922–54

Index

A Confirmation and Discovery of Witchcraft
23, 45, 74, 126, 214

Bacon, Nathaniel 5, 9, 214
Briggs, Pricilla 37–8

Calamy, Edmund 21–2, 45, 65
Clarke, Elizabeth 27–8, 37–8, 44, 86, 141,
144–5, 171, 183–4, 203, 205–7, 210, 212
Cromwell, Oliver 33–4, 39–40, 52–5, 64, 124

Discovery of Witches 7, 15, 20–1, 23–6, 36,
41, 65, 69, 76, 94, 113, 118, 125, 195
Dowsing, William 17, 19–20, 23–4, 37, 64,
78, 118, 123, 195

Edes, John 27

Fairclough, Samuel 21–2, 45
Framlingham 4, 6, 46, 62–3, 65

Gaule, John 22, 35, 45, 64, 66–8, 75, 94,
112, 114, 116, 124
Godbolt, John 21–2, 45, 54, 64, 72–3, 75,
86–7, 90, 148
Gurden, John 5

Hart, John 27
Hopkins, James 3–4, 6–8, 13, 23
will 4–6, 9–13, 16, 74
Hopkins, James (younger) 5–6
Hopkins, John 6, 8–11
Hopkins, Marie 4–6, 76–8, 89
Hopkins, Matthew
birth 5–6, 12
Company 35–9, 41–2, 44–51, 54, 61, 70,
76, 85–7, 94, 105, 111, 114, 116, 119,
122, 197–8
death 3, 10–13, 47, 71, 73–8, 89, 106, 191,
195
fairy tale 74, 77, 81, 107, 117

greyhound 30
lawyer 16, 41, 48, 119, 121
shipping clerk 9, 12, 14–17, 34, 87,
111
Hopkins, Thomas 4, 6, 9, 13
Hunt, Elizabeth 37
Hutchinson, (Bishop) Frances 60–3, 72–4, 78

Lakeland, Mary 16, 56–8, 216
Lilly, William 39–42, 55
Lowes, John 6, 16, 22, 45, 49, 54, 56, 59–65,
72, 75, 86, 107, 116, 118, 124, 153, 162,
199–200, 216

Mills, Frances 37–8

New England 4, 6–7, 9, 12, 77, 89

Oyer and Terminer 21, 45, 54, 62, 86

Philips, Mary 37–8, 70, 109, 112
Purley, Edward 36–8

Rivet, John 26–7

Salem (witch trials) 6, 10, 12, 89
Stearne, John 22–4, 29–38, 44–6, 49–51, 66,
68–70, 74–6, 79, 87, 94, 109, 116, 119,
126, 130, 193–5, 197–8
diary 195–6

Thorn Inn 33–4, 39, 41–2, 46, 55, 80, 83
Thurlowe, John 33, 38–40, 42, 55

West, Anne 27, 184, 207, 214
West, Rebecca 27–33, 146, 168, 170, 183,
197–8, 206–8, 214
White Hart 42, 80
Whorwood, Lady Jane 15
Woolvetter, Henry 26
Wyles, Daniel 6–7